THE LIFE CHANGER

FINDING JOY, PEACE, AND YOUR PURPOSE BY DISCOVERING TRUTH

JOSH PETERSON

ISBN 978-1-68526-497-0 (Paperback)
ISBN 978-1-68526-498-7 (Digital)

Covenant Books
11661 Hwy 707
Murrells Inlet, SC 29576
www.covenantbooks.com

To you.

May this book be a blessing to you.

I'm praying for you.

In loving memory of my sister Nicole Inman,

also known as Hope Warrior.

Contents

Introduction

Where are you on your spiritual journey? Are you searching for answers to your spiritual questions? If you are interested in spiritual things, this book is for you. It's great that you are a spiritual person! It's wise and good for you to be interested in spiritual things. Being spiritual can benefit not only your spiritual well-being but also your mental and emotional well-being. I cite a lot of sources and scholars that are listed in the notes, but this book is written for everyone who is interested in spiritual things.

I think that you will find *The Life Changer* to be one of the most important, interesting, and impactful books that you will ever read. It was written to encourage and challenge you as you search for the meaningful life that God wants you to enjoy. Thank you for taking the time to read this book!

The Life Changer is the result of my lifelong spiritual journey and my search for answers to life's most important questions. My spiritual journey has included talking with people who have a variety of different beliefs. It also has included reading hundreds of books written by Christians and numerous books written by Jews, Muslims, Hindus, Buddhists, and New Agers. I enjoy learning about the spiritual beliefs of those with whom I disagree on fundamental issues. I seek to find common ground with people of different religious backgrounds and worldviews before I discuss how my beliefs differ from their beliefs. Although I am a Christian, I have always sought to understand and appreciate the spiritual and religious beliefs of people who aren't Christians.

This book includes quotes from people from various religions even though I disagree with major points of non-Christian religions. Like the apostle Paul, I will use these quotes to establish common ground between you as the reader and me as the author (see Acts 17:28; 1 Corinthians 15:33; Titus 1:12–13). Many of these quotes are from best-selling authors who have interesting views to share with us. I really seek to get along with people who disagree with

my Christian beliefs. I also desire to be kind, loving, and respect-
ful toward everyone when I talk with them or write to them about
important spiritual truths.

My careful reading of a variety of religious and spiritual books
reflects my desire to follow some wise and timeless advice that I
found years ago in the popular novel *To Kill a Mockingbird*. In this
classic best-selling novel, a man named Atticus Finch tells his daughter Scout, "You never really understand a person until you consider
things from his point of view."[1] When Scout seems confused about
his comments, Atticus adds that understanding another person's
viewpoint is not possible "until you climb into his skin and walk
around in it."[2] Trying to take the perspective of other people has
enabled me to better understand and empathize with them and their
way of seeing the world. My desire to empathize with people who
are different from me helps me to care about them and their spiritual
journey. I feel so blessed that God has given me a desire to understand and empathize with others!

I also feel blessed that God has given me so many life experiences with a variety of people. My experiences with people of various
religions, countries, and classes have enabled me to become a trustworthy guide on spiritual matters.

My life experiences have included knowing many people from
very diverse backgrounds. When I was a teenager and in my early
twenties, I had the privilege to meet and work for some of the rich-
est people in America, including people from billionaire families. I
also had the privilege of meeting governors, senators, and other well-
known politicians and community leaders when I worked at the golf
clubs at two exclusive country clubs. In my late twenties and early
thirties, I spent a lot of time communicating by email with Christians
in India, Pakistan, Uganda, Kenya, Nigeria, and other countries in
Asia and Africa. I also enjoyed spending time talking with Muslims
at a Somali mall in Minneapolis. When I was in my thirties, my wife
Rosy and I felt blessed to have many Hindu neighbors and friends.
We really enjoyed frequently talking with our Hindu friends, and we
often ate dinner with them.

For the last ten years, my work has focused mainly on helping Latinos and Hispanics address their emotional and spiritual needs. I was able to spend a few weeks in Argentina, and my wife and I participated in short-term ministry trips to Brazil and Spain. When I was in my late thirties, my wife and I moved to Uruguay, where we lived near and worked for four years with some of the poorest people in the country. These needy Uruguayans would sometimes search for their food in the garbage dumps, but we always sought to encourage them and minister to their needs. Many of the Uruguayans we met struggled with depression, and we sought to help them to find hope, joy, and purpose in life. During the past five years, we have lived in the Midwest, and most of our work has involved serving the Latinos living near us. God has blessed us with a lot of friends who are Americans, Puerto Ricans, Mexicans, Ecuadorians, Guatemalans, and Colombians. My wife and I also still often talk with our Brazilian and Uruguayan friends. We love the people whom God has brought into our lives!

Despite all of our different backgrounds and life experiences, we all share some important things in common. We all have the same basic needs as human beings. These common needs are physical, emotional, and spiritual. *We all need joy, peace, and a purpose in life*. Addressing these emotional and spiritual needs is just as crucial as addressing our physical needs for food, sleep, and a place to live. Having joy in our lives fills us with a sense that God is in control of our lives no matter what is going on in them. Having peace provides us with emotional and spiritual tranquility through a healthy relationship with God. Having a purpose for our lives energizes us, enables us to focus, and infuses our daily activities with meaning.

We all yearn to enjoy lives filled with meaning, love, and laughter. We strongly desire to find meaning in our lives, to experience God, and to be loved by Him. We long to live a satisfying life that pleases God and makes a positive impact on the world.

Whether you live in America or in another country, God loves you. He loves people of all economic classes, races, and ages. God loves you even if you deny or doubt His existence. God loves you even if you haven't accepted His love for you. He loves you much more than you can imagine and understand. He loves you even though you aren't perfect, and His love is unconditional. He wants you to have a life filled with joy, peace, and purpose. God is actively involved in your life, whether or not you are aware of it. God wants you to know who He is. He wants you to know what He has done and is doing for you. God's desire is that you accept His amazing love for you. God wants you to enjoy a life overflowing with His hope and to experience His presence and forgiveness. God wants you to flourish spiritually.

When we flourish spiritually, we are full of joy, peace, and hope, and we live with a sense of direction and purpose. We know why we are here on this planet and what we want to do with our lives. We also know what God wants us to believe and how God wants us to live our lives.

If you want to flourish spiritually, I encourage you to search for and find the right answers to life's biggest questions. Finding the correct answers to life's biggest questions requires genuinely seeking the truth instead of seeking to prove what you want to be true. As you search for the answers to life's biggest questions, God wants to help you find the answers that will satisfy your mind, heart, and soul.

In this book, I will seek to answer life's biggest questions as well as I can and as God directs me. I pray that you will find my answers to these questions to be intellectually satisfying, emotionally appealing, and theologically sound. Please keep in mind that no one except God has all the answers to all your spiritual questions. I am just writing to share with you what God has put in my heart to share with you. I know that this book will engage your mind and your heart, and I'm sure that applying what you have discovered from this book to your life will satisfy your soul. God will use this book to help satisfy the deepest desires of your soul.

In this book, I will write about five big questions, five big tests, five big facts about Jesus, and five big truths. I will introduce the five big questions in chapter 2, and I will explain the five big tests in chapter 5. I will discuss the five big facts about Jesus in chapter 7 and the five big truths in chapter 9. These four topics will help us to remember essential truths about God, Jesus, ourselves, and our world. Because we can all remember a list of five items, these four topics will make it easier for us to recall what we have learned in our journey to discover the truth.

Would you like to know whether or not your current spiritual beliefs are true? *Knowing whether or not your spiritual beliefs are true will enable you to find the joy, peace, and purpose in life that you are looking for.* My desire is that this book will inspire you as a spiritual seeker to evaluate your current spiritual beliefs and to consider the claims of Jesus. If you are a Christian, this book will provide good reasons for you to keep believing in Jesus's claims. If you are not a Christian, this book will encourage you to consider Jesus's claims. As you investigate Jesus's claims, try to carefully examine the facts, and approach them with an open mind. God will abundantly reward you as you seek the truth about Him and about Jesus. God wants to quench your spiritual thirst with His life-giving truth. He also wants to provide clarity to your quest for spiritual truth. May this book encourage you in your quest for spiritual truth and provide solid answers to your spiritual questions. Knowing the truth will set you free!

Part 1

Finding Common Ground

1

My Story and Nicole's Story

My Story

In the most well-known words he ever wrote, the fifth-century philosopher Augustine writes this about God: "Our hearts are restless until they find their rest in You." Augustine's words still resonate with us. I began to sense that my heart was restless when I was a teenager. I believed in God, but I was too busy doing other things to actively seek Him. I enjoyed attending school, playing sports, and working a variety of fun jobs. I wanted to live a happy life full of meaning. I yearned for peace in my heart and a purpose for my life. I wanted to live a life that made a difference. I also wanted to live a successful and satisfying life. But I was plagued by my not knowing the answers to life's biggest questions: Who am I? Where did I come from? Why am I here? What has gone wrong with the world? What solution can solve the problem? I did not know who I was, why I was on earth, or where I was going after I died. I was unsure about my identity, my purpose, and my destiny. I wondered why God allowed suffering and pain to exist. I often thought about what could solve the problem of evil in the world.

Instead of seeking God, I began my search for happiness and meaning by becoming an excellent student. I took many advanced courses in high school, and I earned better grades than almost all my classmates at a large public school located in a western suburb of Minneapolis, Minnesota. I helped other students with their homework when I had the time to do so. My fellow classmates deeply respected, appreciated, and admired me. My teachers loved me. One of my English teachers told me, "I wish all my students were like you." After earning an academic scholarship to attend a public university, I achieved a high GPA in college. I also joined a fraternity and

3

made some good friends. Despite my academic achievements and enjoyment of college life, I still felt empty inside. I knew something was missing in my life.

While attending a public university, I took an intriguing course titled "The Historical Jesus." I was fascinated with the topic. The course initiated an interesting time in my spiritual journey. As part of the requirements for the course, I read books written by liberal scholars, such as the Jesus Seminar,

> **I didn't know the answers to life's most important questions about our identity, purpose, and destiny.**

Marcus Borg, and John Dominic Crossan. These liberal scholars made it clear that they *didn't* believe in Jesus's virgin birth, some of Jesus's miracles, and Jesus's bodily resurrection from the dead. While taking the course, I felt like I was on an emotional roller coaster. I was sad, angry, and afraid because I had been taught by my parents and church to interpret the Bible literally. I didn't know what would happen if I were to change my beliefs about God or the Bible. Would my family and friends reject me? A sense of confusion flooded my mind. I didn't know what or whom to believe about Jesus. However, I also felt excited about the possibility of interpreting the Bible differently. I even wondered whether reincarnation might be true. I was willing to consider a variety of different spiritual beliefs.

My search for happiness and meaning also included my becoming dedicated to my work as a teenager and young adult. I became an honor caddie and the supervisor of the driving range at two private local golf clubs that were exclusively for only millionaires and billionaires. During my college years, I worked at a local grocery store and as a vendor for a large ice cream company. I worked very hard, and I was paid more than I was supposed to earn for the positions I had. My bosses and my coworkers often praised my work ethic. I had thousands of dollars in my savings account at my bank. It seemed like I should have felt happy and fulfilled with all my success at work and school. However, I was not happy at all. I felt restless inside. I began to struggle with my sleep and worry constantly about what my life would be like in the future.

My lack of inner peace deteriorated into severe anxiety and depression in my early twenties. I worried a lot about what the future would hold for me, and I felt so dissatisfied and discouraged. As a result, I went to a psychiatrist who prescribed the antidepressant medication Zoloft for me. The antidepressant medication seemed to help me emotionally, but after several months of taking it, I decided to stop taking it. I didn't think I needed it anymore. I soon fell into depression again. I couldn't focus enough to complete my college homework, and I had to take a year off from college. I even contemplated suicide. I wondered, "Why am I not happy inside?"

I soon realized that I needed God in my life in order to defeat my anxiety and depression. God led me to begin reading the Bible and many Christian books in order to overcome my depression and to find peace and purpose in my life. I read Psalms 23, 42, 63, and other uplifting Bible passages. I was thirsty for more of God, so I eventually read the entire Bible and many Christian books in my twenties as I sought to find joy, peace, and my purpose. I also turned to the Bible as I sought answers to life's biggest questions about my identity, purpose, and destiny. In addition, after three years of reading the Bible and Christian books on my own, I began attending a church that believed in the Bible as God's inspired Word and Jesus as the divine Son of God. The Christian church members there surprised me by showering me with kindness and encouragement, and I saw that they had peace and purpose in their lives. They knew who they were, why they were on earth, and where they were going when they died. I longed for the peace, purpose, and assurance about going to heaven that permeated those Christians' lives. I knew that they were not perfect people, but I could see God working in their lives. I wanted what they had.

My positive experiences at church and my investigation of the claims of Christianity led me to find what I had been looking for since my teen years. In my search for evidence and answers, I discovered the truth about God and Jesus and compelling answers to life's biggest questions. I knew that Jesus had proved his claims to be God by rising from the dead, and I knew that I needed to get right with God. I needed God's forgiveness for my pride, selfishness, and worry.

I deserved God's punishment and to be banished from His presence, not God's approval or a magnificent mansion in heaven. I realized that I couldn't earn God's approval or my way to heaven by doing good works or by trying to be a good person. I knew that God loved me because Jesus had died for me in my place and rose again. Jesus took the punishment that I deserved, and he conquered the grave. Jesus was ready, willing, and able to offer me forgiveness, peace, joy, purpose in life, and eternal life in heaven. I prayed to God and told Him that I was trusting in Jesus alone as my way to heaven. After I prayed, I no longer felt empty inside. I sensed God's powerful presence and peace, and I knew that He had a purpose for my life.

Since I trusted in Jesus almost twenty years ago, God has enabled me to help hundreds of people to find their joy, peace, and purpose. Jesus has changed my life and the lives of many people whom God has brought into my life. God has given me the opportunity to know people from various countries, cultures, and religious backgrounds.

I enjoy helping other people find their joy, peace, and purpose in a relationship with God.

I've had friends who are Hindus and friends from other non-Christian religions. God has also given me the desire to improve my understanding of non-Christian religions such as Islam, Judaism, Hinduism, Buddhism, and the New Age. I have read many books written by New Agers, Hindus, Buddhists, Muslims, Jews, and atheists. These books have heightened my understanding and appreciation of the spiritual beliefs of people who do not follow Jesus. God loves everyone in the entire world, but not everyone has accepted His amazing love. I enjoy helping other people understand how they can accept God's love and find their joy, peace, and purpose in a relationship with Him.

I'm so glad that I have accepted God's love and trusted in Jesus alone for eternal life in heaven. Trusting in Jesus was the best decision that I have ever made! I'm not a perfect person, but I know that God has forgiven me. I'm just an ordinary person with an extraordinary God. He has been meeting all my physical, emotional, spiritual, and financial needs. God is amazing, and He is doing great things in my life!

Nicole's Story

I will always remember that unforgettable day with mixed emotions. It didn't seem fair. I felt so sad deep inside. It was hard to believe and even harder to accept. It was one of the most difficult days of my life, and yet I felt at peace about what had happened. My sister Nicole Inman passed away that day in December 2020 after battling brain cancer for two and a half years. She had suffered from glioblastoma, which is the most common, complex, treatment-resistant, and deadliest type of brain cancer. I felt both overwhelmed by sadness and filled with a sense of relief. Her suffering was over. In the last two months of her life, Nicole was confined to a wheelchair and unable to speak more than a few words at a time. She went home to heaven when she passed away, and her pain was over. But why did Nicole have to suffer so much the last few months of her life? Why didn't the chemotherapy and radiation treatments stop the cancer from coming back? Those questions would have haunted me if my faith in God weren't strong and unwavering.

Nicole was a happily married woman with a hardworking husband and four wonderful children. God blessed her with two boys and twin girls. She was a Christian with strong, unshakable faith. She was a very kind, caring, energetic, generous, and hardworking woman. Nicole had a magnetic personality, and she radiated warmth and authenticity. For many years, Nicole worked as a youth director at a local church, and she was a soccer coach in her community. She was also a high school teacher for a few years. Nicole was a devoted wife, a loving mother, an outstanding coach, and a gifted teacher. She was loved by her family, church, and community. Nicole was the most unselfish person I have ever known. Why did God only allow her to live into her forties? Her passing seemed so hard to understand.

This book is dedicated to the loving memory of my younger sister Nicole because her story is remarkable and inspiring. I'm sure that you will be encouraged by it. Just before discovering that she had brain cancer, Nicole had led her high school girls' soccer team to the state championship game, and she had won an award as coach of the year in Arkansas. A sudden seizure and a frightening diagnosis of brain cancer didn't cause Nicole to panic or to lose heart. She knew that God was in control and that He had a purpose for her suffering from brain cancer.

Nicole was determined to make good things result from her challenging life circumstances. Nicole set up a *Hope Warrior* blog, and her uplifting blog posts encouraged and inspired the thousands of people who read them. Her blog posts profoundly touched friends, family members, soccer players, students, the local media, and many other people throughout the USA and in other countries. Her heartwarming interviews with local media resonated with thousands of people. Countless people prayed for Nicole and wore "Hope Warrior" T-shirts, which featured seven encouraging Bible verses about trusting in God and not being afraid (Exodus 14:14; Deuteronomy 31:6; Isaiah 35:4; 41:10; John 14:1; Romans 15:13; 1 Peter 5:7). Nicole frequently spoke about her faith with other cancer patients and anyone else whom God brought into her life. In describing her battle with cancer, she said that she was "blessed to be in the front row watching God's handiwork in and through it."[1] While being treated for cancer, Nicole helped her oldest son to earn a full-ride academic scholarship to college, and she helped her twin daughters to earn full-ride soccer scholarships to college.

Nicole also coached her daughters and their high school soccer team to a state title almost a year after being diagnosed with brain cancer. Wow! What an amazing accomplishment! Immediately after winning the title, Nicole went down on her hands and knees on the soccer field and thanked God for providing the victory. God was working in her life in an undeniable and extraordinary way!

God blessed Nicole and her family with an outpouring of love and support from their family, friends, and community. This love and support included many prayers, cards, and donations to pay for expensive medical bills. Nicole was so loved, respected, and appreciated! She believed that God would give her victory over brain cancer. God did enable Nicole to have victory over brain cancer even though it was not the type of victory she wanted to experience at that point in time. She went home to heaven much sooner than she had anticipated.

Nicole's powerful story has not been forgotten since she passed away. It continues to inspire and encourage thousands of people. Despite the ongoing coronavirus pandemic, the encouraging service celebrating Nicole's life was attended by hundreds of people, and many more people from various countries viewed it online. Several days after the celebration service, the U.S. representative for Nicole's district in Arkansas shared Nicole's story on the U.S. House floor. An annual soccer scholarship was also established in her honor by her husband. In addition, Nicole's former high school soccer players dedicated the 2021 spring season to her memory, and they had a special Hope Warrior night at one of their soccer games. Many of the students attending the special night wore pink sunglasses to honor Nicole because she always wore her pink sunglasses while coaching soccer games. Finally, many people today still wear "Hope Warrior" T-shirts and bracelets and pink sunglasses in honor of Nicole's memory. Nicole's awesome story will always live in the hearts of countless people. Her story is still being told by her family members and friends. Nicole is fondly remembered for her heroic battle against brain cancer and for her devout faith.

Although Nicole believed that God would heal her on this earth, God chose to heal Nicole of cancer by taking her to heaven instead. Nicole didn't know that she only had a few months to live. She was convinced that God would heal her on this earth. As I mentioned above, Nicole was also unable to speak more than a few words at a time during the last two months of her life. As a result, Nicole never had the opportunity in the last few months of her life to share what she would have told her family, friends, and anyone else who would listen. I sometimes wish that Nicole would have had the chance to share more words of encouragement and advice during her final days of life in this world.

What would Nicole have said if she had known that God was going to take her home to heaven much earlier than she thought? We don't know for sure, but I think I know some things that Nicole probably would have said. We were close in age (only seventeen months apart), and she was my first best friend. We grew up together and lived in the same house for over seventeen years. I knew Nicole well enough to know what she probably would have said if she had known her time on earth was soon coming to an end.

Nicole loved God, Jesus, and everyone whom God brought into her life. She knew that she served an amazing God, and she wanted other people to know God and to live for Him. Nicole was convinced that Jesus is the way to find life's most important truths and abundant life, and she often took the time to share her faith with other people. She refused to be rushed when she talked with people about her faith at grocery stores, health clinics, and hospitals. Nicole also encouraged me to share my faith with other people.

Besides telling us that she loved us, Nicole would have told us to enjoy life each day by living for God and spending time with family and friends. She would have told us that God loves us and has a wonderful purpose and plan for our lives. Nicole would have also said that hope is the firm belief that God is in control, not just a wish that something good happens. Lastly, Nicole would have told us that the peace, joy, hope, purpose, and forgiveness that God wants us to have are given to every one of us who trusts in Jesus for eternal life in heaven.

The Focus of This Book

The rest of this book will focus on sharing why and how all of us can find what we most want and need by having a life-changing relationship with God. Having this personal and vibrant relationship with God involves knowing Jesus, the Life Changer. Before saying more about Jesus, we need to discuss how most of us seek to satisfy our strongest desires and meet our most important needs. We also need to discover how we

> If we have no purpose in life, God wants to give us one. If we have a purpose that isn't focused on living for God, He wants to give us a new purpose of living for Him.

know that God is real and actively involved in the world. Chapters 2 through 4 will reveal how we can find the life God wants us to live, how we can define truth, and how we can know that God is real.

We will begin our search for spiritual truth by discovering how we can find joy, peace, and our purpose in life. If we have no purpose in life, God wants to give us one. If we have a purpose that isn't focused on living for God, He wants to give us a new purpose of living for Him. But how can we live for God and find joy, peace, and our purpose?

2

How Can We Find Joy, Peace, and Our Purpose?

American culture teaches us to focus our lives on seeking money, material things, and other worldly pursuits. We all want to have our dream job. We like to think that our dream job will enable us to earn good money, get enjoyable tasks done well, and give us a sense of fulfillment. Most of us want to live as well as our neighbors do, and we all want to be as happy as our friends seem to be. Don't their photos posted on Facebook, Instagram, and other social media sites seem to show how happy they really are? We are bombarded every day by television ads, internet ads, and magazine ads. These ads tempt us to buy products and services that are supposed to make us happy. We all want to show other people that we are successful and enjoying life. We all dream of having a new car and a beautiful place to live in. We want all the good things that life has to offer!

But once we get our dream job, find a nice place to live, and buy a new car, something surprising and disappointing tends to occur. We often still feel like something is missing in our lives. We may even feel like we are running on empty. Dream jobs and material things will not satisfy us because they are fleeting—they don't last forever. Rhonda Byrne correctly declares, "It's not possible to find lasting happiness through material things. Every material thing appears and eventually disappears, so if you vest your happiness in a material thing, your happiness will disappear when the material thing disappears."[1] Since pursuing material things makes us feel empty inside, many of us try to fill this void inside with sex, alcohol, and illegal drugs. But seeking pleasure also results in only short-term thrills, not lasting felicity. Deepak Chopra writes, "The greatest hunger in life is not for food, money, success, status, security, sex, or even love from the opposite sex. Time and again people have achieved all of these things and wound up still feeling dissatisfied—indeed, often more dissatisfied than when they began."[2] Our pursuit of worldly things eventually makes us feel like we are stuck in the middle of the desert with no food or water anywhere in sight. We still feel a spiritual hunger and thirst that we seek to satisfy.

Pursuing the things of this world cannot satisfy our souls. Earning money, having material possessions, and enjoying life's pleasures will never be enough to satisfy the desire of our hearts. We struggle with stress, negative thoughts, and questions about our purpose when we go after what the world offers us. Our hearts yearn to find real meaning in life. Harold Kushner writes, "What we miss in our lives, no matter how much we have, is that sense of meaning. We may have all the things on our wish list and still feel empty. We may have reached the top of our professions and still feel that something is missing."[3] Fortune, fame, and anything else in the world fail to bring us true contentment. We all long to make a difference in the world. *We all want to not only survive and succeed but also to make a significant positive impact on the world.* We want to thrive, not just survive. Thriving requires more than having money and a job and more than being in love. Jonathan Haidt provides a helpful illustration: "Just as plants need sun, water, and good soil to thrive, people need love, work, and a connection to something larger."[4] We want and need meaning and purpose in our lives. We hunger for our lives to matter, to make a difference. Kushner writes, "Our souls are not hungry for fame, comfort, wealth, or power. Those rewards create almost as many problems as they solve. Our souls are hungry for meaning, for the sense that we have figured out how to live so that our lives matter, so that the world will be at least a little different for our having passed through it."[5] We want to accomplish significant goals so that we are respected and remembered, not ignored and forgotten.

The classical movie *It's a Wonderful Life* is so inspiring and is considered one of the best movies of all time because it shows that our lives can make a big difference. Have you ever seen it? It's the story of George Bailey, who comes to believe that everyone around him would be better off if he had never been born. He thinks that his life has not really mattered at all. With the help of an angel, George has the opportunity to see what his town and others' lives would have looked like if he had never been born. He sees that without his kind acts and good deeds, his wife and the entire town would have been much worse off. George realizes that he touched many lives and made a difference. He feels a new sense of purpose and joy.

Besides longing for meaning and significance, we all have a God-shaped hole in our hearts that only God can fill. Even if we aren't aware of our need for God, we all want and need God in our lives. If we aren't seeking God, we will experience spiritual emptiness. Nothing and no one can make up for the void we will experience. Many of us desperately try to fill the void by using money, material things, approval from others, friendships, family, sports, our appearance, fame, popularity, etc. But only God can fill the void within. Our homes, cars, friends, and family cannot satisfy our craving for God. Matthew Kelly writes, "You have a God-size hole. You cannot fill it with things, money, power, sex, alcohol, other people, experiences, or accomplishments. Only God can fill that hole. Throw all the money and possessions in the world into the hole and you will find it is still empty and you are still yearning for more."[6] Failure to place God at the center of our lives results in our feeling confused and disillusioned. Not putting Him at the center of all that we do sets us up for what Kelly calls "gnawing dissatisfaction."[7]

> Nothing on this earth can satisfy our souls. Only God can.

Nothing on this earth can satisfy our souls. Only God can. Commenting on our need for God, Gary Thomas points out that nothing and no one except God can compensate for spiritual emptiness: "If what we desire most doesn't satisfy us, we will never be satisfied, even when our 'desires' have been met! That's why finding our fulfillment in God is the cornerstone of a satisfied life."[8] In his most famous sermon, Jesus says that if we make God our top priority in life, God will meet all our needs and bless us with peace in our hearts (see Matthew 6:33).

The many emotional struggles of Hollywood stars and other famous people clearly illustrate our need for making God the center of our lives. Living a life of opulence and achieving worldly success doesn't satisfy them. Divorce, depression, anxiety, drug use, alcoholism, and porn addiction are rampant among the rich, famous, and powerful. Why? Countless wealthy and famous people believe the lie that money, material possessions, and fame make people happy. Many of them have built beautiful mansions and lived luxurious lifestyles yet have still suffered from loneliness, anxiety, and depression. They have sought worldly things instead of spiritual things in their efforts to satisfy their souls. Jay Shetty writes, "Fame, money, glamour, sex—in the end none of these things can satisfy us. We'll simply seek more and more, a circuit that leads to frustration, disillusion, dissatisfaction, unhappiness, and exhaustion."[9] Rather than making people happy, achieving success according to worldly standards can produce misery and make life seem meaningless.

Solomon was a famous king of Israel who struggled during part of his life with the idea that life might be meaningless. Although he was fabulously wealthy and immensely powerful, Solomon came to believe that his life was meaningless. His extravagant lifestyle featured tons of gold, hundreds of wives, and hundreds of horses (see 1 Kings 11:3; 2 Chronicles 9:13–28). The modern equivalent of Solomon's lifestyle would be a multibillionaire living with a massive mansion and hundreds of sports cars. His pursuit of wealth, women, pleasure, work, and idol worship prevented him from seeking God and from enjoying the benefits of finding God. He famously stated, "Everything is meaningless" (see Ecclesiastes 1:2). He felt empty inside! However, King Solomon was not always far from God. At the beginning and the end of his reign, Solomon's life was characterized by his wise living and his ardent pursuit of God. He wrote that God has put eternity in our hearts—a knowledge that we will continue to exist after we die (see Ecclesiastes 3:11). He also wrote that people should trust God, seek His will for their lives, and live for Him (see Proverbs 3:5–6; Ecclesiastes 12:13). Solomon realized that God rewards those who seek Him.

Like Solomon, we all struggle at times with disappointment, discouragement, and disillusionment. We don't always feel satisfied with our lives. People let us down. We don't always feel fulfilled. We sometimes feel empty inside because we try to be happy by pursuing things that won't satisfy our souls. For many of us, our lives consistently lack joy, peace, and purpose. God wants us to overcome our problems, and He longs to fill our lives with His peace and purpose. He desires to surprise us with His comforting presence in the midst of our stressful lives. Louie Giglio writes, "God offers us his presence in the middle of our problems. In his presence we find a deeper sort of solution, one that holds forth fulfillment, peace, a knowledge that he provides, and the hope that he has a wider purpose for our lives than we could ever think up or live out on our own."[10]

How Can We Find Joy, Peace, and Our Purpose?

How can we find the joy, peace, and purpose in life that God wants us to find? There are three things we need to do: 1) place God at the center of our lives by seeking our joy, peace, and purpose in Him; 2) determine if our beliefs about God and about ourselves are true or false; and 3) if necessary, change our beliefs so that our most important beliefs are true instead of false. The famous Greek philosopher Socrates correctly stated, "The unexamined life is not worth living." The apostle Paul, who wrote almost half of the books of the New Testament, also strongly encourages us to engage in self-examination (see 2 Corinthians 13:5). We need to examine our beliefs because holding false beliefs can make us

Deep inside, we all know that deciding to examine the truthfulness of our spiritual beliefs is one of the wisest decisions we could ever make.

slaves to them; they can control our thoughts, feelings, and actions. Having true beliefs enables us to know the truth that sets us free. Evaluating our beliefs is absolutely essential if we want to live our lives as God intended them to be lived. Being willing to change our beliefs is a clear sign of our humility, wisdom, and personal growth. *Deep inside, we all know that deciding to examine the truthfulness of our spiritual beliefs is one of the wisest decisions we could ever make.*

Are you 100% sure that your beliefs about God and about people are true? If what you believe about God and people were not true, would you want to know it?

We all should be willing to evaluate our spiritual views and change them, if necessary, in response to God's leading. We all tend to believe what we want to believe and what our parents and culture teach us. All of us are inclined to believe what seems comfortable and convenient to us. Philip Johnson correctly points out that all of us need to "watch out for the universal human tendency to believe what we want to believe."[11] We are all susceptible to engaging in wishful thinking because of our strong emotional attachments to our beliefs. We may feel too busy to take the time to evaluate our beliefs. In addition, our postmodern world encourages us to be attracted to what is irrational, contradictory, and emotionally appealing. However, taking the time to examine our own beliefs is both helpful and crucial if we want to live an abundant life characterized by joy, peace, and a sense of purpose.

Our spiritual beliefs should be grounded in good evidence, not the result of blind faith. Our spiritual beliefs affect our lives so much that they should be based on solid evidence, not just on our personal experience or personal preference. *Facts—not feelings or experiences—should ultimately determine our spiritual beliefs.* We should be led by God instead of by our feelings as we seek to discover the truth that sets us free. While our feelings may lead us away from the truth, God will always lead us toward the truth that He wants us to discover.

The famous animated movie *The Prince of Egypt* is definitely my favorite animated movie. Have you ever seen it? This thrilling movie features the voices of such famous actors as Val Kilmer, Sandra Bullock, Michelle Pfeiffer, Danny Glover, Steve Martin, and Martin Short. It also includes stunning visuals and the Mariah Carey and Whitney Houston duet "When You Believe." Some people have called it the greatest animated movie of all time.[12] This powerful movie tells the story of Moses, who is a key historical and religious figure not only for Christians but also for Jews and Muslims.

Although *The Prince of Egypt* is filled with memorable lines, one of the most important lines is Moses's statement about how his beliefs and observations were affected by his own desires. He admits to his brother Aaron that because of his wishful thinking, he did not see the slavery that his people were suffering from every day. Moses states, "I did not see because I did not wish to see." For many years, Moses did not see or think about the suffering of his people because he preferred to not see it or think about it. He wanted to think about his life as a prince living in a beautiful palace, not about the lives of slaves working in mud pits.

We don't have to fall into the same trap as Moses fell into many years ago. We don't have to be strongly affected by wishful thinking. Although we can all be affected by wishful thinking, we must realize that our most important beliefs aren't just preferences. They involve our answers to life's most important questions. It really doesn't matter that much if we prefer chocolate or vanilla, fried eggs or scrambled eggs, or hot dogs or hamburgers. It doesn't matter that much what our favorite sport, television show, or hobby is; life is much bigger than what occupies our leisure time. Not knowing our answers to life's important questions can rob us of sleep and reduce our enjoyment of our free time. Our answers to life's biggest questions profoundly impact what we think, feel, choose, and how we live our lives every day. Our answers to life's biggest questions deeply influence our quality of life and how well we handle life's most challenging ups and downs. We can discover solid answers to life's biggest questions! Having solid answers to life's biggest questions enables us to better cope with loneliness, marital problems, financial pressures, emotional struggles, bad habits, and addictions. As a result, we must try to correctly answer these crucial questions.

Every one of us wants and needs to have a worldview that provides adequate answers to life's most important questions.

What Are the Five Big Questions?

What are the five biggest questions that we all need to have answered? *Every one of us wants and needs to have adequate answers to the five big questions. These questions are the following:*

1) *Who am I?*
2) *Where did I come from?*
3) *Why am I here?*
4) *What has gone wrong with the world?*
5) *What solution can solve the problem?*

The first question is about our identity. The second question is about our origin. The third question asks about our purpose—our reason for being alive on earth. The fourth question asks about why there is evil and suffering in the world. The fifth question seeks the best solution to the problem of evil and suffering in the world. Together, our answers to these five questions comprise our worldview. Our worldview consists of our most important beliefs about ourselves, our world, and God.

How would you answer these five questions right now? If you don't know how you would answer them, that's okay. Many people are unsure about how they would answer these questions. Countless people struggle to express what their purpose is and why they believe what they believe. As you're reading this book, you can think more about how you would answer the questions and why you would answer them that way. I will share my answers to these important questions, and you can decide whether or not you agree with my responses. My answers are based on my Christian beliefs and the compelling evidence that I have found for those beliefs.

Before I attempt to answer these questions, we need to make sure that we know whether or not absolute truth exists at all. Many people nowadays don't believe that absolute truth really exists. Some of us think that truth is relative, not absolute. In the next chapter, we'll discuss the issues of what truth is and whether or not truth is absolute.

3

Aren't Your Beliefs True for You but Not for Me?

Is it okay for us to deceive other people if doing so works for us? Is such behavior morally acceptable? In a June 2021 post, a TikTok user named Ashlin showed how she pretended to be pregnant in order to sneak an extra bag on a cheap airplane flight. She posted a video of herself hiding a drawstring bag under her sweater in order to avoid having to pay a fee for too many carry-ons. The viral video has been seen over 27 million times.[1] A follow-up video showed that Ashlin's creative illusion worked so well that she was able to pre-board the flight as a "pregnant" woman. Most of the viewers thought her hack was a brilliant or "genius" thing to do. It seemed so clever, and it worked for her. Ashlin didn't have to pay a fee for her extra bag. Many viewers thought the videos were hilarious and entertaining.[2]

It's easy for many of us to consider what Ashlin did a funny and clever hack that seems like a harmless "white lie." No one was directly hurt by Ashlin's deceptive act. However, we all know that some lies can produce serious negative consequences for those who tell them and other people affected by them. Later on in this chapter, we'll look at one example of a lie that had serious and disastrous consequences. We will see that we all know that lies and certain other behaviors are morally wrong. We will also see that we all know some things are true.

"What is truth?" The Roman governor Pontius Pilate asked Jesus this important question at Jesus's trial before his crucifixion (see John 18:38). Like Pilate, we must ask this crucial question and seek the correct answer to it. We need to know if truth is relative or absolute and how truth should be defined.

As you read this book, you might be thinking to yourself, "What you believe is true for you, but not for me. Truth is relative, not absolute." You might believe that truth is based on what has worked for you in your personal experience. Perhaps you think that truth depends on what culture a person lives in or what religion someone belongs to. You might also believe that truth depends on whether a person lives in modern times or if someone lived thousands of years ago. You might think that what is true depends on the situation that confronts you. If you believe that truth is relative, you are currently a moral relativist; you are comfortable with the idea that what is true depends on various factors. If you are a moral relativist, you are part of a massive shift in America that has occurred in the last three decades. This seismic shift involves a change in beliefs from the acceptance of moral absolutes to the acceptance of moral relativism.

Most people in postmodern America now believe that truth and morality are relative, not absolute. According to two surveys, a majority of Americans now consider truth to be relative. In a survey done by the Barna Group, 57% of Americans said that knowing what is right or wrong is a matter of what works for each person in their personal experience.[3] In an even more recent survey done by George Barna, almost six out of every ten American adults (58%) said that identifying moral truth is up to the individual; there are no moral absolutes that apply to every person, all of the time.[4]

But are there really no moral absolutes? Even if the majority of Americans believe that truth is relative, it is entirely possible that the majority could be wrong. The majority opinion isn't always true. For example, history shows that the majority of people in the world used to hold such false beliefs as the sun revolving around the earth and earth being flat! The majority opinion could also be completely mistaken about the issue of moral absolutes.

All true beliefs must be logical and livable. If our beliefs are not logical and livable, they can't be true. In other words, true beliefs are reasonable instead of contradictory, and they can be followed consistently in real life. The belief that there are no moral absolutes is emotionally appealing to many of us, but it isn't logical. The statement "There are no moral absolutes" is itself a statement of absolute truth and is thus self-defeating. Moreover, the statement "There are no moral absolutes" isn't livable. If there were no moral absolutes, then mass murder, bank robbery, serial rape, and other heinous crimes would need to be permitted instead of punished. Imagine the absolute chaos that would ensue if most Americans frequently killed, raped, stole, kidnapped, and committed adultery! If moral relativists lived in a way that was consistent with their beliefs, having an orderly society would be impossible. If the national, state, and local branches of government fully adhered to moral relativism, there would be no jails or prisons. Murders, rapists, and robbers would be wandering the streets during the day and during the night. Life would be absolutely terrifying every day! Even such simple tasks as going to the grocery store to buy food or leaving your house for any other reason would become scarier than the most frightening nightmares. Who would want to or be able to live in such a terrifying world?

Are There Any Moral Absolutes?

Another problem with the belief that there are no moral absolutes is that there are some types of behaviors that almost everyone considers to be wrong. Since there are such behaviors, then the commonly heard phrase "true for you, not for me" should be rejected as a false belief. Serial rape and robbery are examples of behaviors that everyone knows are wrong.

A South African serial rapist named Sello Abram Mapunya was recently sentenced to 1,088 years in jail for raping and robbing 56 women. His cruel reign of terror lasted over four years. One of

Everyone knows that killing, stealing, lying, and committing adultery are wrong.

his victims was a 14-year-old girl. The packed court gallery cheered and clapped as he was taken away to the holding cells after his sentence.[5] Everyone in the court gallery knew—just like all of us know—that rape and robbery are morally unacceptable criminal behaviors. No one in the court objected to Mapunya's sentence, which he obviously deserved.

Rape and robbery are just two examples of behaviors that everyone knows are wrong. *Everyone in the world also knows that killing, stealing, lying, and committing adultery are wrong.* The

Ten Commandments of Jews and Christians include prohibitions against these four immoral behaviors (see Exodus 20:1–17; Deuteronomy 5:7–21). Muslims,[6] Hindus,[7] Buddhists,[8] and people of other religions also regard these four actions as immoral. Even atheists know that murder, stealing, lying, and adultery are wrong. Atheist Greg Epstein writes, "It is every bit as plain for nonreligious people as for religious ones to recognize that murder, adultery, thievery, and lying—among many such pernicious activities—are wrong."[9]

Why are these four actions and other closely related actions like kidnapping wrong? These destructive actions undermine trust, damage relationships, and bring chaos to society. These actions result in anxiety, fear, depression, and other negative emotions. They can also rob people of their life, liberty, and pursuit of happiness. These immoral actions must be considered wrong in all societies in order for any society to maintain order and to survive instead of suffering from confusion and disorder. Societies must prohibit and punish criminal acts such as murder, rape, robbery, and kidnapping if they want to continue to exist and to protect the lives and freedoms of their law-abiding citizens. Jails and prisons serve as necessary means of punishing the guilty and protecting the innocent.

The mere existence of jails, prisons, and fines shows that people know certain actions are wrong and that truth is absolute. Let's imagine that you are driving on the highway and getting pulled over by a police officer for speeding. What would happen if you told the police officer that speeding is wrong for him or her, but not for you? The police officer would still give you a ticket because you broke the law. You and the police officer would both know that speeding is illegal because it can cause car accidents, damage to property, and loss of human life.

Let's return now to the example of telling lies. Because everyone has told a lie or many lies, lying seems like it's no big deal. Lying often seems like an effective short-term solution to get us out of a difficult situation. Telling lies can help us avoid being judged or punished, but lying can wreak havoc on our personal relationships and result in serious harm to others. Lying may seem innocent and harmless, but lying can damage and even destroy our relationships and our lives and the lives of other people.

In October 2020, a 13-year-old French teen told a lie that led to her history teacher being killed. Her lie sparked a tragic chain of events that led to the murder. The girl lied about her teacher asking Muslim students to leave his classroom so that he could show an irreverent photo of the Prophet Muhammad. She lied in order to hide the fact that she had been suspended from school for repeatedly failing to show up for school lessons. Ten days after her lie, history teacher Samuel Paty was beheaded by an Islamic terrorist named Abdullakh Anzorov. Paty died partly because the teen girl had lied! Paty's family was devastated. Paty left behind a wife and a five-year-old son. The girl lied by telling her father that Paty had told students to leave the classroom so that he could show the rest of the students "a photograph of the Prophet naked." After hearing his daughter's story, Brahim Chnina was infuriated. The father shared a Facebook video in which he denounced Paty and argued that Paty should be fired. He also posted a second social media video in which he accused Paty of "discrimination." The outraged terrorist saw the videos, hunted down Paty, and beheaded him.[10]

Besides knowing that lying is wrong, we know that adultery is wrong. In the last twenty years, Gallup polls about marital infidelity have consistently shown that about 90% of Americans regard married people having an affair as "morally wrong."[11] We know that cheating on one's spouse is wrong because it damages marriages and causes many divorces. Divorces can be necessary at times, but they also contribute to emotional pain for couples and for their families. We also know that marital infidelity is wrong because it involves a lack of loyalty and faithfulness. We know that loyalty and faithfulness are positive qualities that benefit personal relationships and also society as a whole. Failing to be loyal and faithful harms our relationships and our society.

Let's pretend that someone approached you and began asking you some yes-no questions about your moral beliefs. Here are some yes-no questions that he or she could ask:

1) Would it be okay if I stole your car?
2) Would it bother you if I stole your cellphone?
3) Would you object if I killed your best friend?
4) Would you mind if I had sex with your spouse?
5) Would it be okay if your spouse or best friend habitually lied to you?

The answers to these questions are obvious. You would say "no" to questions 1 and 5. You would say "yes" to questions 2, 3, and 4. Your responses to these questions make it clear that truth is absolute.

Why do so many people believe truth is relative when truth is actually absolute? Moral relativism has a strong emotional appeal to many of us. We tend to prefer living our lives how we want to instead of how God or society tells us to live. We want to be our own boss. We want to make our own rules and have our own moral standards. We want the freedom to believe what is convenient for us. We all tend to struggle with wishful thinking, and we can all easily believe what we want to believe. We tend to resist changing our beliefs and lifestyles unless we regard such changes as essential to our emotional and spiritual well-being.

If you are currently a moral relativist, I would suggest that you consider rejecting moral relativism and embracing the idea that truth is absolute. Moral relativism offers a distorted view of truth. The reality is that there are timeless moral truths that transcend cultures. For example, it will always be wrong in all countries and cultures to kill, steal, lie, and commit adultery. Mass murder and identity theft are never justifiable behaviors. People of all countries and cultures also know that torturing babies for fun, raping someone, and kidnapping someone are immoral acts. These immoral behaviors have always been wrong and will always be wrong in every culture and country.

What Is Truth?

Now that we know that there is such a thing as absolute truth, we should define what the word *truth* means. *Truth* can be defined as "that which corresponds to reality." Norm Geisler correctly states, "As applied to the world, truth is the way things really are. Truth is 'telling it like it is.'"[12] Truth describes the way things actually are; truth is accurate. Truth is not that which works for us or what feels good. What is effective for us—such as lying, stealing, or committing adultery—might harm someone else. In addition, someone might feel good while taking revenge and killing someone else. Someone might also feel good while robbing a bank or cheating on their spouse. Our feelings don't determine what is true and morally acceptable; God determines what is true and morally acceptable. He has determined that lying, stealing, killing, committing adultery, and many other harmful behaviors are morally wrong.

> **Truth describes the way things really are in the world; truth isn't whatever works for us or feels good.**

Are You or Is Someone You Know an Atheist?

You might be an agnostic or atheist, or perhaps you just question God's existence from time to time. If you aren't an agonistic or atheist, you probably know someone who is an agnostic or an atheist. As a result, we need to discuss how we know God is real and actively involved in the world. In the next chapter, we will examine some basic yet persuasive reasons for believing in God.

4

Did God Create Us, or
Did We Create God?

Something very surprising happened at Harvard University in August 2021. An atheist was named the president of the university chaplains! Choosing an atheist to be in charge of Harvard's chaplains seems unusual, doesn't it? Greg Epstein, Harvard's humanist chaplain since 2005, was unanimously elected as the chief chaplain even though he is an atheist and the author of the bestselling book *Good Without God*. As the president of Harvard's chaplains, Epstein organizes the activities of more than 40 chaplains from Christian, Jewish, Hindu, Buddhist, and other religious faiths.[1] His selection as the president of Harvard's chaplains confused and disappointed some people who heard about it.[2] Epstein is obviously an intelligent, influential, and popular chaplain and writer. Should we join Epstein and many others in embracing atheism, or should we continue to believe that God exists?

I know from my own personal experience that many atheists are extremely intelligent, friendly, and likable. After I graduated from the University of Minnesota, I often returned to the campus in search of good spiritual conversations with people. I frequently spoke with atheists such as Yannis, Ferris, and their friends at a coffee shop. We enjoyed many interesting and enjoyable conversations about God, Jesus, and the meaning of life. Both men and their atheist friends were smart and kind. I appreciated their willingness to let me share my beliefs with them, and they appreciated my willingness to listen to them. Despite our very different beliefs, I sometimes miss the amicable relationships that I enjoyed with those atheists.

Many agnostics are also very friendly and likable people. For example, tennis player Rafael Nadal is not only an incredible athlete but also an agnostic[3] and a very kind and humble person. He has been my favorite tennis player for many years because he always gives his very best on the tennis court and doesn't let his stardom make him think that he is better than others. Despite being one of the best all-time tennis players, Nadal never boasts about his accomplishments. He is also always looking to improve as a tennis player. James Buddell writes the following about Nadal: "While coaches globally may be unable to replicate the characteristics of Nadal's game in their young charges, they can learn of the Spaniard's spirit and humility. He is an example of everything that is good about the sport—a superstar player, who continually looks to master his craft in spite of his achievements, untouched by his stardom."[4] Although Nadal says that he doesn't know if God exists or not, he is so easy to like and down-to-earth.

Whether or not we currently believe in God, most of us grew up believing in God. Since I was a child, I have always believed in God. I have always believed that God is real and loves everyone. While growing up in Minnesota, I saw many of the beautiful 10,000 lakes in my state and believed that God had created them. Looking at trees, birds, stars, the sun, and the moon convinced me that God is real. I enjoyed catching fish and turtles at our cabin, and I always knew that God had made them. Nature revealed God's existence clearly to me. I also enjoyed positive experiences of God's presence at church while I sang and prayed at worship services. I didn't even know until I was a teenager that countless Americans doubted or denied God's existence. God's existence seemed so obvious to me.

The reality of God's existence became even clearer to me as an adult. After studying the arguments for God's existence, I found most of them convincing. I also came to believe that nature and the universe have been revealing God's existence to people since the beginning of time (see Psalm 19:1–6 and Romans 1:20). Moreover, I gazed in wonder went I went to the incredibly beautiful waterfalls in Foz do Iguaçu, Brazil in 2009. The Iguaçu Falls located on the border of Brazil and Argentina consist of 275 individual falls over 1.7 miles of a spectacular view. Together, these falls make up the largest waterfall in the world. In describing the falls, one writer exclaimed, "The magnificent spectacle of these 275 individual drops has awed tourists, locals and indigenous inhabitants for centuries."[5] The Iguaçu Falls are taller than Niagara Falls and twice as wide.[6] I felt in awe of the falls' beauty, and I wondered how anyone could doubt God's existence after seeing them. Finally, my belief in God was strengthened by His answers to many specific prayers I prayed and by the births of my two children. Like many parents, I consider the birth of my children to be a miracle and a blessing from God.

Although the number of agnostics and atheists is growing in the United States, the vast majority of Americans still believe in God. Some people believe in God based on the arguments for His existence. Some believe in Him based on positive religious experiences at a church, a mosque, or a temple. Many people believe in God because they think they have seen miracles occurring in their lives or the lives of the people they know. Others believe in Him simply by faith. According to the most recent Gallup poll, 81% of Americans answered "yes" when they were asked the question "Do you believe in God?"[7] This poll makes it clear that most Americans still believe in God, but it also reveals that many Americans aren't convinced that God exists.

Many of you reading this book may wonder if God really exists or not. Is God our Creator, or is He is the product of our imagination? More than 15% of Americans are currently either agnostics who doubt that God exists or atheists who deny that God exists.

Do you believe in God? If you are an atheist, you believe that God is a human creation—a fairy tale who is no more real than Santa Claus and Rudolph the Red-Nosed Reindeer. You believe in the theory of evolution as the most accurate scientific explanation for humanity's origin. You believe that humans share a common ancestor with apes and chimpanzees and that this common ancestor lived millions of years ago. If you are an agnostic, you don't know whether or not God exists, and you might be familiar with some weaknesses of the theory of evolution.

In this chapter, I will briefly show why we should have serious doubts about the theory of evolution and why we should believe in God. If you believe in God, this chapter will strengthen your belief in Him. If you don't currently believe in God, this chapter will challenge you to consider the arguments for His existence.

What Is Evolution?

As many of us know, Charles Darwin (1809–1882) is known as the founder of the theory of evolution. He published his theory of evolution in his book *On the Origin of Species* (1859). Darwin argued that evolution occurs by natural selection as the result of our and animals' struggle for survival. He later wrote the book *The Descent of Man*, where he applied this theory of evolution to his belief in human evolution.

Evolution can be considered a historical science rather than an observational science. Science that can be done in a lab is similar to the chemistry experiments many of us did in our high school chemistry class. This type of science is observational science that can be observed, tested, and repeated. Observational science results in modern technology like cars, airplanes, computers, and vaccines. For example, a new type of airbag in cars can be tested many times to make sure that it functions properly before that type of airbag is installed in cars sold to consumers. Unlike observational science, evolution is a historical science that relies more on educated guesses and interesting speculation than on actual observation and testing. Evolution examines past events that can't be directly observed, tested, or repeated. No one alive today was there with a cell phone to take a video of one species evolving from a different species or to see people evolving from an apelike ancestor.

Evolution is a theory that is quite different from a scientific law, like the law of gravity. We can observe the force of gravity causes things to fall to earth. We can all see a ball drop from our hands when we let it go, but no one who is alive today or who was alive in the time of Charles Darwin was there to see humans evolve from an apelike ancestor. Instead of being based on observable past events, evolution is based on an atheistic worldview.[8] This worldview believes that God doesn't exist and that we as human beings evolved from an apelike ancestor.

What Is the Evidence that Atheists Offer for Evolution?

The recent discovery of a huge skull found in China has forced some scientists to rethink their understanding of human evolution. The extraordinary fossilized skull was wrapped up and hidden in a Chinese well almost ninety years ago. The massive skull has been named a new human species: *Homo longi* or "Dragon Man," by Chinese researchers. Some scientists believe that Dragon Man is not only a new human species but also more closely related than Neanderthals are to modern humans.[9] Other scientists disagree that the skull is a new human species. These scientists believe that the huge skull could instead belong to the mysterious Denisovan human lineage. The Denisovan is considered by many scientists to be an elusive human ancestor from Asia known mainly from DNA evidence and from only few remains.[10]

Is Dragon Man scientific proof that humans evolved from an apelike ancestor, or is he really just the cause of wild speculation by scientists? Dragon Man might simply be the skull of a very large and tall human. He doesn't provide any solid evidence for the theory that humans evolved from an apelike ancestor. Such evidence has always proven extremely difficult to find.

Like Dragon Man, other recent fossil findings fail to prove that humans descended from an apelike ancestor. For example, recent findings coming from the so-called Denisovans do not supply solid evidence for evolution. A jaw with two huge teeth was found in a cave at the edge of the Tibetan Plateau in China. Known as the Xiahe mandible, this jawbone was named after the county in China where it was discovered.[11] Does this one jawbone show that humans evolved from an apelike ancestor? Of course not! It's shocking that scientists consider this single jawbone as offering evidence for evolution even though the human body consists of over 200 bones. Similarly, a CNN article written in 2021 describes the current fossil evidence that exists for the Denisovans. The article states, "The only definitive fossil evidence that points to the existence of Denisovans—an enigmatic group of early humans first identified in 2010—comes from five bones from the Denisovan cave in the foothills of Siberia's

Altai mountains. The fragments are so tiny that they can all fit in the palm of one person's hand."[12] The evidence for the so-called Denisovans consists of only five tiny bones. That's not much evidence at all, is it?

One key fact about fossils used to support the theory of human descent from an apelike ancestor is that such fossils are very few in number. Scientists know that there are very few fossils that might link the fossil records between humans and an apelike ancestor. The fossil record, as discovered by paleontologists and anthropologists, doesn't provide any solid evidence that humans evolved from an apelike ancestor. Stephen J. Gould, an atheist and an American paleontologist who spent most of his career teaching at Harvard University, writes, "The extreme rarity of transitional forms in the fossil record persists as the trade secret of paleontology. The evolutionary trees that adorn our textbooks have data only at the tips and nodes of their branches; the rest is inference, however reasonable, not the evidence of fossils."[13] Agnostic Vincent Bugliosi points out that the number of discovered fossil remains of human ancestors is still "extremely scanty."[14] In fact, many people contend that there are no fossils showing a clear link between the fossil record of humans and of an apelike ancestor.

The evidence for human evolution isn't convincing.

The lack of evidence for human evolution from an apelike ancestor has resulted in well-known desperate attempts to provide evidence for it. Such desperate attempts include such hoaxes as Piltdown Man (1912) and Nebraska Man (1922). Piltdown Man consisted of the altered jawbone and some teeth of an orangutan deliberately combined with the cranium of a modern human. Nebraska Man was neither a human nor an ape. He was based on a single tooth belonging to a piglike animal called a peccary!

Java Man (1891–1892) consisted of only a tooth, a skullcap, and a thighbone. Since the skullcap has only three bones, Java Man consisted of only four bones in all. An adult human skeleton is made up of over 200 bones. However, Java Man is still called *Homo erectus* by scientists, and he is considered by many of them to be a "missing link" (transitional fossil) between an apelike ancestor and humans. Doesn't it seem ridiculous to base a human ancestor on only four bones? Many scientists who are atheists know that there is not nearly enough evidence to adequately support the theory that humans evolved from an apelike ancestor.

The quantity and the quality of evidence for evolution aren't impressive. The evidence for evolution isn't persuasive for me or for many of us reading this book. Nevertheless, we need to understand why there are so many atheists and agnostics in the USA and in the world.

Why Are Many People Atheists and Agnostics?

Why are so many people atheists and agnostics if there is so little scientific evidence for human evolution? Countless people all over the world choose to be atheists or agnostics for two main reasons: 1) *the presence of so much evil and suffering in the world* and 2) *the desire to live their lives how they want to live them.* Atheists and agnostics believe that the existence of evil and suffering in the world is inconsistent with the existence of an all-powerful benevolent God. If God is all-powerful and good, why doesn't He eliminate evil and suffering? Isn't He able to do so? Isn't He willing to do so? The apparent inconsistency between the existence of an omnipotent all-loving God and the existence of evil in the world is often called the problem of evil. Atheists and agnostics think that the presence of suffering in the world makes God's existence highly improbable. Many atheists also don't believe in God because they don't want to believe in Him. They don't want to have someone telling them how to live their lives. Many atheists don't want God to tell them how they should live.

The presence of evil in this world is undeniable. Who could honestly deny that evil is real and widespread? We live in a broken world filled with violence, suffering, pain, sadness, and death. Murders, kidnappings, robberies, and rapes occur daily. Many people die each day in car accidents. Every day, millions of people around the world are suffering from viruses, diseases, hunger, malnourishment, starvation, depression, and anxiety. Moreover, wars are currently bringing death and destruction to various countries.

It has been impossible not to wrestle with the problem of evil since the global COVID pandemic began. The global COVID-19 pandemic contributed to and caused the hospitalizations and deaths of millions of people throughout the USA and the world. Several million people in the world have officially died from COVID-19.[15] Millions of people lost their jobs because of the pandemic. A few months after the pandemic began, unemployment figures skyrocketed to record rates as historic job losses mounted in the USA.[16] In 2020, the pandemic caused the worst year for the U.S. economy since 1946.[17] The pandemic also led to soaring levels of anxiety, depression, and drug use. In June 2020, an astonishing 40% of adult Americans reported struggling with their mental health or with substance abuse.[18] U.S. drug overdose deaths rose 30% as they surged to record levels in 2020.[19]

COVID-19 dramatically altered our lives, making them very uncomfortable at times. We all experienced some fear of contracting the virus and various challenges related to being quarantined, being under some form of lockdown, and having to wear masks. Like millions of other people, many of us lost our jobs as a result of the pandemic or vaccine mandates related to the pandemic. Some of my American and Brazilian family members and friends contracted the virus. Four of my wife's and my friends in Brazil died from the virus. One of my mom's cousins died from the virus. Some people you know and love contracted the virus and suffered from it. You probably know at least one person who died from the virus. Perhaps you had the virus yourself. Why didn't God prevent the virus from infecting hundreds of millions of people and killing millions of people? Why does God allow so much suffering in this world?

Why Is There So Much Suffering in the World?

Although God allows suffering, He doesn't cause it. God permits suffering, but He doesn't directly cause suffering in this world and in our lives. God doesn't want us to suffer. Suffering is primarily caused by sinful human thoughts, desires, and actions. Our Creator has given us the ability to think, feel, and choose. Having this ability is such a great privilege. We should all be glad and grateful that we aren't robots or puppets! God doesn't force us to think, feel, and choose what is wrong or what displeases Him. God doesn't tempt us to do evil things (see James 1:13). He doesn't tempt or coerce us to do anything.

All human beings since the beginning of the human race have enjoyed the ability to think, feel, and choose. We all have the free will to choose how we want to live our lives. We get to choose our careers, our friends, our hobbies, and our habits, among numerous other choices. We have this ability because God loves us and wants us to be able to love Him and to have a genuine relationship with Him. Our free will makes it possible for us to choose to believe in God, love God, and live for Him. However, we can also choose to not believe in God, not love God, and not live for Him.

We try our best to live good lives, but none of us is perfect. We don't always think, feel, or do what pleases God. We have all told lies, struggled with selfishness, and been jealous of others. We can all be enticed by our own sinful thoughts and desires to make immoral choices and to engage in wrong behaviors (see Genesis 6:5; Matthew 15:18–20; Mark 7:20–23; James 1:14). These bad choices and wrong actions often cause human suffering. We are responsible for our own choices and the consequences of those choices. Humans—not God—are to blame for human suffering. We sometimes suffer from our own bad choices, and sometimes we suffer from the bad choices of our family members, friends, and even people we don't know. We even suffer from the consequences of the bad choices made by the first humans who ever existed on earth.

> **We as humans are to blame for human suffering.**

The first humans on earth were named Adam and Eve. Their story is found in Genesis 1 to 3, which are the opening chapters of the Old Testament.[20] They lived in a perfect, beautiful place called the Garden of Eden. It was more beautiful than any garden on earth we can imagine. Adam and Eve were created innocent and good by

God, and everything that God created was good. Despite living in a perfect environment, they disobeyed God. They chose to rebel against Him. As a result, Adam and Eve felt terrible. They felt an overwhelming sense of guilt, fear, and shame. In their desperation to avoid being punished by God, Adam and Eve foolishly tried to hide from Him. How could they have hidden from someone who is everywhere and knows everything? They tried to make excuses for their disobedience, and they played the blame game. Eve blamed the serpent that had tempted her to disobey God, and Adam blamed Eve for offering him fruit from the forbidden tree. Their disobedience disrupted the perfect fellowship that they had enjoyed with God and with each other. It eroded the trust in their relationships with God and with each other. Adam and Eve's lives would never be the same.

Besides feeling awful after disobeying God, Adam and Eve were immediately and justly punished by God for their rebellious behavior. They experienced spiritual death—their perfect fellowship with God was ripped apart, and they inherited a tendency to sin. Adam and Eve had been created good, but once they disobeyed God, their good nature was replaced by a sinful nature. Adam's easy and enjoyable work became difficult and stressful. Eve's punishment consisted partly of having pain in childbirth. Moreover, they were expelled from the Garden of Eden, and they would never be able to return to that perfect paradise.

Since Adam and Eve disobeyed God, all of us as their descendants have felt the ripple effects of their disobedience. Our jobs can frustrate us, be filled with seemingly insurmountable obstacles, and make us want to scream or rip our hair out. Women continue to suffer from painful labor that sometimes lasts up to 24 hours. Although labor is different for every woman, labor usually feels like extremely strong menstrual cramps that can take a woman's breath away and make a woman unable to talk. In addition, due to Adam and Eve's sin, from the moment of our birth, we all inherit a tendency to disobey God (see Psalm 51:5; Romans 5:12, 18–19).

My wife Rosy endured more than 19 hours of painful labor while giving birth to our daughter. She suffered from such a large vaginal tear that she almost needed a blood transfusion. A slow yet steady stream of blood was pouring out of her, and I thought for a moment that she might die. It was scary! Rosy's first experience of giving birth left her barely able to walk. She was very weak for a month even though she took liquid iron supplements to strengthen her body. My wife's stressful birth experience made us reluctant to try to have more kids for several years afterward. Moreover, it didn't seem fair that Rosy had to suffer so much just because Adam and Eve disobeyed God.

Why do we suffer for the sins of Adam and Eve? Our suffering for the disobedience of Adam and Eve doesn't seem fair, but it actually is fair. It's fair for us to suffer for their disobedience because we also would have disobeyed God. Tommy Mitchell writes, "If we are honest with ourselves, we will realize that Adam is a fair representative for all of us. If a perfect person in a perfect place decided to disobey God's rules, none of us would have done any better."[21] We want to think that we wouldn't have disobeyed God if we had lived in the Garden of Eden. This false idea is wishful thinking that comes from the pride in our hearts, not from an honest assessment of who we really are as human beings. We all try our best to be good persons, but we fail to always do the right thing. We all give in to temptation sometimes. Can any of us honestly say that we have never given in to the temptation to lie when we were faced with a difficult situation? Don't we all act selfishly at least some of the time? If it had been any of us in the Garden of Eden, the result would have been the same.[22] We all would have disobeyed God eventually.

What Good Can Come from Our Suffering?

God allows us to suffer because He cares so much about us. Our suffering can be good for us.

God permits us to suffer because our suffering produces spiritual blessings and hidden benefits, and suffering can promote greater good in our lives. Our suffering is never pointless or gratuitous. Suffering and trials build our character, and they can draw us closer to God. They foster patience, perseverance, hope, and character development (see Romans 5:3–5; James 1:2–4). God enables us to endure challenging trials that test our patience and perseverance. Instead of always rescuing us from trials, God sometimes gives us the opportunity to pass through them and learn from them. When we fail a test at school, get into a car accident, get sick, or experience any other unexpected trial in our lives, God is inviting us to talk to Him and spend more time with Him. Scripture tells us to call out to God when we are going through hard times; He wants to help us (see Psalm 50:15). God often uses difficult circumstances to draw us much closer to Him. In fact, many of us will not even consider seeking God or spending more time talking to Him unless something bad happens to us.

> **Our suffering produces spiritual blessings and hidden benefits, and it can promote greater good in our lives.**

Millions of people every year seek God and find peace with Him as the result of experiencing the death of a loved one, a divorce, or a job loss. God is always ready, willing, and able to turn our pain into our gain—into our emotional and spiritual benefit. Our pain and disappointments can be divine appointments to encounter God in a powerful way.

God is the perfect Father. He is more loving, kind, and wise than any human father could ever be. Like any good father, God knows that He must let us learn from our mistakes, our hard times, and our failures. If God never allowed us to suffer or to fail, we couldn't grow and learn from our suffering and failures. If we never failed, we could never learn from our failures! If we don't learn from our failures and mistakes, we will repeat them. Stressful life experiences such as failures can frustrate and confuse us, but such failures also teach us important lessons about ourselves. J. K. Rowling writes, "Failure taught me things about myself that I could have learned no other way."[23] Experiencing failures and hard times at least once in a while gives us the opportunity to experience spiritual and personal growth and to become emotionally stronger people. Setbacks can become comebacks if we consider them opportunities for learning and growth. Our trials can become triumphs if we allow God to work in our lives. God wants to bless us with a new perspective and a fresh start.

Millions of us actually benefited in some ways from the global COVD-19 pandemic. First of all, the pandemic resulted in many of us trying to put our priorities in the correct order. We had more time to seek God and to read the Bible and Christian books if we wanted to do so. Millions of us worked from home and had more opportunities to spend time with our families. The virus also served to remind us that our priorities should be God first, family and friends second, our job third, and sports and other hobbies and forms of entertainment fourth. We all struggle with putting our priorities in the right order, and the pandemic forced us to reevaluate how we are spending our time and money. Secondly, many of us came to know God and have a vibrant personal relationship with Him during the global pandemic. Being forced to think more often about the possibility of getting the virus and dying encouraged millions of us to think about where we would spend eternity if we died. I personally know over 50 people who came to know God in a personal relationship with Him during the pandemic. Isn't that awesome?

Besides using the pandemic to draw people to Himself, God sometimes uses a variety of diseases and natural disasters to help people see their need for Him. Many people come to know God while suffering from illnesses that force them to spend time at home, a nursing home, or a hospital. Some of us need to be confronted with the possibility of dying in order to seek God and make our peace with Him. For example, in 2009, my wife Rosy and I talked to an 87-year-old man named Clarion who was near death and clinging on to life when we visited him in a nursing home in Roseville, Minnesota. A few friends and relatives told us that Clarion was neither a Christian nor a spiritual person. However, after we prayed for Clarion and shared the good news about Jesus with him, he opened his eyes and said to God, "I love you! I believe!" He had made peace with God by trusting in Jesus.

Some people have come to know God as the result of natural disasters such as storms, tornadoes, earthquakes, floods, tsunamis, and hurricanes. Fearing death, many people cry out to God for help, and they begin to read the Bible because of the natural disasters happening around them. For example, Martin Luther (1483–1546), arguably the most influential person who lived in the 1500s, was nearly struck by lightning when he was caught outside in a storm in Germany. He vowed to become a monk during that thunderstorm in July 1505. He kept his vow. As a result of carefully studying the Bible, he trusted in Jesus. Luther would begin the Protestant Reformation in 1517, and he translated the Bible from Latin into German, making it accessible to laypeople. He emphasized that people make their peace with God by trusting in Jesus, not by doing good works. God has used Luther's belief in salvation by faith alone to make a huge positive difference for hundreds of millions of people during the last 500 years.[24]

The most well-known story of God using suffering to accomplish a greater good is the amazing story of Jesus of Nazareth. According to the New Testament, Jesus lived a perfect life, performed many remarkable miracles, died on the cross for our sins, and rose again. By taking upon himself all the billions of sins humans have ever committed, Jesus suffered on the cross more than any person in human history has ever suffered. Jesus's infinite suffering on the cross demonstrates that God loves us despite our many sins (see Romans 5:8; 1 John 4:10). If Jesus did indeed rise from the dead, the ultimate solution to the problem of evil is found in his death and resurrection.[25] According to Christians, Jesus's resurrection shows that God exists, and it makes it clear that Jesus has defeated sin, suffering, and death. Gary Habermas and Michael Licona argue persuasively, "If the tomb was empty because Jesus rose from the dead, then God exists and eternal life is both possible and available."[26]

Countless people who believe in Jesus and who have suffered have also experienced the hidden blessings of suffering. For example, the family of pregnant blogger Emily Mitchell felt blessed by God even though she passed away suddenly from a pulmonary embolism in December 2020.[27] Emily was a parenting blogger, and her Instagram account still has 174,000 followers.[28] Her husband and four kids experienced an outpouring of love and support after her sudden passing. Using a fundraiser, Emily's family also received more than $175,000 in donations and the opportunity to share her faith and their faith with thousands of people.[29] Her family wrote that they knew Emily was in a better place, and they shared the following Bible verse: "For God so loved the world that he gave his one and only Son, that whoever believes in him shall not perish but have eternal life" (John 3:16).[30] Emily's story and her faith have encouraged thousands of people, including me and my family.

Another encouraging story of a Christian enduring suffering is the story of Brayden Auten. Brayden was a healthy and active 8-year-old boy until his life changed in April 2019. Brayden came home from his elementary school in Wisconsin with a stomachache, diarrhea, and a yellow tint in his eyes. As his condition worsened, his eyes and skin turned yellow.[31] Doctors at a hospital named Children's Wisconsin in Milwaukee discovered that an unknown virus was attacking Brayden's liver. The mysterious virus threatened to kill him. The doctors diagnosed Brayden with liver failure, and they put him on the list to receive a liver transplant. Brayden's health deteriorated every day as he fought for his life and waited for a liver donor. No match could be found for a liver donor, and time was running out. Brayden's family kept praying for God to provide a matching liver donor.

God wasn't going to let Brayden die. Just a few weeks after Brayden was admitted into the hospital, God provided Brayden with a liver donor named Cami Loritz. Cami was a nurse at a transplant care unit of another hospital in Milwaukee. She signed up to be a living donor, and she underwent surgery to have a portion of her liver removed. Brayden received her liver donation the same day that doctors operated on Cami.[32] Since that day, Brayden and his family have considered Cami to be an answer to prayer and a member of their family.[33] The family soon took beautiful photos with Cami, including photos in which Brayden wore a T-shirt that said, "Saved by Jesus and an Organ Donor," and Cami wore a T-shirt that said, "Saved by Jesus to be an Organ Donor."[34] Brayden's faith in God clearly grew because God met his need for a liver donor by having Cami serve as that donor.

God often uses pain and suffering to help those who already believe in Him to grow in their faith. God is much more interested in our character than in our comfort. God often wants us to leave our comfort zone and follow Him wherever He leads us to go. God is always with those who truly believe in Him, and He has promised to never leave nor forsake believers (see Deuteronomy 31:6; Hebrews 13:5). According to the Bible, pain and suffering produce spiritual growth in those who believe in God and seek to live for Him (see Romans 5:3–4; 2 Corinthians 1:8–10; James 1:2–4). Pain and suffering result in character formation, perseverance, and hope for believers. The spiritual growth resulting from passing through hard times involves knowing God better and enjoying Him more. Frank Turek writes, "Comfort tends to stagnate us. But pain produces growth, which enhances our capacity to achieve our ultimate purpose—to know God and enjoy Him forever."[35]

Does Satan Cause Some of Our Suffering?

Are our human sins really responsible for all the suffering that exists in the world? What about evil spirits or demons like Satan? Do they contribute to some of our suffering?

In the most famous story of suffering in the Old Testament, a righteous man named Job suffers terribly because Satan causes him to suffer. The first two chapters of Job make it clear that the death of Job's children and animals and his physical ailments result from the activity of Satan in his life. Similarly, in some of the cases of demonic possession in the Gospels, demons cause their victims to experience physical suffering. The problems and pain of Job and of the demonic possessed are due to Satan and other demons, not due to human sin.

Whether or not you believe in Satan, he and other demons are still actively contributing to the suffering of people all over the world. In 2017, two MS-13 gang members in Houston kidnapped and murdered a 15-year-old girl as a satanic sacrifice. Miguel Alvarez-Flores and Diego Hernandez-Rivera killed the teen girl during a satanic ritual in which they offered her soul to Santa Muerte, the saint of death.[36] These gang members killed the girl because she had struck the gang's shrine to the satanic saint.[37] At their initial court hearing, one of the murderers shocked observers by smiling and waving at TV cameras. This grinning killer was considered to be diabolical (i.e., devilish) by other gang members.[38] The evil and bizarre behavior of the two killers can only adequately be explained by their being under demonic influence or possession.

In an even more gruesome murder, a self-described Satanist in California tortured and beheaded a cellmate in 2019. Jaime Osuna, who was already serving a life sentence for torturing and killing a woman, beheaded and dissected the body of his cellmate at Corcoran State Prison.[39] Osuna's wicked and grisly murder of his cellmate defies any other explanation besides his being under demonic influence or demonic possession. His heinous murder shows that Jesus was right when he said that Satan afflicts us with suffering by seeking "to kill and destroy" (see John 10:10).

Many other examples of murderers acting under satanic influence could be given. One final example should be sufficient to demonstrate that Satan is still active in the world today. In January 2021, Netflix released a four-part documentary miniseries about serial killer Richard Ramirez. It was called *Night Stalker: The Hunt for a Serial Killer*.[40] Ramirez terrorized neighborhoods in Los Angeles and San Francisco during the 1980s, killing 13 people, most of whom he had also sexually assaulted. Besides being a serial killer and serial rapist, Ramirez was a kidnapper, a child abuser, and a burglar. Ramirez left behind satanic symbols such as pentagrams at his gruesome crime scenes. During a court appearance in 1985, he also displayed a pentagram he had drawn on the palm of his left hand.[41] Just before displaying it, he shouted out, "Hail Satan!"[42] Ramirez claimed to be a devil worshipper, and his brutal crimes can only be adequately explained as being influenced by Satan.

What about Adolf Hitler and the Crusades?

What about all the suffering caused by Adolf Hitler, who seemed to be a Christian? Doesn't that suffering make God's existence seem unlikely? It's true that Adolf Hitler ordered the mass murder of 6 million Jews during the Holocaust. By the end of World War II, two-thirds of European Jews and more than one-third of all the Jews in the world had been murdered by Hitler.[43] He also ordered the mass murder of 5 million other people for racial, political, ideological, and behavioral reasons.[44] Moreover, Hitler made public statements in which he claimed to believe in God, and many people assumed that he was a Christian.

Was Hitler actually a Christian? No, he wasn't a Christian! Hitler actually hated Christianity, and he didn't believe in Jesus's deity or in Jesus's resurrection from the dead.[45] Hitler intended to destroy Christianity in Germany and to replace it with paganism. He established a National Reich Church, demanded that the Bible no longer be published or distributed in Germany, ordered that his racist book *Mein Kampf* ("My Struggle") take the place of the Bible in churches, and required that crosses in churches be removed and replaced by the Nazi swastika.[46] Seven hundred pastors who protested these changes were either murdered or disappeared into concentration camps. These protesting pastors were then replaced by Nazi "pastors" who sought to destroy Christianity.[47] Instead of being a Christian, Hitler was actually a pantheist. He often described God as an impersonal force, and he called nature eternal and all-powerful. He often used the word *nature* as a substitute for the word *God*.[48]

Have you ever heard of Dietrich Bonhoeffer? He was one of the German pastors who protested against the changes that Hitler and the Nazis were forcing upon churches and pastors. Bonhoeffer was arrested and taken to a concentration camp, and he was eventually hanged by the Nazis in a concentration camp. Bonhoeffer was a devout Christian pastor and author who wrote the classic book *The Cost of Discipleship*. I read his inspiring book years ago, and I encourage you to consider reading it. It's a great book!

What about the Crusades? Don't they show that Christians have been responsible for a lot of suffering in this world? Don't the Crusades provide proof against Christianity and theism? The Crusades were religious wars that were designed to retake the city of Jerusalem and other lands that were controlled by Muslims. The Crusades were provoked by the Muslim takeover of land that Christians had previously controlled for centuries. These religious wars did involve atrocities, rapes, and looting by people who claimed to be Christians. However, Jesus would never have ordered his followers to kill, rape, and steal from other people. In his most famous sermon, Jesus clearly states that he is opposed to killing and other acts of violence done in his name (see Matthew 5:39, 44). Jesus never formed his own army because he rejected the use of violence to kill innocent people (see Matthew 26:51–52; Luke 22:50–51; and John 18:10–11). Jesus commanded his followers to love and forgive people, not to seek vengeance and kill them (see Luke 6:27–35; 23:34)! Jesus also pointed out that many people who claim to know and follow him don't really know and follow him (see Matthew 7:21–23). Thus, many of the Crusaders weren't real followers of Jesus. In other words, many of the Crusaders weren't really Christians because they weren't living for Jesus.

The truth is that more murders in recent human history have been committed by people who call themselves atheists than by people who call themselves Christians. Mao Zedong of China, Joseph Stalin of the former Soviet Union, Pol Pot of Cambodia, and other communist leaders killed millions of people in the 20th century. These victims were murdered or starved to death. Mao Zedong was responsible for about 40 million deaths, and Stalin was responsible for about 20 million deaths.[49] Stephen Kotkin, a professor of history and international affairs at Princeton University, writes:

> Since 1917—in the Soviet Union, China, Mongolia, Eastern Europe, Indochina, Africa, Afghanistan and parts of Latin America—communism has claimed at least 65 million lives, according to the painstaking research of demog-

raphers... Though communism has killed huge numbers of people intentionally, even more of its victims have died from starvation as a result of its cruel projects of social engineering.[50]

Communism, also called Marxism, has been responsible for millions more deaths than any other religion in human history. R. J. Rummel, a former history professor, declares:

Of all religions, secular and otherwise, that of Marxism has been by far the bloodiest—bloodier than the Catholic Inquisition, the various Catholic crusades, and the Thirty Years War between Catholics and Protestants. In practice, Marxism has meant bloody terrorism, deadly purges, lethal prison camps and murderous forced labor, fatal deportations, man-made famines, extrajudicial executions and fraudulent show trials, outright mass murder and genocide.[51]

Mao Zedong, Joseph Stalin, and other communist leaders who killed millions of people were atheists and rational men. They weren't crazy or insane. They were men who realized that if God doesn't exist, we can do whatever we want. If God is just a product of human imagination, there are no rules or moral absolutes that we must follow. In the classic novel *The Karamazov Brothers*, the atheist Ivan says that if God doesn't exist, "everything is permitted."[52] Murder, rape, torture, robbery, kidnapping, and anything else we can think of are permissible if God doesn't really exist. If atheism is true, even mass murder and genocide are permissible.

Many Atheists Don't Want to Believe in God

We have seen that the presence of evil and suffering in the world doesn't make God's existence unlikely. God's existence is compatible with the presence of evil and suffering in the world. But atheists deny God's existence not only because of the presence of evil in the world but also because they don't want to believe in God. *Many atheists don't want to have someone telling them how they should live their lives.* They don't want to be held accountable to anyone for how they choose to live. Many atheists realize that there is not enough evidence to justify their beliefs, but they refuse to consider believing in God because they don't want to believe in Him. Countless atheists are committed to their antisupernatural bias even though this commitment defies common sense. Richard Lewontin, an atheist and a former professor of zoology and biology at Harvard University, writes:

> Our willingness to accept scientific claims that are against common sense is the key to an understanding of the real struggle between science and the supernatural. We take the side of science in spite of the patent absurdity of some of its constructs, in spite of its failure to fulfill many of its extravagant promises of health and life, in spite of the tolerance of the scientific community for unsubstantiated just-so stories, because we have a prior commitment to materialism. It is not that the methods and institutions of science somehow compel us to accept a material explanation of the phenomenal world but, on the contrary, that we are forced by our a priori adherence to material causes to create an apparatus of investigation and a set of concepts that produce material explanations, no matter how counterintuitive, no matter how mystifying to the uninitiated. Moreover that materialism is absolute for we cannot allow a divine foot in the door.[53]

Lewontin clearly states that he and many other atheists will not consider the possibility of God's existence because of their commitment to antisupernatural explanations for scientific claims. Like Richard Lewontin, other atheists who are committed to their bias against the supernatural won't consider the possibility of God's existence. Such atheists won't even consider the evidence for God's existence.

Why Do Most of Us Believe That God Exists?

We should all be grateful that many atheists aren't so closed-minded. Countless atheists and agnostics reading this book are wise and open-minded enough to at least consider the main arguments for His existence. Let's briefly discuss the main arguments for God's existence.

Moral Values Require a Law Giver: The Moral Argument

The most powerful argument for God's existence is the moral argument. The moral argument contends that absolute moral values exist because God exists. We know that absolute or objective moral values exist because everyone knows that killing, lying, stealing, committing adultery, and other immoral acts are wrong. Even atheist Greg Epstein of Harvard University admits that these objective moral values exist.[54] All of us also know that kindness, creativity, fairness, gratitude, self-control, and courage are virtues. Regardless of whether we are atheists or theists, we know that these things are virtues. Adherents of all religions know that these things are virtues.[55] We all know that certain things are objectively right and certain things are objectively wrong. Atheist Alex Rosenberg writes, "All cultures, and almost everyone in them, endorse most of the same core moral principles as binding on everyone."[56]

The main arguments for God's existence are powerful and persuasive.

All of us know that it's wrong to deprive another person of his or her rights as a human being. We know that we have dignity and rights as human beings. According to the Universal Declaration of Human

Rights (1948), we all have inherent dignity and the right to life, liberty, and protection from discrimination.[57] Therefore, it's wrong for an individual to do anything that would take away the rights of another person. There are never any heated debates in courtrooms about whether murder, rape, kidnapping, torture, and sexual slavery are right or wrong. Everyone knows that these actions are wrong because we have the right to life and liberty. Murder robs people of their life. Rape, kidnapping, torture, and sexual slavery rob people of their freedom. We all agree that these actions are wrong because they do not show the proper respect for the rights that all of us have as human beings.

Where do these objective moral values come from? Do they come from God, or are they merely the result of evolution? The moral argument correctly contends that our objective moral values and duties come from God. The moral argument can be stated this way:

1) If objective moral values and duties exist, God exists.
2) Objective moral values and duties exist.
3) Therefore, God exists.[58]

These objective or absolute moral values are the results of God giving all of us a conscience (see Romans 2:14–15). Having a conscience is part of our being made in God's image and likeness. As persons made in God's image, we are moral, rational, social, and emotional beings who can choose to do what is right or what is wrong.[59]

Evolutionists have admitted that the existence of objective moral values and duties presents a serious problem for the theory of evolution. Richard Dawkins, the world's most prominent atheist, admits that "it is pretty hard to defend absolutist morals on grounds other than religious ones."[60] Nevertheless, some atheists have tried to argue that our sense of right and wrong is the result of evolution by natural selection. These atheists have contended that cooperation is a major feature of evolution.[61] However, the reality is that competition for scarce resources and the struggle to survive are the hallmarks of evolution. Evolution by natural selection involves the survival of the fittest; it involves much more emphasis on competition than on cooperation. Atheists Martin Nowak and Roger Highfield write, "At its heart, natural selection undermines our ability to work together… Natural selection is after all about competition, dog-eat-dog and winner takes all."[62] In addition, science describes what occurs; it doesn't and can't prescribe what should occur. Moral values do tell us what we should do and how we should live. Therefore, theories from science such as evolution can't result in moral values and duties. Atheist Alex Rosenberg honestly admits, "Science has no way to bridge the gap between is and ought."[63]

Science can't tell us how we should live. Neither can evolution, which claims to be a scientific theory. If evolution is true, then we are all competing against one another for such scarce resources as food, water, shelter, and clothes. If life is really about "the survival of the fittest," we can kill one another, steal from one another, and lie to one another in our efforts to acquire whatever we need to live. If evolution is true, we can also commit adultery in our efforts to reproduce and have our genes survive into the next generation.

If God doesn't exist, anything would be acceptable for us to do. In other words, if atheism is really true, then anything goes. While referring to evolution's founder, Charles Darwin, atheist Alex Rosenberg exclaims, "If Darwinism is true, then anything goes!"[64] There would be no rules to tell us how we should live. There would be no crimes and no punishments. If atheism is true, we could all kill our neighbors, steal from them, and not worry about going to jail for doing it. We could steal from our employers, cheat on our tests, and rape any attractive person whom we meet. But if atheism is true, we would also live with perpetual chaos and constant fear. We couldn't sleep at night. If God doesn't exist, we wouldn't know if we were living our lives well or living them poorly.

It gets even worse if atheism is true. If God doesn't exist, we wouldn't even know why we were here on this earth. Without God's existence, our lives would lack value, purpose, and meaning.[65] We could only live for ourselves instead of living for God. Many of us would probably become depressed and contemplate suicide.[66]

The moral argument makes it clear that we as human beings are different from animals. We have a sense of right and wrong that apes, chimpanzees, and other animals completely lack. Are there any jails or prisons for animals? No, of course not. The idea of an ape or a chimp being held in jail for months or years by another ape or chimp is humorous and ridiculous, isn't it? Unlike humans, animals don't hold one another accountable for bad behavior. Why are there jails and prisons for humans but not for animals? In the animal world, there is no such thing as immoral behavior. It's completely acceptable for animals to harm and kill one another. Animals don't have a conscience, they don't have free will, and they don't think before they act. We freely choose to do what we know is right or what is wrong, and thus we are responsible for and held accountable for our actions. If we choose to kill, rob, rape, or kidnap someone, we deserve to go to prison as moral beings. In contrast to us as humans, animals are controlled by instinct; they react to things around them without thinking about their reactions. Moreover, we seek not only to survive but also to achieve success and to make a significant impact on the world. Animals care only about their struggle for survival; they don't care about success and significance. Lastly, we as humans seek meaning and purpose in life, and if we fail to find any meaning and purpose in life, we may become depressed and contemplate suicide. Unlike us, animals do not seek any meaning and purpose in their lives, and regardless of how difficult their lives become, they don't contemplate suicide. *We are so different from animals because we don't share a common ancestor with apes, chimpanzees, or any other type of animal.*

The moral argument for God's existence is powerful and persuasive for the vast majority of us. Objective moral values and duties exist, so God must exist. God is the Moral Lawgiver. But the moral argument is just one of several arguments for God's existence. Let's take a look now at a few of the other arguments.

The Universe Requires a Cause: The Cosmological Argument

A second major argument for God's existence is the cosmological argument. One version of the cosmological argument can be stated the following way:

1) Whatever begins to exist has a cause.
2) The universe began to exist.
3) Therefore, the universe has a cause.[67]

This argument says that every effect requires a cause, and it implies that the cause of the universe must be God. For me and other people who agree with this argument, creation requires a Creator. God is the Creator required by the existence of our awe-inspiring universe.

For almost 100 years, scientists have known that the universe began to exist at some point in the past. Have you ever heard of Edwin Hubble, the American astronomer? In 1929, Hubble discovered that the stars near the earth are not moving away from us, but the distant galaxies are moving away from us. He also discovered that the galaxies farther away from us are retreating at a faster rate than the nearer galaxies. His findings made it clear that the universe is expanding.[68] Because the universe is expanding, it can't be eternal. The universe must have had a beginning. Moreover, the second law of thermodynamics tells us that the universe is becoming less ordered. This law says that "there is a natural tendency of any isolated system to degenerate into a more disordered state."[69] This law means that the universe is wearing out. If the universe is wearing out, it must have had an extremely ordered beginning. Both the findings of astronomy and the second law of thermodynamics make it clear that the universe had a beginning, and this beginning was very ordered.

We know that the universe had a beginning, but who or what caused the universe to begin? Scientists who are agnostics and atheists have started to recognize that the universe having a beginning presents problems for their disbelief in God. Robert Jastrow, an agnostic[70] who was the founder and director of the NASA Goddard Institute for Space Studies, points out that the Bible's account of creation in Genesis 1 seems compatible with the findings of astronomy. Jastrow writes, "Now we see how the astronomical evidence leads to a biblical view of the origin of the world. All the details differ, but the essential element in the astronomical and biblical accounts of Genesis is the same; the chain of events leading to man commenced suddenly and sharply, at a definite moment in time, in a flash of light and energy."[71] Furthermore, Jastrow clearly states that supernatural forces seem to have been the cause of the universe's origin. Responding to an interviewer's question about the universe's origin, Jastrow states, "That there are what I or anyone would call supernatural forces at work is now, I think, a scientifically proven fact."[72] Wow! What a stunning statement by one of the most important astronomers of our time. Despite his agnostic views, Jastrow admits that the universe's beginning seems to indicate that a supernatural power such as God caused the universe to exist.

Does this cosmological argument really make sense or not? It does make sense because the universe is so enormous and amazing. The universe consists of 100 billion galaxies. Our own galaxy, the Milky Way, contains as many as 400 billion stars![73] Isn't that astounding? Our universe is an immense effect that requires a sufficient cause. The universe couldn't have simply come from nothing, and it couldn't have created itself.[74] Every effect requires a cause, and an enormous effect requires a sufficiently powerful cause. Our immense universe must have been caused by someone who is or something that is extremely powerful. Science journalist Fred Heeren correctly writes, "The idea that the entire universe came from nothing is irrational, not just to the Western mind, but to the human mind. Logic demands a cause for every effect. The universe is an effect that demands a very great cause."[75] The only great enough cause for the universe is an all-powerful God.

Things much smaller and less complex than the universe need to be made. Airplanes, cars, computers, homes, buildings, home appliances, and many other things of various sizes and complexity are made by humans. Has anyone ever seen an airplane, car, or any other man-made thing create itself? No! If smaller and less complex items such as these all need to be made by humans, the universe must have been created by God. The universe is simply too enormous and too complex to have been the result of Darwinian evolution or blind chance.

Some atheists contend that God Himself requires a cause or a creator. They like to ask this interesting question: Who created God?[76] This seems like a good question that is difficult to answer. But this question can be answered in an intellectually satisfying way. Because God is eternal, He doesn't need a cause or a creator. He never began to exist. God has always existed, and He will always exist. He is self-existent, timeless, and infinite. Logic tells us that God, as the cause of the universe, must be greater than the universe because a cause must be greater than its effect. God is an eternal, all-powerful, and supremely intelligent Being who is the Creator and the First

Cause. The universe being created by such an awesome God is the only adequate explanation for the universe's origin.

Design Requires a Designer: The Teleological Argument

We've seen that the cosmological argument and the moral argument provide logical and convincing reasons for believing in God's existence. Let's consider one final argument for God's existence: the argument from design. This final argument is often called the teleological argument.[77] The teleological argument implies that design requires a Designer. The Designer is a supremely intelligent Being who is able to design the universe with remarkable precision. This Designer is God, who has designed a finely tuned universe.

Scientists have discovered fine-tuning in the universe that makes life possible on earth. This discovery has led many theologians, scientists, and other people to seek an explanation for such cosmic fine-tuning. William Lane Craig offers the following teleological argument that takes cosmic fine-tuning into account:

1) The fine-tuning of the universe is the result of either physical necessity, chance, or design.
2) It is not the result of physical necessity or chance.
3) Therefore, it is due to design.[78]

What is some of the evidence for a fine-tuned universe? There is more evidence for a fine-tuned universe than we can possibly discuss in this book. According to Hugh Ross, a Canadian astrophysicist (a scientist who studies the physics of the universe), life on earth and anywhere else in the universe would be impossible without the fine-tuning of hundreds of the universe's features. Ross writes, "More than a hundred different parameters for the universe must have values falling within narrowly defined ranges for physical life of any conceivable kind to exist."[79] In his book *The Creator and the Cosmos*, Ross provides a list of 60 conditions as evidence for the fine-tuning of the universe.[80] His book also includes a list of an additional 150 features of the Milky Way galaxy, solar system, and earth that must be present for life to exist on earth.[81] The fine-tuning of the many laws of physics makes life on this planet possible. For example, the constants of the four fundamental forces—the gravitational force, the electromagnetic force, the strong nuclear force, and the weak nuclear force—make earth able to sustain life. If these constants for the fundamental forces were slightly altered, the earth couldn't be inhabited by living things. If any of the other hundreds of constants for various features of the universe were altered, there could be no life at all on this planet. There could be no human life on our planet without the fine-tuning of the universe. Such fine-tuning makes our planet the only planet in our solar system suitable for human life.

How did the universe become so fine-tuned that life is possible on earth? The fine-tuning of this planet couldn't have resulted from mere accident or chance. Fine-tuning requires a fine-tuner. Josh and Sean McDowell write:

> The laws of physics that govern the universe are exquisitely fine-tuned for the emergence and sustenance of human life. The slightest changes in any number of physical constants would make our universe inhospitable. The most compelling and reliable explanation for why the universe is so precisely fine-tuned is that an Intelligent Mind made it that way. Simply put, the fine-tuning of the universe points to a Fine-Tuner.[82]

Who is this amazing Fine-Tuner? The Fine-Tuner who has designed the universe and everything in it is God. The design of the universe means that God must exist, and He designed the universe.

Like the moral argument and the cosmological argument, the argument from design is compelling. The arguments for God have convinced many skeptics to reconsider their views about God. The moral argument shows that a moral lawgiver must exist. Moral laws require a Moral Lawgiver. The cosmological argument makes it clear that a First Cause must exist. Creation requires a Creator. Lastly, the argument from design—also called the teleological argument—

demonstrates that a Designer or Fine-Tuner must exist. *God is the Moral Lawgiver, the First Cause, and the Designer. He is the only Being who is pure enough, powerful enough, and wise enough to create the universe and everything in it.*

Many Leading Scientists Have Believed in God

Partly because the arguments for God are logical and persuasive, many men who were leading scientists during their lifetimes have strongly believed in God's existence. Please see the impressive list below of fifteen leading scientists who were theists. Among these brilliant scientists who believed in God were some of the most important and famous scientists in human history. These brilliant scientists are listed in the order of their birth. Except for Isaac Newton[83] and perhaps René Descartes,[84] all of the other scientists on this list were Christians. Have you heard of some of the famous scientists on this list?

Table 1. Leading Scientists Who Believed in God

Name of Scientist	Most Famous Accomplishment
Francis Bacon (1561–1626)	first person to define the scientific method
Galileo Galilei (1564–1642)	father of modern science
Johannes Kepler (1571–1630)	discoverer of the laws of planetary motion
René Descartes (1596–1650)	inventor of analytic geometry
Blaise Pascal (1623–1662)	founder of probability studies, hydrostatics
Isaac Newton (1642–1727)	discoverer of the universal law of gravitation
Gottfried Wilhelm Leibniz (1646–1716)	coinventor of calculus (with Newton)
Michael Faraday (1791–1867)	discoverer of electromagnetic induction
James Prescott Joule (1818–1889)	discoverer of the first law of thermodynamics
Gregor Mendel (1822–1884)	founder of the science of genetics
Louis Pasteur (1822–1895)	inventor of vaccines and pasteurization
Joseph Lister (1827–1912)	founder of antiseptic medicine and surgery

| William Mitchell Ramsay (1851–1939) | famous archeologist |
| William Foxwell Albright (1891–1971) | famous twentieth-century archeologist |

Do some leading scientists living today believe in God? Yes, some of them do believe in God! Many leading scientists living today are atheists, but some leading scientists are theists.

Dr. Francis Collins, the director of the National Institutes of Health from 2009 to 2021, used to be an atheist, but he has now believed in God for many years. Collins describes his intellectual journey from atheism to theism in his most popular book.[85] Collins writes that he is a Christian and that he has given his life to Jesus.[86] Collins has been one of the most prominent scientists in the United States for decades. Before working in his most recent position, he led the Human Genome Project from 1993 to 2008. Collins is so important that he was Dr. Anthony Fauci's boss for many years.[87] Dr. Fauci is the director of the National Institute of Allergy and Infectious Diseases, and he has been interviewed numerous times as one of the lead members of the White House's COVID-19 Task Force and Response Team. Besides affirming his belief in God, Dr. Collins asserts that atheism is the "least rational" of all possible worldviews.[88]

Atheism Isn't Rational, but Theism Is Rational

We have seen in this chapter that atheism is irrational. It is based more on speculation and wishful thinking than on solid evidence. Atheism is somewhat emotionally appealing because it seeks to answer why there is so much pain, suffering, and evil in the world. However, atheism is neither intellectually satisfying nor theologically sound. Many atheists don't want to believe in God simply because they don't want to be accountable to Him for how they live. They want to live in a way that makes them feel good and that they think will make them happy. The truth is that all of us would prefer to believe that God will not hold us accountable and would never punish us for not believing in Him or living for Him. In other words, atheism is much more likely to be motivated by wishful thinking than theism is to be motivated by it. Edward Feser writes, "Atheism is hardly less plausibly motivated by wishful thinking than theism is. For while it is hard to understand why someone would want to believe that he is in danger of everlasting hellfire, it is not at all hard to see why one would desperately want not to believe this."[89]

If you are someone who denies or doubts God's existence, please keep reading this book. If you disagree with anything that I have written in this book so far, please keep reading. You will be so glad that you continued reading this book. God loves you so much, and He wants you to know Him. He wants to fill your life with His joy, peace, and purpose. God will reward your continuing to seek Him and the answers to life's biggest questions. God will help you to discover the answers to your most important questions. Rick Warren writes, "You were made by God and for God… It is only in God that we discover our origin, our identity, our meaning, our purpose, our significance, and our destiny."[90]

While atheism isn't rational, belief in God is rational. Theism is based on solid arguments for God's existence. We have examined only three of several well-known arguments for God's existence. Each of these arguments presents logical reasons for believing in God. Other arguments for God's existence—such as the breathtaking beauty of the earth's mountains, trees, flowers, and waterfalls—are also persuasive for many of us. God has revealed His existence and His power to us through the universe and everything in it, including the beauty of nature (see Psalm 19:1–6; Romans 1:18–20).

Besides being intellectually satisfying, theism is emotionally appealing and theologically sound. We long to believe that our lives have value, purpose, and meaning, and they do. Our lives do have value because God has made us in His image. Our lives have purpose and meaning because God has made us to live for Him. Finally, theism makes sense to us because we have a yearning for immortality. We want to live forever, and we don't want to die. God has given each of us this yearning for immortality and an immortal soul.

Answers for Some of the Five Big Questions

Do you remember the five questions that I mentioned at the beginning of chapter 1? The five big questions are the following:

1) Who am I?
2) Where did I come from?
3) Why am I here?
4) What has gone wrong with the world?
5) What solution can solve the problem?

You now have solid answers to questions 1 to 3, and I will provide good answers for questions 4 and 5 later on in this book.

Here are our answers for questions 1 to 3:

1) You are a person with an immortal soul, a conscience, and the capacity to think, feel, and choose. As a result, you have physical, emotional, spiritual, social, and financial needs.
2) You were created by God in His image.
3) You are here on earth to live for God. As a result, you have a longing for God and for immortality.

In addition to wanting to live forever, we all want to know if what we believe is true or not. In the next chapter, we will discover how we can know if our most important beliefs are true or false. I will describe the five big tests and how we can use them to evaluate our most important beliefs. The next chapter is going to be a very important and interesting chapter for all of us!

Part 2

Discovering What Is True

5

How Can We Know if Our Beliefs Are True?

Wouldn't we all like to know if what we believe is true or false? How can we know if what we believe is true or false? This chapter will describe five big tests that we can use in order to determine if our main beliefs about ourselves, the world, and God are true or not. In other words, these tests help us to determine if our worldview is correct or incorrect. Let's get started!

In December 2019, a White woman in Iowa ran over and tried to kill two children with her car because of their race. Nicole Poole Franklin was driving her car in Des Moines, Iowa, when she saw a 12-year-old boy who is Black on the sidewalk walking with his sibling. She drove over the curb toward both children, striking the boy but not his sibling. Due to God protecting him, the boy suffered cuts and bruises but didn't need to go to the hospital. After striking the boy, Poole Franklin drove away from the scene and saw a 14-year-old girl whom she believed was Hispanic walking on the sidewalk. She drove over the curb, struck the girl, and drove away. The girl limped to a nearby school to ask for help, and she was taken to the hospital. The injured girl was treated at the hospital for serious injuries, including a concussion and bruises.[1]

Poole Franklin admitted to the police that her hit-and-runs were intentional and motivated by negative beliefs about Blacks and Hispanic people. Poole Franklin pled guilty to federal hate crime charges in April 2021, and she was sentenced in August 2021 in federal court to 25 years in prison for the 2019 attacks. Poole Franklin's federal sentence is running concurrently with a 25-year state sentence for attempted murder charges.[2]

Were you outraged by reading about Pool Franklin's attempts to kill two children? I'm infuriated when I read about what she did.

We should be angry at what she did. Poole Franklin's attempts to kill the two children were wrong for at least two reasons. First of all, we all know that trying to murder someone is wrong. Attempting to kill anyone of any gender, class, or race is wrong because people have inherent value as beings made in God's image. People also have the right to life, and no person can take the life of another human being. Secondly, we should all know that racism is wrong. Every person of every race on earth is a human being with intrinsic value and the right to life. We are God's special creation, and God abhors racism in any form. Racism causes division among people, hurts interpersonal relationships, leads to violent acts, and provides justification for genocide. The Holocaust, in which Adolf Hitler and the Nazis killed 6 million Jews in Europe from 1941 to 1945, dramatically illustrates how immoral and dangerous racism is to the human race.

The Five Big Tests

As I have already asserted, spiritual beliefs that are true are intellectually satisfying, emotionally appealing, and theologically sound. True beliefs satisfy the mind, heart, and soul. They give us sufficient reasons for trusting in God, who is our Creator and the Designer of the universe. True beliefs accurately describe us, our world, and God.

Since postmodernism began to dominate American culture,[3] most people have held key beliefs that are emotionally appealing but not intellectually satisfying or theologically sound. We have seen that relativism and atheism are excellent examples of beliefs that are emotionally appealing to many of us. Relativism and atheism appeal to so many of us because they are regarded as relevant worldviews in today's world of countless different beliefs and widespread suffering. Relativism and atheism seem tolerant and open-minded. Nevertheless, relativism can't be true because it's irrational and self-contradictory. Similarly, atheism must be considered false because it is based more on wishful thinking than on scientific evidence.

The following five big tests assume that God exists, but they don't assume that any particular form of theism is true or false. The tests don't assume that Christianity, Judaism, Islam, Hinduism,

Buddhism, or New Age beliefs are true or false. However, the tests do presuppose that God must be worthy of our worship and service. If God weren't worthy of our worship and service, would it be rational to worship Him and live for Him? Of course not! If God didn't deserve to be served and worshipped, we would all choose to live for ourselves instead of for Him.

> We can use five tests to help us determine if our beliefs about God, ourselves, and our world are true or false.

The five big tests are easy to understand, and each of them has two parts. Below are the five tests. Please read the descriptions of the tests carefully.

Test 1: The Human Reason Test

Would you want to believe something that doesn't accurately describe how the world really is? Of course not! We all want our worldview to be rational, and we want our beliefs to accurately describe how things really are in the world.

The human reason test helps us to determine if our main beliefs are intellectually satisfying. Our beliefs satisfy us intellectually if they are *rational*. The two parts of this test are the consistency test and the correspondence test. *The consistency test* states that in order for a belief to be true, it must contain no contradictions.[4] A true belief cannot contradict itself. *The correspondence test* points out that in order for a belief to be true, it must correspond to reality.[5] A true belief must describe the way things really are in the world, not how we wish things were in the world.

Test 2: The Contemporary Living Test

Would you want to believe something that is outdated and unlivable? Would you want someone to accuse you of being racist or sexist? Of course not! We all want our beliefs to be relevant and livable in the twenty-first century. We want our beliefs to enable us to enjoy many positive experiences with a variety of people and with

God. In addition, none of us wants to have beliefs that seem to promote racism, sexism, or classism. We know that our beliefs must adequately address racism, sexism, and classism in our contemporary world.

The contemporary living test helps us to determine if our beliefs are *relevant* in today's world. This test states that in order for our beliefs to be true, they must be emotionally appealing to us as human beings. True beliefs can be emotionally appealing if they promote respect for human beings. In other words, true beliefs can't promote immoral thinking and disrespectful behavior. For example, true beliefs can't promote racism, sexism, or classism, which are all morally wrong.

The two parts of the contemporary living test are the human dignity test and the livability test. *The human dignity test* states that in order for our beliefs to be true, they must show the proper respect for human beings. True beliefs will acknowledge that all humans should be treated with love, respect, and appreciation. True beliefs will also acknowledge that human beings are morally responsible beings who have free will; we aren't puppets or robots. We are also not highly developed animals who have evolved from an apelike ancestor. God's existence must be acknowledged in order for us to have an adequate moral foundation for treating people with love, respect, and appreciation. *The livability test* states that in order for our beliefs to be true, they must be practical and livable.[6] True beliefs don't just sound appealing to us; they can also be lived out in the real world. We have seen that relativism isn't livable, so it must not be true.

Test 3: The Divine Glory Test

Would you want to have beliefs about God that fail to show Him the proper respect that He deserves? Would you want to have beliefs about God that misrepresent or diminish Him? Of course not! We all want to have beliefs about God that accurately describe what He is like.

The divine glory test enables us to determine if our beliefs about God are theologically sound. Our beliefs about God are theologically sound if they provide us with sufficient reasons for serving and wor-shipping God. Our beliefs about God must demonstrate a *reverent* attitude toward Him, our amazing Creator.

The two parts of the divine glory test are the divine greatness test and the divine goodness test. *The divine greatness test* says that in order for our beliefs about God to be true, they must acknowl-edge that He is all-powerful, all-knowing, and present in all places at all times. God is omnipotent, omniscient, and omnipresent. *The divine goodness test* says that in order for our beliefs about God to be true, they must recognize that God is loving, holy, just, and merciful. God can't lie, steal, or be unfair. If our beliefs imply that God can be deceptive or dishonest, our beliefs about Him are false, and they need to be changed. God is completely perfect and always fair, not just somewhat holy and usually fair. He isn't like an indulgent grand-father or a genie in a bottle who always gives us whatever we want. God knows better than we do what is good for us. As a result, God sometimes permits us to go through difficult times so that we can grow spiritually by drawing closer to Him.

Test 4: The Honest Reporting Test

Would you want to have beliefs that are based on dishonest reporting? Would you want your most important beliefs to be based on made-up stories or fairy tales? Of course not! We all want our spiritual beliefs to be based on true stories, not fairy tales. The honest reporting test enables us to determine if our beliefs are based on hon-est accounts in the scriptures that we regard as sacred.

The two parts of the honest reporting test are the cover-up test and the simplicity test. *The cover-up test* says that whatever is embar-rassing to the person or group sharing the embarrassing information is very likely to be true.[7] A person won't share potentially embar-rassing information about himself or herself, a cherished group, or a cherished cause unless it is true. Why? Sharing such information could be counterproductive. For example, no one would be likely to admit to lying, stealing, betraying a friend, or acting like a coward unless these embarrassing actions were true. Would you make up a story that makes you or one of your friends look dishonest, disloyal, or treacherous? Of course not. *The simplicity test* says that a simple and short description of an event is more likely to be true than a complicated and long description of an event.[8] This test is reflected in the acronym KISS: "Keep It Short and Simple" or "Keep It Simple and Straightforward." Simple and short descriptions or explanations of events may not have a lot of details, but they are also unlikely to be embellished with fanciful details. Our beliefs are much more likely to be true if they are based on stories of events that are told in a simple and brief way. Moreover, the simplest explanation of an event is usually the right one. J. Warner Wallace correctly writes, "The truth will usually be straightforward."[9]

Test 5: The All-Inclusive Test

Would you want to have beliefs that are based on very little evidence? Would you want to have beliefs that can't be corroborated by any sources outside of the scripture(s) that they come from? Of course not! All of us would like our beliefs to be supported by evidence from such sources as secular historians and science.

The all-inclusive test makes it possible for us to determine whether or not our beliefs are based on solid evidence. Like the other four main tests above, the all-inclusive test has two parts: the comprehensiveness test and the corroboration test. *The comprehensiveness test* states that a belief is more likely to be true if it explains more of the evidence than another competing belief does.[10] For example, an explanation for the existence of evil in the world is probably true if it accounts for more of the evidence than another explanation does. *The corroboration test* says that a belief is more likely to be true if there is outside evidence to corroborate it.[11] For example, secular sources and scientific sources can provide outside evidence to corroborate a belief that we have about our sacred scripture(s) or a belief that we have about God. Secular historians and archeologists are especially great sources to consult to see if they can provide any additional evidence for our spiritual and religious beliefs.

How Do the Five Big Tests Work?

The five big tests enable us to determine if our spiritual beliefs are intellectually satisfying, emotionally appealing, and theologically sound. True beliefs must not only be emotionally appealing but also intellectually satisfying. In addition, our beliefs about God must not only be intellectually satisfying and emotionally appealing but also theologically sound. Our beliefs are true if they accurately describe us, our world, and God.

The five big tests also help us to determine if our spiritual beliefs are true by enabling us to minimize wishful thinking. Wishful thinking involves thinking and believing what we want to think and believe even though our beliefs are not logical and are not supported by solid evidence. We can all struggle with thinking and believing what we want to think and believe about ourselves, God, and our world. In other words, wishful thinking can strongly influence our worldview. It can cause us to misunderstand who we are, who God is, and what the world is like. The tests help us to determine if our key beliefs are logical, livable, and supported by good evidence. *The five big tests make it easier for us to resist the temptation to believe what is comfortable and convenient for us to believe.*

> **The five big tests enable us to determine if our spiritual beliefs are intellectually satisfying, emotionally appealing, and theologically sound.**

The vast majority of us want to believe that our current worldview is correct, but the five big tests encourage us to be wise and not assume that our current worldview is right. These tests encourage us to carefully examine our current worldview so that we can each determine whether our most important beliefs are true or false. It's wise and healthy to search for answers to life's biggest questions and to consider if our current answers need to be changed. *Self-examination is a beneficial and necessary activity for each and every one of us.*

Are All of the Five Big Tests Equally Important?

Yes, all five of the big tests are equally important. Why? If a belief is logical but not livable, it will probably fail to be taken seriously by the vast majority of people. All of us want our beliefs to be practical, livable, and beneficial to us. In addition, if a belief is livable but not based on solid evidence, it is unlikely to be true, and it is potentially harmful to us. Ideas have consequences, and holding certain false beliefs involves us being incorrect about the answers to life's most important questions. Lastly, if we have beliefs about God that are emotionally appealing but not theologically sound, our beliefs about Him will also be irrational and irreverent. All of us can hold beliefs that suffer from serious flaws if we don't carefully evaluate our beliefs and change them when necessary.

Does a Worldview Need to Pass All Five Big Tests?

Yes, in order for a worldview to be true, it needs to pass all of the five big tests. Different worldviews are provided by atheism, postmodernism, Christianity, Judaism, Islam, Hinduism, Buddhism, the New Age movement, and other religions. Almost all of these worldviews can be understood as passing at least one of the five tests, but not all of these worldviews pass all five of the tests. We'll discuss more various worldviews and religions in chapter 8.

At this point in our quest for truth, we need to know that atheism and postmodernism don't pass all five tests. The inadequacies of these two worldviews were already clear even before I introduced the tests in this chapter. We can choose to believe in atheism or in postmodernism, but we should know that these worldviews aren't true. Atheism fails to pass the human reason test, the divine glory test, and the all-inclusive test. Atheism passes the honest reporting test because some scientists have admitted that there are very few fossils that can be regarded as possible proof for human evolution from an apelike ancestor. Atheism could be considered to pass the contemporary living test if more atheists would admit that moral absolutes exist. Postmodernism (i.e., relativism) could be considered as passing the honest reporting test if relativists would admit that their view has some weaknesses. For example, relativists could say that at least some truth is absolute. It seems clear that relativism fails the other four tests because it isn't rational, and there isn't enough evidence for truth being relative.

If a worldview doesn't pass some of the five big tests, it won't satisfy us intellectually, emotionally, and spiritually. For example, atheism and relativism both fail to satisfy us intellectually and spiritually. Moreover, both atheism and relativism can only partially satisfy us emotionally. Atheism errs in assuming that miracles are impossible and in asserting that God doesn't exist. Relativism errs in contending that moral values are relative instead of absolute. Both atheism and relativism are clearly false worldviews that no one should believe in today's world. Both of these worldviews result from our tendency to believe what we want to believe.

> **If our worldview is true, it will pass all of the five big tests.**

Which Is the Easiest Test for a Worldview to Pass?

The easiest test for any worldview to pass is the honest reporting test. This test requires a worldview to tell the truth about the evidence in favor of it and to be willing to share information that could be considered embarrassing and counterproductive. Atheism passes this test even though it fails to pass the other four tests. For example, Charles Darwin, the founder of the theory of evolution, points out that there are very few fossils linking an apelike ancestor to humans.[12] Darwin also clearly states that it seems completely absurd that the human eye, with all of its many parts, could have been formed by natural selection.[13] Furthermore, Darwin admits that there are some significant differences between human beings and animals. He writes, "Obviously no animal would be capable of admiring such scenes as the heavens at night, a beautiful landscape, or refined music."[14] Similarly, Richard Dawkins, the world's most prominent atheist, admits that living things have the appearance of being designed. He writes, "Biology is the study of complicated things that give the appearance of having been designed for a purpose."[15] Even Dawkins acknowledges that living things seem to be designed.

Although the honest reporting test is the easiest test to pass, it's possible that a worldview could have embarrassing stories that present huge problems for that worldview. If any worldview has excessively embarrassing stories, these stories could invalidate their own worldview by making it fail one or more of the other four tests. For example, if any worldview has stories in which their God or gods do something sinful, those stories would prevent that worldview from passing the divine glory test. Moreover, not all worldviews pass the honest reporting test.

Which Are the Hardest Tests for a Worldview to Pass?

Two of the five big tests are difficult for any worldview to pass. The first test that is challenging for any worldview to pass is the contemporary living test. The second test that is hard for any worldview to pass is the divine glory test.

Let's discuss the contemporary living test first. Why is it so hard to pass? *In order to pass the contemporary living test, a worldview must be ahead of its time.* The sacred scriptures or most important books of worldviews were written centuries ago. Obviously, the world has changed in various significant ways since ancient times, since the Middle Ages, and even since the 1800s. For example, racism, sexism, and classism were accepted by a much higher percentage of people many years ago than they have been in the last several decades. We need to remember that Black men couldn't legally vote in the USA until 1870, and women earned the right to vote in the USA in 1920. Racism and sexism still affect life today, but these forms of prejudice and discrimination exerted much more influence on society decades ago than they do now.

The rampant nature of racism and sexism in earlier times can be clearly seen in the writings of Charles Darwin. In 1859, Charles Darwin wrote his most important book, *On the Origin of Species*. The subtitle of the book seems to imply that Darwin was a racist. The subtitle was *By Means of Natural Selection or the Preservation of Favored Races in the Struggle for Life*. Darwin's implied racist views become openly expressed racist views in his book *The Descent of Man*, which was first published in 1871. In *The Descent of Man*, Darwin describes some races as being "less civilized," "savage," and "savage races" that will be replaced by "civilized races."[16] Moreover, Darwin clearly states his belief that women are inferior to men. He claims that women are less courageous, creative, and intelligent than men.[17] Darwin's racist and sexist views are abhorrent to God and the vast majority of us as human beings. Because Darwin is the founder of the theory of evolution, the entire theory of evolution seems to condone racism and sexism. Therefore, Darwin's racist and sexist statements provide yet another good reason for rejecting the theory of evolution.[18] Without the theory of evolution supporting it, atheism itself becomes virtually impossible to believe in and defend.

The recent case of George Floyd illustrates how wrong racism is and how dangerous it can be to us and to society. Most people have heard about and read about the story of George Floyd. He was a Black man who was murdered in May 2020 by a White police officer in Minneapolis, Minnesota, while in police custody. Floyd was being placed under arrest after a store clerk called 911 to report that Floyd used a counterfeit bill to buy cigarettes.[19] After arriving at the scene, officer Derek Chauvin knelt on Floyd's neck and back for several minutes. As he was dying, Floyd was heard saying, "I can't breathe" more than 20 times.[20]

He was begging to be allowed to breathe. Floyd died due to a lack of oxygen to his brain from being pinned to the pavement with a knee on his neck.[21] Chauvin was found guilty of all three charges against him, including second-degree unintentional murder. He was sentenced to 22.5 years in jail.[22]

The bystander video of Floyd's final minutes of life sparked massive protests and chaotic violence in various cities throughout the United States. The unrest spread to some 140 cities in at least 21 states and in the District of Columbia. Although some of the protests were peaceful demonstrations, many of them turned violent.

Riots involving looting, arson, and vandalism resulted in significant property damage. The estimated cost of the riots sparked by Floyd's death was between $1 billion to $2 billion for insurance companies.[23] Furthermore, at least 6 people were killed in the riots,[24] and more than 10,000 protesters were arrested.[25]

The contemporary living test emphasizes that racism is wrong. Some worldviews today don't clearly reject racism. As a result, these worldviews feature incorrect and immoral beliefs which none of us should embrace.

Like the contemporary living test, the divine glory test is difficult for any worldview to pass. Why is it hard to pass the divine glory test? First of all, every person who believes in God has at least some tendency to create God in his or her own image. God is certainly real and relevant to our lives today, but we all tend to think of God as being more similar to us than He actually is to us. For example, some of us want to believe that God engages in deceptive behavior because we all tell lies occasionally. Many of us want to believe that God can lose His temper because we lose our temper once in a while. Some of us want to believe that God can gossip, steal, and have lustful thoughts because we gossip, steal, and have lustful thoughts. Secondly, many of us want to believe that we are more like God than we really are as human beings. We want to believe that we can have superhuman abilities and that we can be like the superheroes we loved as kids. Who doesn't want to fly like Superman, swing through the air like Spiderman, and fight like Captain America? Wouldn't it be nice to be able to fly around instead of having to drive our car wherever we need to go? That would be awesome! It would be cheap, convenient, and fast! We all want to be like God and our favorite superheroes. Desiring to have the same powers and knowledge as God is part of our human nature.

Which Worldview Is the Most Testable Worldview?

The most testable worldview is the Christian worldview. It's easier to determine if the Christian worldview is true or false than it is to determine if the Jewish, Muslim, Hindu, Buddhist, New Age, atheist, and postmodern worldviews are true or false. It's more challenging to determine if non-Christian worldviews are true or not.

Why is the Christian worldview the most testable worldview? There are at least three reasons. First of all, more has been written about the Bible than about any other book in the history of humankind. Secondly, more has been written about Jesus than about any other person in the history of the human race. Finally, the truth of Christianity depends on the death, burial, and resurrection of Jesus. The apostle Paul, who wrote more books of the Bible than any other person, points out that if Jesus was not raised from the dead, Christianity is false (see 1 Corinthians 15:14, 17). On the other hand, Paul makes it clear that if Jesus died, was buried, and rose again from the dead, then Christianity is true (see 1 Corinthians 15:1–8, 20–28, 42–58). Christianity encourages everyone to investigate its claims, especially its claim about Jesus's resurrection from the dead. Craig Hazen writes, "If Jesus did not come back from the dead after being executed by a Roman crucifixion team in first-century Jerusalem, then, according to the apostle Paul, Christianity is simply not true. It openly invites people to investigate its claims objectively."[26]

Let's examine the Christian worldview first because it's the most testable worldview. We'll examine the main claims of the Christian worldview in the next two chapters. After determining whether or not the Christian worldview is true, we'll examine the other most widely held worldviews. Let's continue our exciting quest for truth!

6

Can We Trust the Story of
Jesus in the Gospels?

According to Christians, the story of Jesus is the greatest story ever told. It's found in the Gospels, which are the first four books of the New Testament. As reported in the Gospels, God becomes a man in the person of Jesus of Nazareth. Jesus is miraculously born of a virgin named Mary about the year 5 or 6 BC. Mary is a righteous Jewish woman who eventually has more children with her husband, Joseph. Jesus becomes a carpenter until God calls him to begin his three-year public ministry as an itinerant Jewish preacher and prophet. For over three years, Jesus announces the arrival of God's kingdom, teaches about God's kingdom, and performs extraordinary miracles. His remarkable miracles include such things as casting demons out of people, opening the eyes of the blind, healing lepers, walking on water, calming a storm, and raising dead people back to life. Many people follow Jesus because of his astonishing miracles and powerful teachings. As a result, the Jewish leaders begin to see Jesus as a significant threat to their power and influence. After claiming to be divine and Israel's promised Messiah ("the Christ"), he is accused of blasphemy by the Jewish leaders. In about the year AD 33, Jesus is crucified by the Romans at the request of the Jewish leaders and some other Jewish people. He is crucified with two thieves, and his death is agonizing. However, after dying and being buried in a rich man's tomb, something jaw-dropping occurs. Jesus miraculously rises from the dead!

The risen Jesus then appears in his glorified body on various occasions and in several different places to his disciples and many of his other followers. He instructs his disciples and followers to tell everyone about his teachings, his life, his death, and his resurrection.

Can we trust the amazing story of Jesus found in the Gospels of the New Testament? Or is this story just a fairy tale that was fabricated by his disciples decades after his death? We all have to admit that the biblical story of Jesus is full of astounding claims. To many of us, the biblical story of Jesus seems too good to be true. But is the biblical story of Jesus reported in the Gospels true, or is it false? We'll see that there are convincing reasons for considering the story to be true.

The Gospels Are Historically Reliable Sources

Although their claims about Jesus seem very difficult to believe, the four Gospels themselves are historically reliable sources. How do we know that they are historically reliable? We know that they are historically reliable for at least five reasons:

1) Secular and Jewish historians tell the same basic story about Jesus that the Gospels tell about him.
2) Luke, the author of one of the four Gospels, was an excellent historian.
3) The authors of the Gospels provide eyewitness testimony about Jesus.
4) The Gospels are ancient biographies of Jesus's life.
5) The Gospels pass all of the five big tests that can be used to determine if they are trustworthy or untrustworthy.

Secular, Jewish, and Christian Sources Tell the Same Basic Story about Jesus

Secular, Jewish, and Christian sources tell the same basic story about Jesus. They all agree about when he lived and where he lived.

> **The Gospels are historically reliable sources that tell the truth about what Jesus said and did.**

They agree that he had a reputation of being a miracle worker. They also agree that Jesus was worshipped as being divine. Finally, some of these different sources mention that Jesus died by crucifixion.

According to the Roman historian Tacitus (c. AD 56–c. 118), Jesus lived in Judea during the reign of Tiberius, the Roman emperor from AD 14 to 37. Writing around AD 115–117, Tacitus states that Jesus was executed by the order of Pontius Pilate, who ruled as the governor of Judea from AD 26 to 36. Tacitus also writes that a "pernicious superstition" about Jesus spread from Judea to Rome after Jesus died (*Annals* 15.44). This so-called superstition was most likely the Christian belief that Jesus rose from the dead.[1]

One of Tacitus's friends was Pliny the Younger (c. AD 61–113). Pliny was the Roman governor of a region in northwest Turkey. He mentions Jesus in a letter that he wrote to Emperor Trajan in about the year AD 112. Pliny was seeking advice from Trajan about how to deal with the Christians living in his region. In his letter, Pliny points out that Christians get together on a fixed day before daylight to worship Jesus as a god—as divine (*Epistles* 10.96–97). Pliny is clearly referring to the Christian tradition of worshipping on Sundays. Early Christians began to worship Jesus on Sundays because they believed that he rose from the dead.

Besides Tacitus and Pliny, one ancient Jewish source also clearly mentions key facts about Jesus. This famous Jewish work that refers to Jesus is *Antiquities of the Jews*, which was written by the Jewish historian Josephus about the year AD 93–94. Josephus mentions Jesus twice. Describing Jesus sixty years after he died, Josephus (AD 37–c. 100) says that Jesus had a reputation as a miracle worker, was crucified by the order of Pilate, and continued to have many followers after his death (*Antiquities of the Jews* 18.63–64).[2] Josephus also describes how Jesus's brother James was condemned to death by stoning, and he writes that Jesus was called Christ (*Antiquities of the Jews* 20.200). Jesus's followers called him Christ because they regarded him as the Messiah, the promised One predicted by the Old Testament prophets.

Tacitus, Pliny the Younger, and Josephus were just three of many non-Christian ancient writers whose works mention key details about Jesus. These non-Christian works refer to such important details as Jesus's reputation of being a miracle worker, his crucifixion under Pontius Pilate, and his being worshipped as divine by early

Christians. Gary Habermas summarizes the ancient non-Christian sources that mention Jesus:

> At least seventeen non-Christian writings record more than fifty details concerning the life, teachings, death, and resurrection of Jesus, plus details concerning the earliest church. Most frequently reported is Jesus' death, mentioned by twelve sources. Dated approximately 20 to 150 years after Jesus' death, these secular sources are quite early by the standards of ancient historiography.[3]

Luke, the Author of One of the Gospels, Was an Excellent Historian

The second reason we can trust the Gospels as historically reliable sources is that one of them was written by an excellent historian. Luke was the medical doctor and traveling companion of the apostle Paul, who was the most important early Christian. He wrote the Gospel of Luke about three decades after Jesus's public ministry, probably sometime between AD 58 and 65. Luke honestly admits in the introduction to his Gospel that he was not an eyewitness to Jesus's ministry, but he claims that his account is based on eyewitness testimony. He has done careful research drawing on many eyewitness accounts from various people who personally knew Jesus (see Luke 1:1–4). Commenting on Luke's introduction, Andreas Köstenberger writes, "Luke is not only an evangelist and theologian; he is also a careful historian."[4] Luke shows no interest in inventing stories about Jesus that didn't actually occur. Luke wants his readers to know the truth about Jesus so that they believe in him and follow him. After quoting Luke's introduction (1:1–4), Köstenberger states, "Luke provides an account of a careful historian motivated by a desire to present an accurate narrative of the events surrounding Jesus' birth, life, death, and resurrection in order to strengthen his readers' faith."[5]

Luke not only claims to be a careful historian, but he also shows himself to be a careful historian. Luke wrote a sequel to his Gospel called Acts, most likely between AD 60 to 65. In the book of Acts, Luke describes the early Christian movement. His description of the early Christian movement includes many people, cities, customs, and circumstances. The many facts in the book of Acts provide us with the opportunity to evaluate Luke as a historian. Luke demonstrates impressive accuracy in his careful reporting of historical information in Acts. Luke is so accurate that he records 84 facts in Acts 13–28 that have been confirmed by historical research and by archeology.[6] Historian A. N. Sherwin-White describes Luke's historical accuracy in Acts by saying, "For Acts the confirmation of historicity is overwhelming... [A]ny attempt to reject its basic historicity even in matters of detail must now appear absurd."[7] Moreover, Sir William Mitchell Ramsay, one of the greatest archeologists who has ever lived, regarded Luke as a great historian. Ramsay had initially doubted the reliability of Acts and the rest of the New Testament until his extensive archaeological and historical studies convinced him of their historical accuracy. Ramsay writes, "Luke's history is unsurpassed in respect of its trustworthiness."[8] Ramsay also asserts, "Luke is a historian of the first rank... This author should be placed along with the very greatest of historians."[9]

Although Luke has been proved to be historically accurate, some scholars today continue to doubt his trustworthiness. These doubts have arisen because Luke reports a census in his Gospel that they regard as being inaccurately reported. Luke seems to state that a census of the entire Roman Empire took place in the year that Jesus was born (see Luke 2:1–3). Jesus was probably born in 6 or 5 BC. However, an empire-wide census of Caesar Augustus took place in 7 or 8 BC and in AD 6. This difference in dating isn't an issue for Luke's accuracy as a historian. The earlier census may have taken several years to complete because it was massive, and Luke is clearly aware of the more famous census of AD 6 (see Acts 5:37). Commenting on the census that Luke reports in his Gospel, Norm Geisler writes, "Luke has proven himself an amazingly reliable historian... There is no reason to doubt him here."[10]

Like Norm Geisler, many scholars today continue to regard Luke as an excellent historian. Luke didn't make up stories about

Jesus or about the early Christians. Luke's goal was to provide accurate accounts of Jesus and of his followers. Luke sought to be an excellent historian, and he succeeded in achieving that goal. Readers today can still trust what Luke wrote. Craig Keener states, "Far from writing with the creative freedom of a novelist, Luke writes his work based on historical information available to him… We should therefore approach Luke's historical work with great confidence."[11]

What are the implications of Luke being an excellent historian? There are two main implications: 1) Because Luke was an excellent historian, we know that the story of Jesus that he reports in the Gospel of Luke must be accurately reported. 2) Since Luke's Gospel reports the same basic story of Matthew and Mark, all three of these Gospels must accurately report the story of Jesus. Norm Geiser and Frank Turek write, "Since Luke is telling the truth, then so are Mark and Matthew because their Gospels tell the same basic story. This is devastating to skeptics, but the logic is inescapable."[12]

The Authors of the Gospels Provide Eyewitness Testimony about Jesus

How was Luke able to be so accurate as a historian? He was able to be so accurate by basing his Gospel and the sequel to his Gospel on eyewitness testimony. The Gospel of Luke is based primarily on the eyewitness testimony of Jesus's twelve disciples. Jesus's twelve disciples spent every day with Jesus for more than three years. They lived with Jesus, talked with Jesus, heard him teach, and watched him perform miracles. The most prominent and outspoken of Jesus's twelve disciples was Peter. As the leader and spokesperson of the Twelve, Peter claims to be an eyewitness to Jesus's ministry, death, and resurrection. Peter's claims to be an eyewitness are recorded repeatedly by Luke and by Peter himself (see Acts 2:32; 3:15; 4:18–20; 5:30–32; 10:39–40; 1 Peter 5:1; 2 Peter 1:16).

It's possible that Luke knew Jesus's disciples Peter and John and other prominent early Christians such as Jesus's mother Mary and Jesus's brother James. Luke was Paul's medical doctor and traveling companion, and Paul clearly knew Jesus's disciples.[13] Whether or not

Luke personally knew all the most prominent early Christians, he did know Paul, whom Luke seems to have stayed with for up to two years. Staying with Paul for such a long time would have given Luke plenty of time to speak with members of the Jesus movement from Judea who had been around since the movement's beginning (see Acts 24:27).[14]

Like the Gospel of Luke, the Gospel of Mark is also based on eyewitness testimony of Jesus's ministry, death, and resurrection. Early Christian leaders known as the Church Fathers state that Mark wrote his Gospel based on the teaching and preaching of Peter.[15] Mark's basing his Gospel on Peter's teaching and preaching makes sense because Peter calls Mark his spiritual "son," and Mark spent some time with Peter when Peter was in Rome (see 1 Peter 5:13). Mark, who was sometimes called "John Mark," was the cousin of Barnabas, Paul's fellow missionary (see Colossians 4:10–11). Mark traveled with Paul and Barnabas on a missionary trip as their helper (see Acts 12:25; 13:4–5). Mark was a coworker of both Peter and Paul, and he was well-known among the earliest Christians (see Acts 12:1–19).[16] Early Christians sometimes gathered at the house of Mark's mother, whose name was Mary. Because he was so well-connected to the early Christian movement, Mark was able to write his Gospel based on eyewitness testimony.

The Gospels of Matthew and John are not only based on eyewitness testimony, but they are also written by eyewitnesses who personally knew Jesus. Matthew and John were two of the twelve disciples of Jesus. Before they followed Jesus, Matthew was a tax collector, and John was a fisherman. Matthew and John were eyewitnesses of Jesus's ministry, death, and resurrection. Matthew was also called Levi,[17] and he writes his Gospel in order to show that Jesus is the promised Messiah of the Old Testament. John claims to be an eyewitness of Jesus's ministry, death, and life. John makes this important claim several times in his Gospel (see John 1:14; 19:33–35; 20:24–30; see also 1 John 1:1–2).

Why should we even consider the Gospel writers' claim to provide eyewitness testimony about Jesus? We have good reasons to believe that the traditional authors of the four Gospels—Matthew, Mark, Luke, and John—did indeed write the Gospels named after them. External evidence from the early Church Fathers and internal evidence from each of the Gospels themselves makes this fact clear. For example, Irenaeus (c. AD 130–202) writes that Matthew, Mark, Luke, and John wrote the Gospels named after them.[18] Irenaeus's testimony about the authors of the four Gospels is very significant because he was a disciple of Polycarp (AD 69–155), who was himself a disciple of John. Similarly, Tertullian (c. AD 155–220) writes that Matthew, Mark, Luke, and John wrote the Gospels named after them.[19]

The internal evidence for the traditional authorship of the Gospels is also persuasive. Such internal evidence exists for all four Gospels. For example, one reason we believe that Matthew wrote the Gospel named after him is that it contains various unique references to financial transactions that are not found in the other Gospels (see Matthew 17:24–27; 18:23–35; 20:1–16; 26:15; 27:3–10; 28:11–15). As a former tax collector, Matthew's high interest in money and finances shows up in his Gospel. Another example of internal evidence relates to the author of John. One reason we believe that John wrote the fourth Gospel is that the author of that Gospel describes himself as being closely associated with Peter (see John 20:2–10; 21:1–14, 20–23). In the early Christian movement, the only person described as being closely associated with Peter is John (see Acts 3:1–4:23).[20] Moreover, the author of the fourth Gospel was a fisherman (see John 21:1–7), and we know that John was a fisherman (see Mark 1:16–20; Luke 5:3–10).

Much more internal evidence for the traditional authorship of the Gospels has already been explained in recent books and articles. Please refer to them if you want more evidence.[21] Because the traditional authors wrote the Gospels, we should be willing to consider their claim to provide eyewitness testimony about Jesus.

Besides claiming to provide eyewitness testimony, the four Gospels make it clear that they actually do provide such testimony. The way that the Gospels handle parallel accounts demonstrates that they are eyewitness accounts, not fabricated stories. The four Gospels feature parallel accounts of some of the same events in Jesus's life. These parallel accounts often contain the same basic story but differ in their details. We should expect parallel accounts of Jesus's miracles, death, and resurrection to differ in their details. Why would they have different details? Because if they didn't have different details, we would know that the four Gospel writers had talked to one another in an effort to make sure that they told the same exact story. Such collusion would have made their parallel accounts of Jesus's miracles and death both deceptive and unreliable. The difference in the details of parallel accounts in the Gospels shows that the four Gospel writers were not guilty of collusion. For example, the small differences in the Gospels' reporting of Jesus's resurrection also indicate that the Gospel writers were seeking to tell the truth. Louis Markos writes:

> Modern skeptics think they can dismiss the historical reliability of the resurrection because the various testimonies recorded in the four Gospels show slight discrepancies. In making this argument, the skeptics show that they know little of how a trial works. Were the testimonies in the Gospels carbon copies of one another, an impartial judge would count that evidence for collusion and throw out the testimony. If, on the other hand, the testimonies varied widely on important points, he would dismiss them as unreliable. What an experienced and discerning judge looks for are testimonies that complement, rather than copy, one another, agreeing on the major points, but showing the kinds of variations one would expect from witnesses who have different personalities, memories, and points of view. And that is exactly what we find in the Gospels.[22]

An illustration can help us understand how eyewitness testimony works. Have you ever witnessed a crime or a car accident? Let's imagine that there were four witnesses to a bank robbery. Two of those witnesses were inside the bank at the time of the robbery, and two of them were outside the bank walking on the sidewalk across the street. Would the four witnesses agree on all the details of the robbery? Of course not! They would tell the police the same basic story about the robbery, but each of their stories would contain some different details. The eyewitnesses would probably disagree on such things as the exact height of the robber(s) and the exact description of the getaway car. The four eyewitnesses would agree on major points and disagree on minor points. The minor differences between the eyewitness accounts would show that they were honestly reporting what they saw happening.

The differences between the four Gospels' parallel accounts of the same events often provide what scholars call "multiple attestation" of events. For example, stories that are found both in the Gospel of John and in any of the other three Gospels are multiply attested. Why? Because John's Gospel is different enough from the other three Gospels, John must *not* have used them as sources to write his Gospel. In other words, John wrote his Gospel independently of the other three Gospels, which are often called the Synoptic Gospels.[23] Some stories about Jesus that are found in all the Synoptic Gospels and in John include the following: 1) the cleansing of the temple; 2) the feeding of the 5,000; 3) the triumphal entry into Jerusalem; 4) the betrayal by Judas Iscariot; 5) Peter's denial of knowing Jesus; 6) the trial before Pontius Pilate; 7) the crucifixion of Jesus as the King of the Jews; 8) the death and burial of Jesus; and 9) the resurrection of Jesus. All of these stories are very likely to be true events based on eyewitness testimony because they are multiply attested and independently reported in the Synoptic Gospels and in John's Gospel.

In addition to having multiply attested stories, the Gospels were written early enough to contain eyewitness testimony. The Gospels were all written within 30 to 60 years of Jesus's life on earth. The Synoptic Gospels were all likely written before AD 66, and the Gospel of John was probably written between AD 80 and 90. None of the Synoptic Gospels mention the destruction of the temple in Jerusalem, which Jesus had predicted[24] and which occurred in AD 70. The temple was destroyed by the Romans during the Great Jewish War (AD 66–73). If the Synoptic Gospels had been written during or after this war, they would certainly have mentioned the destruction of the temple. Moreover, if the book of Acts had been written after the temple's destruction, Acts would have also mentioned this crucial fact. The temple was the most important feature of Judaism during the first century AD. Moreover, the temple was the center of Jews' religious, political, and economic life for over a thousand years. David Fiensy writes:

> The temple and the land gave Judaism its center and focus… Judaism was still a religion of sacrifice and offering, holy place and priest. Each day bloody offerings of animals were made in the temple. People made regular pilgrimages from various parts of Palestine and even outside Palestine to worship in its sacred precincts. Nearly every Jew paid the yearly temple tax as well as tithes to priests and Levites. The temple was the glue that held all Jews together.[25]

Because the temple was so important, it seems inconceivable that the Synoptic Gospels and Acts would have failed to mention its destruction if they had been written after this tragic and monumental event.

Some scholars have mistakenly argued that the modern children's "telephone game" serves as a good analogy for the writing of the Gospels. In this internationally popular game, children try to pass a message to one another without changing it. Players form a line or a circle, and the first player whispers a message to the second player. The second player repeats the message to the third player, and so on. When the last player receives the message, he or she announces it to the whole group. The first person compares the original message to the last version of the message, and the players laugh because the last version of the message is usually very different from the original version. The telephone game can be very fun to play, but it can't serve as an appropriate analogy for the writing of the Gospels. Unlike the telephone game, the Gospels were written to provide accurate information to readers instead of to entertain players. The Gospel writers sought to accurately record and pass on what Jesus taught and did. Craig Evans writes, "Jesus taught his disciples, and his disciples taught those who came after them. What was taught could be adapted, even expanded, but not distorted."[26] Furthermore, the authors of the Gospels wrote their books soon enough after Jesus's life for them to accurately remember what Jesus said and did.

How could the Gospel writers have accurately remembered Jesus's sayings and deeds a few decades or so after his life on earth? First of all, the Gospel writers lived in a primarily oral culture, and people in ancient oral cultures often excelled at remembering what they heard. Secondly, some of Jesus's disciples and other early hearers may have taken notes when he taught and preached. Thirdly, as a Jewish rabbi, Jesus would have expected his disciples to memorize his teachings by using repetition. Fourthly, Jesus often spoke in easily memorizable forms.[27] Some of these forms included proverbs, parables, paradoxes, and similes. We can see great examples of these forms in his famous Sermon on the Mount (see Matthew 5–7). Fifthly, the Gospel writers witnessed some unforgettable, life-changing miracles such as healings. These miracles were inherently memorable events.[28] Finally, there were at least 20,000 eyewitnesses to Jesus's life, death, and ministry who were still alive thirty years after his life on earth. These eyewitnesses' continued presence in the communities out of which the Gospels were written would have ensured that the Gospel writers told the truth about what Jesus said and did.[29] Paul Rhodes Eddy states, "If the early Jesus movement was typical of other orally dominant cultures in this regard—and we have no reason to think otherwise—then all members of the community would have had a stake in, and thus to some degree a responsibility for, preserving the essential elements of the original Jesus tradition."[30] It would have been impossible for the Gospel writers to get away with lying about what Jesus said and did when 20,000 eyewitnesses to Jesus's life were still alive at the time when they wrote!

We have seen that the four Gospels found in the New Testament are based on eyewitness testimony. Therefore, the Gospels are reliable historical accounts of Jesus's words and deeds. They truthfully and accurately report the teaching, miracles, death, and resurrection of Jesus.

The Gospels Are Ancient Biographies of Jesus's Life

Do you enjoy reading biographies? Many of us enjoy reading biographies of famous people. Biographies of presidents, movie stars, famous athletes, business leaders, and religious leaders can make fascinating reading during our spare time. The most recent biography that I read was about the life of Mahatma Gandhi.[31] I really enjoyed reading it.

As ancient biographies of Jesus's life, the Gospels provide eyewitness testimony about Jesus. They are ancient biographies of Jesus's life with historical facts and true stories. Brant Pitre writes, "The four Gospels are not just any kind of ancient biography. They are historical biographies, two of which explicitly claim to tell us what Jesus actually did and said and to be based on eyewitness testimony (Luke 1:1–4; John 21:20–24)."[32] The Gospels are not a form of folklore, and they don't contain myths. The Gospels are thus far different from the tales of Greek mythology and the story of Rudolph the Red-Nosed Reindeer.

> **The Gospels are ancient biographies of Jesus's life that are based on eyewitness testimony.**

A majority of scholars today regard the Gospels as being similar to Greco-Roman biographies. The Gospels contain such common characteristics of Greco-Roman biographies as:

1) The life of the main character isn't always covered in chronological order.
2) There is little psychological analysis of the main character.
3) We learn about the main character's ancestry and then move quickly along to the beginning of his public life.
4) The main subject's character is revealed through his words and deeds as a model for readers either to imitate or to avoid imitating.[33]

The Gospels point out that Jesus is a model for readers to imitate (see Mark 10:43–45; John 13:14–15). They make it clear that everyone should seek to imitate Jesus by living a godly life.

The four Gospels are historical biographies written by authors who were committed to accurately reporting the words and deeds of Jesus. In the first century, accurately reporting what Jesus said meant recording either Jesus's exact words or at least carefully summarizing Jesus' words. Ancient historians could summarize a person's words,[34] but they couldn't make up something that the person never said.[35] Accurate reporting of Jesus's words didn't allow for inventing anything that he never actually said. Similarly, accurate reporting of Jesus's deeds didn't permit inventing any miracle that Jesus never performed. The Gospel writers couldn't just make things up; they couldn't just put words in Jesus's mouth. Why? The Gospel writers were not only evangelists but also writers of historical biographies. In addition, because they regarded Jesus as God's Son and the Savior of the world, they wouldn't have put words in his mouth.

There is absolutely no evidence that the Gospel writers put any words in Jesus's mouth. If they had invented some sayings of Jesus, those invented sayings would have addressed the needs of the early Christians. The early Christians needed to know how to deal with such practical and controversial issues as baptism, circumcision, women's role in the church, eating meat sacrificed to idols, and appointing leaders. After Jesus's time on earth had ended, the Jerusalem Council in Acts 15 and the Pauline epistles had to address these crucial issues because the Gospels don't record Jesus saying anything about them. Craig Evans states:

> Given such a high regard for Jesus' words, it is not likely that early Christians would have freely invented sayings and then attributed them to Jesus. In fact, the oft-heard assertion that many of the sayings were generated by questions and issues that the early church faced is called into doubt by the observation that many of these questions and issues (as seen in the New Testament

letters) are nowhere addressed by the sayings of
Jesus. There was disagreement over the question
of circumcision, eating meat sacrificed to idols,
spiritual gifts, Jew-Gentile relations, and qualifi-
cations for church office, but not a saying of Jesus
speaks to any of these questions.[36]

The Gospels Pass All of the Five Big Tests

We have already discussed four reasons why the Gospels should
be considered reliable sources about Jesus. Let's quickly review these
four reasons:

1) Secular and Jewish historians tell the same basic story about
Jesus that the Gospels tell about him.
2) Luke, the author of one of the four Gospels, was an excellent historian.
3) The authors of the Gospels provide eyewitness testimony
about Jesus.
4) The Gospels are ancient biographies of Jesus's life.

We will now discuss the fifth and final reason why the Gospels
should be regarded as reliable sources about Jesus. *The fifth reason
why the Gospels are trustworthy is that they pass all of the five big tests
that can be used to determine if they are trustworthy or untrustworthy.*
Let's evaluate the Gospels using the five tests in the order from the
easiest-to-pass test to the hardest-to-pass test.

The Gospels pass the honest reporting test with flying colors. Let's
discuss the first part of this test now—the cover-up test. In chapter
4, we described the cover-up test as pointing out that whatever is
embarrassing to the person or group sharing the embarrassing information is very likely to be true.

The Gospel writers demonstrate amazing honesty in their
reporting of the teaching and miracles of Jesus. They show their
remarkable honesty by reporting embarrassing facts about themselves
and even about Jesus himself. It would have been counterproductive

and absurd to invent these embarrassing things, so we know that the Gospel writers didn't invent any of them. For example, the Gospels report Peter—the spokesperson of the disciples and an early church leader—denying three times that he knew Jesus (see Matthew 26:69–75; Mark 14:66–72; Luke 22:54–62; John 18:15–18, 25–27). The Gospels also report Jesus calling Peter "Satan" when Peter doesn't understand Jesus's prediction of his own death and resurrection (see Matthew 16:21–23; Mark 8:31–33). Moreover, the Gospels report that the disciples slept when Jesus asked them to pray and deserted Jesus when they were afraid (see Matthew 26:36–45, 56; Mark 14:32–41, 50). In addition, Mark's Gospel describes the disciples as being slow to understand, selfish, and worldly minded (see Mark 4:13; 6:52; 8:17, 21; 9:10, 32).[37]

The Gospels also report embarrassing things about Jesus. They report Jesus not knowing the day or hour of his return,[38] Jesus being betrayed by one of his disciples,[39] and Jesus being executed by crucifixion.[40] Jesus's not knowing the time of his return made it harder for early Christians to claim that he was divine. Jesus's being betrayed by Judas made him look like he didn't always make good decisions because Jesus had chosen Judas to be one of his twelve disciples. Lastly, Jesus's crucifixion made it more difficult for Christians to evangelize Jews. According to Jews, crucifixion was normally a sign of being cursed by God (see Deuteronomy 21:23; Galatians 3:13).

At this point, it's helpful to ask the following: Do any of the Gospel stories report any embarrassing details that make the Christian worldview too difficult to believe? The answer is no. The Gospels do report Jesus being born in a manger, being baptized by John the Baptist, and being accused of doing miracles by the power of Satan. These are all very surprising stories, but they don't make it too hard for us to trust in the Gospels or to believe in the Christian worldview. These three stories provide more evidence of the Gospel writers' truthful reporting. The honesty of the Gospel authors is simply astonishing.

Instead of being born in a palace, Jesus was born in a simple cave. That cave was a stable.[41] He was then placed in a manger—a feeding trough for animals. The baby Jesus was soon visited by shepherds, who were told of Jesus's birth by angels and who shared the good news of his birth with many people (see Luke 2:6–18). Having shepherds receive the birth announcement and then tell people about Jesus's birth would have been considered shocking to first-century Jews. Why? Shepherds were considered second-class citizens and untrustworthy in first-century Palestine. Shepherds couldn't have their testimony admitted in court during the time of Jesus.[42] However, all of these details about Jesus's birth make the Gospels more trustworthy. If the story had all been made up by early Christians, the birth of Jesus would have been announced to priests or kings rather than to shepherds. His birth was announced to shepherds in order to emphasize that Jesus came to earth for everyone, including those who are poor and ostracized.

Like the story of Jesus's birth, the story of Jesus's baptism in the Gospels would have surprised first-century Jews. Jesus's baptism involved him submitting to baptism by John the Baptist (see Matthew 3:13–17; Mark 1:9–11; Luke 3:21–22). John's baptism was for sinners—certainly not for someone whom Christians considered to be the sinless Son of God. Nevertheless, Jesus's baptism doesn't imply that he was a sinner. Jesus was baptized in order to set an example of obedience for his followers to imitate. Jesus clearly wanted his followers to repent of their sins and to be baptized.

Jesus also wanted his followers to witness his power over demons. The authors of the Gospels frequently report Jesus's casting demons out of people. Shockingly, they also report Jesus being accused of using the power of Satan to perform his exorcisms (see Matthew 12:22–24; Mark 3:22; Luke 11:14–15)![43] These accusations make it clear that the authors of the Gospels were being completely honest in their reporting of Jesus's exorcisms. They were not trying to hide any facts about the exorcisms from their readers. These accusations reported in the Gospels also acknowledge that Jesus was able to cast demons out of people.

The Gospels are full of more surprising stories that would never have been fabricated by the early Christians. These surprising stories make it clear that Jesus had to deal with a lot of criticism, opposition, and misunderstanding. All of these surprising stories must be true reports about Jesus, and they make the Gospels more credible to us as readers. For example, they report that Jesus was accused of being "a glutton and a drunkard, a friend of tax collectors and sinners" (see Matthew 11:19; Luke 7:34). The Gospels also report that Jesus was accused of being demon possessed by some of the Jews who heard him speak (see Mark 3:22; John 8:48, 52). Lastly, the Gospels report that Jesus's siblings didn't believe in him (see Mark 3:20–21; John 7:5). The truth is that Jesus wasn't an out-of-control party animal, but He was willing to associate with anyone because He loved everyone. Jesus's exorcisms displayed his compassion for people, and they demonstrated that the kingdom of God was arriving in his ministry (see Matthew 12:28; Luke 11:20). In addition, Jesus's siblings did eventually believe in him and join the early Christian movement (see Acts 1:12–14).

The Gospels easily pass the first part of the honest reporting test. We will see in the next chapter of this book that the Gospels also definitely pass the second part of the honest reporting test. The Gospel writers tell their stories about Jesus in a very honest, simple, and straightforward manner. Let's move on to the next big test.

Besides easily passing the honest reporting test, the Gospels also pass the human reason test. The human reason test states that a true belief must contain no contradictions, and it must correspond to reality. The Gospels acknowledge that true statements have no contradictions and that truth is what corresponds to the way things really are.

There are no contradictions in any of the key beliefs taught in the Gospels. For example, there is no contradiction in the Christian belief that Jesus is both human and divine. God could choose to become a man in Jesus if he wanted to do so. He is all-powerful and thus able to take on human form. The Gospels claim that God did become a man in the person of Jesus (see John 1:1–2, 14).[44] The Gospels record Jesus as claiming to be divine (see Matthew 11:27; Mark 2:5–12; Luke 5:17–26; 10:22; John 8:58; 10:30; 14:6). He clearly claimed to have a special relationship with God as God's Son. For example, when the Jewish leaders asked Jesus about his identity, he claimed to be the Son of Man riding on the clouds and sitting at the right hand of God (see Matthew 26:63–65; Mark 14:61–64).[45]

Jesus was claiming to be a divine person whom God would vindicate. Jesus was also claiming that he would eventually judge these same Jewish leaders who sought his death. Moreover, there is no contradiction in the Gospel teaching that God is one God in three persons—God the Father, God the Son (Jesus), and God the Holy Spirit.[46] The three persons of the Godhead share the same divine essence and attributes, but they are distinct persons who enjoy perfect fellowship with one another.

If God actually became a man in Jesus, it's true that Jesus is divine and God's Son. If Jesus really rose from the dead, he showed himself to be both divine and God's one and only Son. The truth about Jesus that reveals who he is will become evident when we discuss the issue of his resurrection in the next chapter.

We've already used two of the five big tests to evaluate the Gospels. Let's finish evaluating them by using the other three tests.

In addition to passing the human reason test, the Gospels pass the contemporary living test. As we saw in chapter 5, the contemporary living test has two parts. The first part is the human dignity test, which says that true beliefs will acknowledge that everyone should be treated with love and respect. The second part is the livability test, which says that true beliefs are practical and able to be applied to one's life.

In the Gospels, Jesus loves and respects people of all ages, classes, and races. Jesus loves everyone who comes across his path—men, women, children, the poor, the wealthy, Jews, Samaritans, etc. He talks with and offers forgiveness to everyone who will believe in him, even to outcasts who have lived immoral lifestyles. For example, he talks with a Samaritan woman who was living an immoral lifestyle, and he invites her to believe in him (see John 4:1–26). Jesus consistently demonstrates love and respect toward Samaritans even though Jews hated them. For example, he tells the famous parable of the Good Samaritan (see Luke 10:25–37), and he heals ten men of leprosy, including a Samaritan (see Luke 17:11–19).

In the Gospels, Jesus displays such a high view of children, poor people, and women. Jesus claims that we need to be willing to believe in him like children trust in him. He loves children and blesses them (see Matthew 19:13–15; Mark 10:13–15; Luke 18:15–17). In his famous Sermon on the Plain, Jesus says, "Blessed are you who are poor, for yours is the kingdom of God. Blessed are you who are hungry now, for you shall be satisfied" (Luke 6:20–21a). Many of Jesus's friends and followers are women. For example, Jesus often spends time with Mary and Martha, and he teaches them the Scriptures (see Luke 10:38–42; John 11:1–44).

It's clear from the Gospels that Jesus greatly respected and appreciated women. Ron Rhodes correctly writes:

> It is undeniable that Jesus had a very high view of women. In a Jewish culture, where women were discouraged from studying the Law, Jesus taught women right alongside men as equals (Matthew 14:21; 15:38). And when He taught, He often used women's activities to illustrate the character of the kingdom of God, such as baking bread (Luke 13:20, 21), grinding corn (Luke 17:35), and sweeping the house to find a lost coin (Luke 15:8–10).[47]

The Gospels point out that everyone can follow Jesus. In other words, the Gospels provide excellent examples of the fact that being a follower of Jesus is livable. One example of someone who flourishes while following Jesus is the Samaritan woman at the well. After believing in Jesus, she tells the people in her town about him, and many of the townspeople also believe in Jesus (see John 4:28–29, 39–42). A second example of a believer in Jesus who shows that following Jesus is livable is Zacchaeus, a former tax collector who changes his ways after Jesus goes to his house and speaks with him. Jesus changes Zacchaeus from being a greedy man to being a very generous man (see Luke 19:1–10). Other examples of Jesus followers who flourish while living for Jesus include the previously mentioned Mary and Martha and the four Gospel writers of Matthew, Mark, Luke, and John. John follows Jesus so well that he not only writes his Gospel but also four other books of the New Testament—the three

Epistles of John and Revelation. Moreover, John lives 60 more years after Jesus's life on earth, and he lives to be over 90 years old. John's amazing life demonstrates that being a follower of Jesus is livable.

The Gospels not only pass the contemporary living test but also the all-inclusive test. As we discovered in chapter 4, the all-inclusive test has two parts: a) the comprehensiveness test; and b) the corroboration test. The comprehensiveness test says that a belief is more likely to be true if it explains more of the evidence than another competing belief does. The corroboration test says that a belief is more likely to be true if there is outside evidence to corroborate it. Let's evaluate the Gospels now by using these two parts of the all-inclusive test.

The Gospels don't encourage us to embrace two common yet ineffective solutions to the comprehensiveness test. One ineffective solution to the problem of evil and suffering is denying that suffering and evil are real. We all know that cancer, disease, and death are real; they aren't illusions. We've all experienced some suffering in our lives, and we've all seen loved ones die. Who hasn't read an obituary, been to a funeral or memorial service, or experienced some type of suffering? We have all seen other people suffer, and we have all experienced difficult times. Another ineffective solution to the problem of evil and suffering is trying to earn our way to heaven by living a good life. We will never be good enough to be 100% sure that we are good enough for God and that we are going to spend eternity with Him. The reality is that we can't be good enough for God because He is perfect and we aren't perfect.

The Gospels pass the comprehensiveness test by providing the best solution to the problem of evil and suffering. *The best solution to the problem of evil and suffering is found in the amazing story of Jesus of Nazareth.* As reported in the Gospels, Jesus's life is the story of God using suffering to accomplish not only a greater good but also the best possible result. The Gospels record that Jesus lived a perfect life, performed many miracles, and gained many followers. The Gospels also report that Jesus experienced rejection by the Jewish leaders, died on the cross for our sins in our place, and rose again. According to the Gospels, Jesus died for us as our substitute, taking the punishment we deserved for our sins—our lies, lust, pride, selfishness, etc. By taking upon himself all of the countless sins humans have ever committed, Jesus suffered on the cross more than any person in human history has ever suffered. Jesus's infinite suffering on the cross demonstrates that God loves us despite our many sins (see John 3:14–16; 8:31–36; 15:13; see also 1 John 4:10; Romans 5:8). If Jesus did actually rise from the dead, the ultimate solution to the problem of evil is found in his death and resurrection. According to the Gospel writers, Jesus's resurrection shows that God exists, and it makes it clear that Jesus has defeated sin, suffering, and death. Jesus himself provides us with victory over sin, suffering, and death. In his comments on Jesus's death and resurrection, Millard Erickson writes, "God himself became the victim of evil so that he and we might be victors over evil."[48] The Gospels clearly state that at the moment we trust in Jesus, we have eternal life and the certainty of spending eternity with God in heaven (see John 3:36; 5:24; 10:28).

According to the Gospels, Jesus offers wonderful benefits to us not only in the afterlife but also in the present life. Because of Jesus's death and resurrection, anyone can have eternal life, joy, peace, and a purpose in life. Jesus says in the Gospels that he wants to give us abundant life (John 10:10), peace (John 14:27; 16:33), and a new purpose in life (John 13:34–35; 17:3). Jesus provides the best solution to the problem of evil. He does this by giving everyone who trusts in him eternal life, forgiveness of their sins, joy, peace, and a purpose in life.

Besides passing the comprehensiveness test, the Gospels pass the corroboration test. They pass the corroboration test by receiving confirmation of key facts from non-Christian historians and from archeological findings.

As we saw at the beginning of this chapter, secular historians and the Jewish historian Josephus corroborate the Gospel's basic story about Jesus. Josephus writes that Jesus had a reputation as a miracle worker, was crucified by Pontius Pilate, and continued to have a following after his death (*Antiquities of the Jews* 18.63–64). The Roman historian Tacitus reports that Jesus was executed by Pilate and continued to have a following after his death (*Annals* 15.44). Josephus, Tacitus, and the Gospels all agree that: 1) Jesus started a Christian movement; 2) Jesus was executed by Pilate; and 3) Jesus's execution didn't stop the movement. The book of Acts also agrees with all of these facts (see Acts 13:26–52). Furthermore, the Roman historian and magistrate Pliny the Younger reports that Jesus was worshipped as divine by his followers (*Epistles* 10.96–97). The Gospels also report Jesus as being worshipped as divine by his followers (see Matthew 2:11; 14:22–33; John 9:17, 35–38).

Like non-Christian historians, archeological findings also corroborate the Gospel's most important facts about Jesus. First of all, a 1961 archeological finding corroborates the existence of Pontius Pilate. The so-called Pilate Stone was discovered in Caesarea, Israel, in a staircase near the theater. The inscription, dated between AD 26–36, refers to this Roman governor with his name, his title, and a dedication to the reigning emperor Tiberius.[49] Secondly, the 1968 discovery of the remains of a crucified man named Yehohanan in Jerusalem provides archeological evidence that crucifixion victims could be buried in a Jewish family tomb. Yehohanan's ankle bone was found in a bone box in a rock-cut tomb thousands of years later with a nail still in it! Jewish custom permitted criminals condemned to death by Roman law to be buried in family tombs. This very important discovery shows that Jesus could have been given a proper Jewish burial in a tomb, just as the Gospels report.[50] Moreover, because Jesus was crucified in a time of peace between the Romans and the Jews, he would have been given a proper Jewish burial in a tomb.[51]

Archeological evidence exists not only for Jesus's crucifixion and burial but also for Jesus's resurrection. Yes, that's right! There is actual archeological evidence that supports the Gospels' claim that Jesus rose from the dead! Isn't that both shocking and exhilarating?

The correct location of Jesus's tomb in Jerusalem's Old City was known to early Christians and then passed down to other Christians since his death and resurrection in about AD 33. The location of Jesus's tomb is in the Church of the Holy Sepulchre, which was constructed in about AD 326. Scientific tests done in 2016 and in 2017 and reported to *National Geographic* prove that this ancient church was originally built in the fourth century.[52] The church was built on the site of Jesus's tomb, which itself was newly made in Jesus's day. Commenting on this location for Jesus's tomb, archeologist Dan

Bahat emphatically states, "We may not be absolutely certain that the site of the Holy Sepulchre Church is the site of Jesus' burial, but we certainly have no other site that can lay a claim nearly as weighty, and we really have no reason to reject the authenticity of the site."[53] *The fact that the tomb inside the Church of the Holy Sepulchre is empty constitutes indirect evidence that Jesus rose from the dead.* The empty tomb inside this ancient church fits the description of Jesus's tomb in the Gospels. According to the four Gospels, Jesus's tomb was a new tomb that was just outside the city walls, hewn out of rock, single-chambered, having a bench on which to lay the body, and sealed with a large stone.[54] Archeologist Titus Kennedy states, "Due to the significance of the resurrection in Christianity, the tomb of Jesus has been remembered, revered, and preserved for almost 2,000 years."[55]

In addition to having archeological evidence for Jesus's resurrection, we also have recent archeological evidence for other key people and places named in the Gospels. For example, we have archeological evidence for the existence of Caiaphas, the high priest who asked Jesus to tell the Jewish leaders in the council if he was the Son of God or not. Caiaphas was the high priest in Jerusalem from AD 18 to 36. Matthew, Luke, and John mention Caiaphas by name in their Gospels, and Luke also mentions him by name in the book of Acts (see Matthew 26:3, 57; Luke 3:2; John 11:49; 18:12–28; Acts 4:6). In 1990, the burial cave of Caiaphas and his family was discovered by accident. The roof of the cave collapsed when workers were making a water park. Caiaphas's bone box, which is called an ossuary, was found inside the cave with his name inscribed on it.[56] Moreover, a more recent archeological find that provides evidence for the truthfulness of the Gospels is the Pool of Siloam. The Pool of Siloam was the huge pool where Jesus cured the blind man as recorded in John 9:1–11. This important and unexpected archeological find of the over 225-feet-wide pool was made in 2004. Coins found at the discovery site indicate that the Pool of Siloam existed at the time of Jesus.[57]

Archeology has also provided substantial manuscript evidence for the Gospels and for the rest of the New Testament. New Testament manuscripts are handwritten copies based on the original writings.

The vast majority of the manuscripts were made prior to the invention of the printing press in the 15th century. The oldest fragment of a New Testament manuscript is the John Rylands Papyrus (P52) which was found in Egypt. This fragment contains John 18:31–33, 37–38. It has been dated to about AD 125,[58] which is only 35 to 45 years after the Gospel of John was written. Some other early manuscripts include the following: 1) the Chester Beatty Papyri (AD 200), which contains major portions of the New Testament; 2) Codex Vaticanus (AD 325–350), which contains the Gospels, Acts, and the vast majority of the New Testament; and 3) Codex Sinaiticus (AD 350), which contains almost all of the New Testament except for a small number of verses.

> **The Gospels pass all of the five tests that we can use to determine if they are telling us the truth about Jesus.**

The Gospels and the rest of the New Testament enjoy far better manuscript evidence than any other ancient work. *The New Testament manuscripts have much earlier manuscript dates that are closer to the originals, and they have a much larger number of manuscripts than any other ancient work.* The New Testament has about 25,000 manuscripts, including hundreds of manuscripts written within 500 years of the originals. Other ancient works by Homer, Caesar, Plato, Herodotus, Aristotle, and other writers have a much smaller number of manuscripts that were mostly copied 700 to 1,400 years after the originals.[59]

The manuscript evidence for the New Testament also shows that the New Testament has been accurately preserved. The professional scribes who wrote the manuscripts of the New Testament did an outstanding job. The 25,000 manuscripts of the New Testament and over 36,000 quotes of the New Testament by the early Church Fathers[60] show that the New Testament has been accurately preserved. In fact, the New Testament we have today is 98–99% identical to the original text. There are many variants in the New Testament manuscripts, but the vast majority of them are minor issues such as spelling, word order, and differences in style.[61] Only two variants in the entire New Testament involve disputed passages of more than two verses (see the notes in most English Bibles about Mark 16:9–20 and John 7:53–8:11). Furthermore, no key doctrine or command in the New Testament is affected by any variants. Craig Blomberg writes, "It cannot be emphasized strongly enough that no orthodox doctrine or ethical practice of Christianity depends solely on any disputed wording. There are always undisputed passages one can consult that teach the same truths."[62]

Because the New Testament has been accurately preserved, we know that it has not changed over time. We know that the Gospel writers did record Jesus as performing miracles, claiming to be divine, dying on the cross, and rising again. We also know that the early Christians who were eyewitnesses to Jesus's life believed in his divinity and in his resurrection from the dead. These key beliefs weren't invented hundreds of years later by people who weren't eyewitnesses to Jesus's life, death, and resurrection. These key beliefs were held and taught by the earliest followers of Jesus. Many of these early followers of Jesus had personally known him during his more than three years of public ministry. These early followers knew the truth about what Jesus said and did, and four of them wrote down the truth about Jesus in the four Gospels.

The Gospels not only pass the all-inclusive test, but they also pass the divine glory test. The Gospels portray God in a way that is theologically sound—in a way that makes Him worthy of our worship and our service. They describe God as being great and good and thus deserving our worship and service.

During the last few years of her life, my sister Nicole's favorite song was "Is He Worthy?" by Chris Tomlin. It was the first song that I sang along with many other people at Nicole's celebration of life service in December 2020. This beautiful song is based on a biblical passage written by John, the author of the fourth Gospel and four other books in the New Testament. The song is based on what John wrote in Revelation 5. It implies that in order for us to worship Jesus, we must be sure that he is actually worthy of our worship. Similarly, the popular song called "Revelation Song" implies that God and Jesus should be worshipped because they are worthy of our worship.[63] The words of these songs bring us to a very important question: Is the God of the Gospels worthy of our worship and our service? The short answer to this question is: "Yes, He is!" Let's now discuss why He is worthy.

The Gospels pass the divine glory test by giving us sufficient reasons for serving and worshipping God. The Gospels describe God as coming to earth in the man Jesus of Nazareth. Therefore, if Jesus is worthy of our worship, then the God of the Gospels deserves our worship. The Gospels portray Jesus as good and great and thus worthy of being called the Son of God and worthy of our worship.

The Gospels portray Jesus as the most approachable, loving, and compassionate person in human history. Jesus takes the time to talk with children, with outcasts, and with everyone else who approaches him. He is never too busy to talk with people, encourage them, and teach them. Jesus helps many people by addressing their spiritual, emotional, and physical needs. He casts out demons from people, showing his power over the forces of darkness. He heals the blind, the deaf, the paralyzed, and those with leprosy. Jesus's miracles and teaching are motivated by his deep love for people and the compassion he feels for them (see Matthew 9:36; 14:14; 15:32; 20:34; Mark 6:34). His parables and sermons engage the minds, capture the hearts, and nourish the souls of thousands of people who hear him teach. Jesus speaks some of the most moving words that anyone has ever said, such as: "Blessed are those who hunger and thirst for righteousness, for they shall be satisfied. Blessed are the merciful, for they shall receive mercy. Blessed are the pure in heart, for they shall see God" (Matthew 5:6–8). Jesus shares some of the most memorable and impactful stories that have ever been told, such as the parable of the Good Samaritan (Luke 10:25–37) and the parable of the lost son (Luke 15:11–32). The Gospels show how exciting and encouraging it is to be around Jesus, who has an effervescent personality!

Besides portraying Jesus as an amazing person, the Gospels describe him as being a uniquely divine person who is God's Son. In the Gospels, Jesus clearly shows that he is a divine person. Jesus demonstrates his divine nature by showing his power and control over nature. He walks on the water, calms a storm, turns water into wine, and feeds thousands of people with only five loaves of bread and two fish.[64] Jesus also demonstrates his divine nature by raising three people from the dead: the widow of Nain's son (Luke 7:11–17), Jairus's daughter (Mark 5:35–43; Luke 8:49–56), and Lazarus (John 11:1–44). Moreover, Jesus also reveals his divine nature by predicting his own death and resurrection[65] and the destruction of the temple in Jerusalem. Finally, Jesus demonstrates his divine nature by rising from the dead three days after he was crucified. His resurrection from the dead is multiply attested in all four Gospels (see Matthew 28:1–10; Mark 16:1–8; Luke 24:1–12; John 20:1–18).

Jesus's death and resurrection reported in the Gospels clearly portray God as being both great and good. As a result, the Gospels pass the two parts of the divine glory test: a) the divine greatness test; and b) the divine goodness test. The Gospels depict God as being great in that Jesus knows the future and is able to do all things, including raising himself from the dead (see John 10:17–18). Only God, as an omniscient and omnipotent being, can know and control the future and raise the dead. Jesus is the God-man in the Gospels who is omniscient and omnipotent; He is able to predict his death and to raise himself from the dead. Furthermore, the Gospels also depict God as being good in that Jesus's death and resurrection demonstrate God's holiness, love, and justice. Because God is holy, He must punish human sin. Because God is loving, He chooses to have Jesus die in our place, taking the punishment for our sins that we deserve. Because God is just, Jesus rises again from the dead, making forgiveness of sins and eternal life available to everyone who trusts in Jesus as the way to heaven.

Jesus's death and resurrection as reported in the Gospels clearly show that God is great and good. They demonstrate that God is in control and that He loves us. Moreover, if Jesus really rose from the dead, then we can be 100% sure that the Gospels are trustworthy. All of this is exciting, but is it too good to be true?

How Can We Be Sure That Jesus Rose from the Dead?

But how can we be sure that Jesus of Nazareth really died, was buried, and rose from the dead? No one was at the tomb of Jesus with a cell phone making a video of what happened on Easter Sunday, and there were no hidden cameras recording what happened that day. However, we can still examine the evidence for Jesus's resurrection and determine what most likely happened on Easter Sunday. We'll address the extremely important issue of Jesus's resurrection in the next chapter. This is the most important issue in the Gospels and in all of sacred literature, so please read the next chapter carefully!

7

Did Jesus Really Rise from the Dead?

Did you ever participate in Easter egg hunts as a child? When I was a child, I enjoyed participating in Easter egg hunts with my sister Nicole and my other siblings. They were so much fun! My parents hid plastic eggs of various colors outside in our yard, and my siblings and I would try to find as many hidden eggs as fast as we could find them. We were so excited when we found the hidden eggs, and we loved to eat the jelly beans and chocolate candies that were inside them! Although I truly enjoyed the Easter eggs hunts, I knew that Easter wasn't really about the Easter bunny and Easter egg hunts. I knew that Easter is really about something much more important. I knew that Christians celebrate Easter because of their belief in the resurrection of Jesus.

The most crucial issue in the Gospels and in the Christian worldview is the resurrection of Jesus of Nazareth. If Jesus really rose from the dead, then the Gospels are trustworthy and true. If he rose from the dead, then the Christian church began as a result of his resurrection. Christians today maintain that Jesus's resurrection from the dead provides the only adequate explanation for the faith of the early Christians and for the existence of the Christian church. J. P. Moreland writes, "The resurrection of Jesus of Nazareth from the dead is the foundation upon which the Christian faith is built. Without the resurrection, there would have been no Christian faith, and the most dynamic movement in history would never have come to be."[1]

The resurrection of Jesus is not only the most important issue in the Christian faith but also the most important religious issue that we can examine. Why is the issue of Jesus's resurrection so important? If Jesus's resurrection occurred, it validates the Christian faith and Jesus himself. If Jesus rose from the dead, he is divine and God's Son, and everyone should believe in him. If Jesus didn't rise from the dead, he isn't divine, and no one should believe in him. Because the issue of Jesus's resurrection is so crucial, we all must know the truth about it.

Some of us may consider the idea that Jesus rose from the dead as too difficult to believe. But Jesus's rising from the dead could have really happened if God intervened and a divine miracle occurred. If God exists, miracles are possible. Therefore, God certainly could have raised Jesus from the dead even if his resurrection seems strange and shocking to some of us.

Did Jesus really rise from the dead? Is there enough evidence to conclude that Jesus really rose from the dead? The resurrection of Jesus is either a historical fact or it's a horrible lie. One writer correctly states, "The Resurrection is either history or hoax, miracle or myth, fact or fantasy."[2] We will see in this chapter that there is sufficient evidence to conclude that Jesus's resurrection is indeed a historical fact; Jesus did actually rise from the dead. But before we directly discuss the resurrection, we need to know whether or not he died on the cross and was given a proper burial. In order for us to determine if Jesus rose from the dead, we must know whether or not Jesus died and was properly buried.

> The resurrection of Jesus is either a historical fact or a horrible lie. We need to know if Jesus is alive or dead.

Did Jesus Really Die on the Cross?

Some of you reading this book may doubt that Jesus really died on the cross. Some movies and books have argued that Jesus actually survived his crucifixion instead of dying on the cross. Did Jesus really die on the cross, or did he survive his crucifixion?

One author who argued that Jesus didn't actually die on the cross is the late psychic Sylvia Browne. She became well-known in 2020 because her book *End of Days* really seemed to predict the COVID-19 global pandemic. In her 2008 book, Browne wrote about a pneumonia-like virus that she predicted would spread around the world in about 2020.[3] Did she know that the global pandemic was coming? No! Should people consult a psychic as soon as possible to know what will happen in the future? No, that wouldn't be a good idea. Browne's book *End of Days* is filled with false prophecies about U.S. presidents, the common cold, cancer, diabetes, Parkinson's, multiple sclerosis (MS), retirement funds, the stock market, and other topics.[4] Despite these false prophecies, Browne appeared frequently on TV and radio as a guest on various talk shows and news shows before she passed away in 2013. She also wrote more than 40 books, including a New Age book about Jesus.

In her book *The Mystical Life of Jesus*, Browne makes various interesting yet false claims about Jesus. For example, she argues that instead of dying on the cross, Jesus survived his crucifixion and went into hiding. He was revived in the cold tomb after having his wounds treated and being given food and water. Browne claims that the revived Jesus then secretly took a ship across the ocean, settled down in France, became a father, and died there as an old man![5] The truth is that Browne's views about Jesus are much more entertaining than they are accurate. Virtually all scholars agree that Jesus died on the cross, and thus he couldn't have survived his crucifixion and settled down in France. Scholars also agree that there is no evidence that Jesus was ever married or a father.[6]

Both conservative and liberal scholars agree that Jesus died by crucifixion. He died an excruciating death. Before being crucified, Jesus was brutally whipped, and a crown of thorns was placed on his head. The leather whip used to beat Jesus had pieces of bone or metal woven into it. The whip tore into Jesus's flesh and muscle, weakening him through blood loss. The Roman soldiers who crucified Jesus drove seven-inch nails into his wrists and feet, and one of them thrust a spear into his side (see John 19:33–34). Jesus didn't somehow survive being whipped and being nailed to a cross. The Roman soldiers were experts at using crucifixion to execute people. The soldiers made sure that Jesus was dead because they faced death if they allowed him or any other prisoner to survive crucifixion. Like other victims of crucifixion, Jesus died of asphyxiation (suffocation), loss of bodily fluids, and multiple organ failure.[7] John Ankerberg and John Weldon write:

Indeed, survival from crucifixions was unknown; just as today, men simply do not survive the firing squad, electric chair, lethal injection, or gas chamber. Because the law has decreed the prisoner's death, even if a first attempt fails, procedures are repeated until death occurs. Death by crucifixion was just as certain as by any modern method of execution; there was no escape.[8]

Even very liberal scholars assert that Jesus must have been executed because the non-Christian historians Tacitus and Josephus report his execution by Pilate.[9] John Dominic Crossan, the most influential liberal scholar of the last thirty years, writes, "Jesus' death by execution under Pontius Pilate is as sure as anything historical can ever be."[10]

Did Jesus Receive a Proper Jewish Burial?

There is simply no chance whatsoever that Jesus survived his crucifixion. He definitely died on the cross, and his death was agonizing. But was Jesus's body buried after he was crucified? If Jesus was buried, what type of burial did Jesus receive?

Some liberal scholars and skeptics have recently argued that Jesus's body was not given a proper Jewish burial. According to them, Jesus's body was either left on the cross or buried in a shallow grave. If Jesus's body was left on the cross or buried in a shallow grave, scavengers such as dogs and crows would have eaten it.[11] Bart Ehrman, a popular author and an agnostic, states, "Crucified criminals were normally not allowed a decent burial, but were either left on their crosses to rot and be devoured by scavengers or tossed into a common grave. This was part of the humiliation."[12] Crucified criminals suffered a gruesome and painful death, and their bodies were often not properly buried.

The fact that crucified criminals didn't usually receive a proper burial doesn't actually tell us what happened to Jesus's body after his crucifixion. We need to briefly examine some more evidence about

Roman and Jewish burial customs to know what happened to Jesus's body. As we examine the evidence, we need to take into account that Jesus was crucified during a time of peace between the Romans and Jews. We also need to remember that he was crucified on the eve of Passover, a major Jewish holiday.

Evidence from both Roman law and from the Jewish historian Josephus indicates that Jesus must have received a proper Jewish burial on the eve of Passover. Roman law during Jesus's time stated that the bodies of persons condemned to death should be given to relatives or to anyone who requested the bodies in order to bury them.[13] Family and friends could be given the bodies of condemned persons. Josephus writes that the Roman governors in Israel during the first-century respected Jewish customs, including their custom of always burying their dead loved ones (*Jewish War* 2.220; *Against Apion* 2.211). The Roman governors wanted to keep the peace, and they knew that refusing to allow the Jews to bury their dead loved ones could result in riots.[14] Refusal to permit the Jews to bury their loved ones could have resulted in riots because leaving bodies hanging on crosses would have defiled their land (see Deuteronomy 21:23). Moreover, Josephus writes that the Jews who were sentenced to crucifixion were taken down from their crosses and buried before sunset so that the land wouldn't be defiled (*Jewish War* 4.317). Craig Evans summarizes the Roman and Jewish evidence for Jesus's burial:

> Those crucified or executed by other means were
> buried and, in fact, from the Jewish point of view
> had to be buried to prevent the defilement of the
> land. There is simply no chance that the bod-
> ies of Jesus and the two men crucified with him
> would have been left hanging on their respective
> crosses, just outside the walls of Jerusalem, on the

Evidence from non-Christian historians and Roman law indicates that Jesus died by crucifixion and was given a proper burial.

eve of Passover, unburied and subject to scaveng-
ing birds and animals.[15]

In order for Jesus to receive a proper Jewish burial, he needed to
be buried by family or friends. Because he had been crucified, Jesus
couldn't be buried right away in his family's tomb. Jews considered
crucifixion a shameful death, and they would only allow a crucified
person's bones to be placed in the family tomb after his or her flesh
had decomposed.[16] Such decomposition would take up to a year. As
a result, Jesus needed to be buried in the tomb of one of his friends
or followers.

According to all four Gospels, Jesus was buried by one of his
friends or followers—a man named Joseph of Arimathea. Joseph of
Arimathea was a member of the Jewish high priest's council, which
was called the Sanhedrin. He was a disciple of Jesus who was willing
to make sure that Jesus was properly buried. Joseph's burial of Jesus
in a new rock-cut tomb is described in all four Gospels (see Matthew
27:57–60; Mark 15:43–47; Luke 23:50–56; John 19:38–42). After
asking Pilate for Jesus's body, Joseph took Jesus's body down from the
cross and wrapped it in linen cloth. The Gospel of John records that
a man named Nicodemus helped Joseph to put Jesus's body in the
new tomb. The new tomb belonged to Joseph himself, not to Jesus's
family.

The Gospel accounts of Jesus's burial by Joseph of Arimathea
are trustworthy for at least three reasons. First of all, Jesus's burial
by Joseph is multiply attested in all four Gospels. Therefore, it is
very likely to be true. Secondly, Jesus's burial by Joseph of Arimathea
wouldn't have been invented by the early church, and it couldn't
have been invented by the early church. As a respected member of
the Sanhedrin, Joseph was a well-known person. His burial of Jesus
couldn't have been fabricated by the church without being detected by
eyewitnesses to Jesus's death and his burial. Such detection of a false
story would have been embarrassing and harmful to the Christian
movement. Finally, we know that Joseph's burial of Jesus wasn't made
up by the church because no other competing burial story exists. No

Christian or non-Christian source has a story of one of Jesus's twelve disciples, family members, or the Romans burying Jesus.[17]

For the reasons listed above, most scholars consider the Gospels' story that Jesus was buried by Joseph of Arimathea to be a true story. Because Joseph was a well-known person, his existence couldn't have been made up. Making up Joseph's existence would be like trying to fabricate the existence of a well-known public figure such as a U.S. Supreme Court member. We couldn't say that someone specific like Mike Smith was a member of the U.S. Supreme Court thirty years ago unless he was in fact a member of the U.S. Supreme Court at that time. Joseph was a member of the Great Sanhedrin, which was the Supreme Court for Jewish people. The Great Sanhedrin included 70 men and the high priest, who were all public figures. Therefore, making up Joseph of Arimathea's existence as a member of the Great Sanhedrin would have been impossible. J. P. Moreland correctly writes:

> Most scholars believe that Joseph of Arimathea was a real, historical person and that Jesus was actually buried in his tomb. According to the Gospels, he was a member of the Sanhedrin, a group of seventy-one leaders whose members were very well known... No one could have invented a person who did not exist and say he was on the Sanhedrin if such were not the case. Almost everyone knew who was on the Sanhedrin.[18]

We can be absolutely certain that the story of Jesus's death, burial, and resurrection was not invented by the early church decades after his life on earth. How can we be so sure about this? An ancient oral tradition preserved in one of the apostle Paul's letters reports the death, burial, and resurrection of Jesus. This tradition is found in Paul's letter 1 Corinthians, which was written in AD 53 or 54. This very early oral tradition recorded in 1 Corinthians 15:3–4 states the following: 1) Jesus died; 2) Jesus was buried; and 3) Jesus rose again. It is very likely that Paul received this oral tradition from Jesus's disciple Peter and from Jesus's brother James while visiting them in Jerusalem three years after his conversion (see Galatians 1:18–19). Because Paul was converted a year or two after Jesus's crucifixion, he received this oral tradition within about five years of Jesus's death from two people who knew Jesus.[19] Dozens of critical scholars agree that Paul received this oral tradition about five or six years after Jesus's crucifixion.[20]

This early oral tradition recorded in 1 Corinthians 15 became a creed—a formal statement of key beliefs—among early Christians. This creed shows what the early Christians believed from the time of Jesus's death. The early church believed that Jesus died, was buried, and rose again. Commenting on this Christian creed, Gary Habermas correctly states:

> Paul received creedal material in Jerusalem just five years or so after Jesus' crucifixion that was actually formulated earlier, perhaps dating all the way back to shortly after the death of Jesus. But regardless of where we date this creedal tradition itself, the underlying content of the gospel message regarding the death and resurrection of Jesus goes back to the beginning. In other words, it was the central message of the early apostolic church from its inception.[21]

Did Jesus Really Rise from the Dead?

Why did the early Christians believe that Jesus rose from the dead? Was their belief in Jesus's resurrection based on solid evidence, or was it just wishful thinking? It's virtually certain that Jesus died and was given a proper Jewish burial, and early Christians believed that Jesus had risen from the dead. It's now time for us to discuss the exciting evidence for Jesus's resurrection!

The early Christians believed that Jesus rose from the dead for two main reasons. The first reason was that Jesus's tomb was discovered as empty by some of his female followers on Easter Sunday morning. The empty tomb serves as indirect evidence for Jesus's resurrection.

The second reason was that many of Jesus's disciples and other followers reported experiencing the risen Jesus after he died. In other words, many early Christians reported Jesus as appearing to them alive after his death. The appearances of Jesus after his death serve as direct evidence for his resurrection.

Let's briefly examine the evidence for the empty tomb and for the appearances of the risen Jesus. We'll see that the evidence for the empty tomb and for the risen Jesus's appearances is compelling. This powerful evidence has convinced countless people to believe in Jesus's resurrection, including many people who used to regard his resurrection as a hoax.

The evidence that Jesus's tomb was discovered empty on Easter morning is persuasive. Why is this evidence so clear and convincing? First of all, each of the four Gospels reports that Jesus's tomb was first discovered as empty by a group of women, not by some men (see Matthew 28:1–8; Mark 16:1–8; Luke 24:1–8; John 20:1–2, 11–18). In ancient Roman and Jewish cultures, the testimony of women was considered questionable and untrustworthy. Women's testimony was generally not permitted in a court of law during Jesus's time. Their testimony often counted for nothing; it tended to be regarded as worthless. The belief that women's testimony was untrustworthy appears often in ancient Jewish literature.[22] Therefore, the Gospel writers must be telling the truth when they report that Jesus's tomb was discovered as empty by female disciples. If the Gospel writers had been making up the story of the empty tomb, they would have reported male disciples such as Peter and John discovering the empty tomb first. Reporting females discover the empty tomb first would have been potentially counterproductive and embarrassing to the cause of the early Christian movement. William Lane Craig persuasively states:

> If the empty tomb story were a legend, then it
> is most likely that the male disciples would have
> been made to be the first to discover the empty
> tomb. The fact that women, whose testimony
> was deemed worthless, were the chief witnesses

to the fact of the empty tomb can only be plausibly explained if, like it or not, they actually were the discoverers of the empty tomb. Hence, the Gospels are most likely giving an accurate account of this matter.[23]

The Gospels' report of the tomb being found empty on Easter morning is also compelling due to the location of the tomb and enemy attestation of the empty tomb. Because Jesus's tomb was located in Jerusalem, it would have been impossible for the Christian faith to survive and spread in Jerusalem if Jesus's body had still been in the tomb. If Jesus's body had still been in the tomb, the Jewish leaders would have produced his corpse and paraded it in the streets in response to any claims that Jesus had risen from the dead. However, the empty tomb was attested to by Jesus's enemies—the Jewish leaders and the Romans (see Matthew 28:11–15). Jesus's followers, the Jews, and the Romans all agreed that Jesus's tomb was empty. Everyone knew that the tomb was empty. Many years after Jesus's death, the Jews still acknowledged that Jesus's body was not in the tomb.[24]

Convincing evidence has made it clear that Jesus's tomb was indeed found empty on the Sunday after his crucifixion. But did Jesus really appear to his disciples after rising from the dead? If so, were his appearances to them bodily appearances or merely spiritual appearances?

According to the Gospels, the risen Jesus appeared to many people in his resurrected human body in the days following his crucifixion. The Gospels report the risen Jesus as appearing to different people at different locations over a period of forty days. The Gospels report nine different occasions in which the risen Jesus appears to various individuals or groups. In all of these appearances, Jesus has a physical human body. Jesus doesn't make his appearances as a spirit or as a ghost. The risen Jesus isn't like Casper the Friendly Ghost from the animated cartoon series on TV and in several movies! The risen Jesus proves that he has a physical body by inviting his disciples to touch him and by eating a piece of broiled fish in their presence (see Luke 24:36–43; John 20:26–29).

Like the Gospels, the books of Acts and 1 Corinthians also report the risen Jesus appearing to various people in the days after his crucifixion. In Acts, the risen Jesus appears to his disciples and to the apostle Paul (1:3–8; 9:1–19). Jesus again proves that he has a physical body by eating with his disciples (1:3–5). In 1 Corinthians, Paul writes that the appearances of the risen Jesus include his appearing to Peter, the twelve disciples, more than 500 disciples at one time, his brother James, and Paul himself (15:3–8). Paul also implies that Jesus's resurrection appearances were bodily appearances (15:35–57). Adding up the total number of Jesus's resurrection appearances recorded in the New Testament results in twelve total resurrection appearances.[25]

Why should we believe that the Gospels, Acts, and 1 Corinthians are accurately reporting Jesus's resurrection appearances? How do we know that these reports of Jesus's resurrection appearances aren't the inventions of the early Christians?

The Gospels' resurrection accounts are trustworthy because they pass the contemporary living test and the honest reporting test. By reporting women as the first witnesses to Jesus's resurrection, the Gospels pass the contemporary living test. As we discussed in chapter 5, the two parts of the honest reporting test are the cover-up test and the simplicity test. All four Gospels pass the cover-up test by having women being the first people to discover the empty tomb and to see the risen Jesus (see Matthew 28:1–10; Mark 16:1–8; Luke 24:1–10; John 20:1–2, 11–18). Since women's testimony in first-century Palestine wasn't usually accepted in a court of law, the Gospels must be telling the truth about women being the first to find the tomb empty and to see the risen Jesus. The Gospels' resurrection accounts also pass the simplicity test. They are told in a very simple and straightforward way. They lack any fanciful details, creative embellishments, and theological statements. For example, unlike one extrabiblical source, the Gospels' resurrection accounts don't describe huge angels or a talking cross.[26]

The Gospel reports of Jesus's resurrection are also trustworthy because they pass the human reason test and the all-inclusive test. They pass these tests by having accounts that are consistent with reliable eyewitness testimony. Reliable eyewitness testimony from more than one witness features the same basic facts in all accounts but also some variations in the details. The Gospel accounts of Jesus's resurrection contain no contradictions; they complement one another by telling the same basic story with differing details. If there are no differences in the details of the eyewitness accounts, the eyewitnesses must be guilty of collusion. Since the time of the early church father John Chrysostom (c. AD 347–407), Christians have correctly argued that the Gospel accounts of Jesus's resurrection differ in their details because the four Gospel writers were not guilty of collusion.[27] For example, Simon Greenleaf, one of the founders of Harvard University's law school, wrote a book in which he argued that the differences in details between the Gospel accounts of Jesus's resurrection show that the four Gospel writers didn't collude with one another.[28] Greenleaf's book is titled *The Testimony of the Evangelists, Examined by the Rules of Evidence Administered in Courts of Justice* (1846). Many scholars today continue to correctly point out that the Gospel reports of Jesus's resurrection are trustworthy because the Gospel writers didn't collude with one another.[29]

Besides passing the other four of the five big tests, the Gospel accounts of Jesus's resurrection unquestionably pass the divine glory test. Jesus's death and resurrection demonstrate that God is a good God who loves us and would do anything that He can do for us. Jesus's resurrection also demonstrates that God is a great God who is all-powerful and who can perform miracles. *The resurrection of Jesus is the most important and impressive miracle that God has performed in human history.*

The Gospel accounts of Jesus's resurrection pass all of the five big tests. Isn't that exciting?

Another reason why the Gospel reports of Jesus's resurrection appearances are trustworthy is that some of them are multiply attested in independent sources. In other words, some of Jesus's resurrection appearances are reported by different writers who wrote independent reports of the same event. The four multiply attested appearances of the risen Jesus are: a) the appearance to the female disciples (Matthew 28:8–10; John 20:11–17); b) the appearance to Peter (Luke 24:33–34; 1 Corinthians 15:3–5); c) the appearance to the Twelve (Luke 24:36–43; John 20:19–20; 1 Corinthians 15:3–5); and d) the appearance to the disciples in Galilee (Matthew 28:16–17; Mark 16:7; John 21).[30] Because these resurrection appearances are multiply attested, it is virtually certain that they actually occurred. In addition, the appearance of Jesus to the female disciples must be historical. There is no chance that the early Christians would have invented the story that Jesus appeared first to female disciples instead of to male disciples. Inventing that story would have been counterproductive to the Gospel writers' attempts to evangelize Jews in Palestine's patriarchal society.

Not only are the Gospel reports of Jesus's resurrection trustworthy, but the reports of Jesus's resurrection in Acts and 1 Corinthians are also trustworthy. Acts was written by Luke. We discovered in chapter 6 of this book that Luke was a very accurate historian. As a result, anything Luke writes in Acts and in the Gospel of Luke about Jesus is likely to be true. Luke reports in the book of Acts that the early Christians preached the resurrection of Jesus from the dead because the risen Jesus appeared to them (1:1–11; 2:24; 3:26; 9:1–6; 10:40; 13:33; 17:31). The reports of Jesus's resurrection in 1 Corinthians 15 are also trustworthy. As we learned earlier in this chapter, the tradition and creed found in 1 Corinthians 15:3–8 about Jesus's resurrection appearances go back to within five or six years of Jesus's crucifixion. The apostle Paul wrote 1 Corinthians 15:3–8 only after meeting and talking with Jesus's disciples Peter and John and Jesus's brother James (see Galatians 1:18–19; 2:1, 9). Paul received the tradition found in 1 Corinthians 15 from these three key Christian leaders, and he wrote the words contained in the tradition about twenty years after Jesus's crucifixion. Moreover, Paul also wrote about Jesus's resurrection before he wrote the tradition about it in 1 Corinthians 15 (see Galatians 1:1; 1 Thessalonians 1:10). *Because the belief in Jesus's resurrection goes back to the earliest Christians, there is no chance that Jesus's resurrection was made up by Luke, Paul, or any of the other New Testament writers.* The more than 500 eyewitnesses of the risen Jesus knew that Jesus rose from the dead (see 1 Corinthians 15:6).

Would the Early Christians Have Died for a Lie?

Some of you reading this book may still not be convinced that the Gospel writers, Peter, Paul, and James are telling the truth about what really happened to Jesus's body after he was crucified. Many people have died for a lie that they have mistakenly believed was true. However, Jesus's disciples knew the truth about whether Jesus really rose from the dead or didn't rise from the dead. If Jesus had not risen from the dead, his disciples and other key Christian leaders would have known the truth. Would the early Christians have been willing to die for what they knew was a lie? Would any group of people die for a belief that they knew was false? No, of course not!

Peter, Paul, James, and countless other early Christians were martyred for their belief that Jesus rose from the dead. Peter was crucified, Paul was beheaded, and James was stoned to death. The Gospel writer Mark was dragged by a rope through the streets until he died. The Gospel writer Matthew was killed by a sword wound for his faith in Jesus. All of the other twelve disciples besides John were also martyred for their faith. Only John died a natural death from old age.[31] These brave and honest men died for their faith because they were convinced that Jesus had risen from the dead. Josh McDowell and Sean McDowell write, "Jesus' followers could not have faced torture and death unless they were convinced of his resurrection."[32] His followers were convinced that his resurrection had really occurred because his tomb was empty and because the risen Jesus had appeared to them after his crucifixion. They were telling the truth. Gary Habermas and Michael Licona write, "The disciples' willingness to suffer and die for their beliefs indicates that they certainly regarded those beliefs as true. The case is strong that they did not willfully lie about the appearances of the risen Jesus. Liars make poor martyrs."[33]

Five Big Facts about Jesus: Other Explanations?

You might be thinking to yourself, "Wait a minute. Are there any other possible explanations for what happened on and after Easter Sunday? Could there be good alternative explanations for the known facts about Jesus? What are the alternative theories to explain what happened to Jesus after he was crucified?"

Before we discuss the alternative theories, let's discuss how we should evaluate them. Alternative theories to the resurrection of Jesus must explain five important facts about Jesus. *There are five big facts about Jesus and his impact on other people*:

1) Jesus was crucified by the Romans.
2) Jesus's tomb was discovered empty on Easter Sunday.
3) Jesus's disciples believed that he rose from the dead and appeared to them.
4) The church persecutor Paul was suddenly changed into a dedicated follower of Jesus.
5) The skeptic James, the brother of Jesus, was suddenly changed into a dedicated follower of Jesus.[34]

Four of these five big facts about Jesus are accepted by virtually all scholars who study the subject of Jesus's resurrection. Only the fact about the empty tomb isn't accepted by almost all scholars. The scholars who study Jesus's resurrection include many liberals, agnostics, and atheists. Nevertheless, 70–75% of all scholars who study Jesus's resurrection accept the empty tomb as a historical fact.[35] Moreover, we have already examined persuasive reasons for accepting that Jesus's tomb was indeed empty.

Earlier in this chapter, we discussed the first three of these five important facts. Let's discuss the last two facts now. The last two facts are that the church persecutor Paul and the skeptic James suddenly changed into dedicated followers of Jesus. Why did Paul and James suddenly change?

According to the New Testament, Paul and James suddenly changed due to their experience of seeing the risen Jesus. Because

Jesus appeared to him, Paul soon changed from a persecutor of Christians to a Christian missionary and an eloquent author of New Testament books. Jesus's appearance to Paul is recorded in Acts 9:1–6 and 1 Corinthians 15:3–8. Paul became not only a follower of Jesus but also the author of almost half of the books of the New Testament. Paul also suffered beatings, imprisonment, and martyrdom for his faith in Jesus (see Acts 24:27; 28:16–17, 30; 2 Corinthians 11:23–28; 2 Timothy 4:6). Similarly, Jesus's brother James didn't initially believe in Jesus (see Mark 3:20–21; John 7:5). However, soon after Jesus's death and resurrection, James joined the early church and became the leader of the church in Jerusalem (see Acts 1:12–14, 15:4–29). In addition, James wrote a book of the New Testament and was stoned to death for his faith in Jesus. James was willing to die for his faith in Jesus because he was convinced that the risen Jesus had appeared to him (see 1 Corinthians 15:3–7).

Skeptics have offered several different alternative theories to the resurrection of Jesus. The stolen body theory argues that Jesus's disciples stole his body while the Roman guards were sleeping. The swoon theory maintains that Jesus didn't really die on the cross; he only fainted as a result of blood loss and exhaustion. He was later revived in the tomb. The wrong tomb theory contends that the women who reported the tomb as being empty had mistakenly gone to the wrong tomb that morning. The hallucination theory asserts that the appearances of Jesus were auditory and visual hallucinations that Jesus's disciples saw. The myth theory argues that the idea of Jesus's resurrection was taken from the Greco-Roman mystery religions. Finally, the substitution theory claims that Jesus wasn't really crucified; an innocent bystander was crucified in his place.

Although these alternative theories appeal to some people, none of them can explain all five of the most important facts that we know about Jesus. The stolen body theory, the swoon theory, and the wrong tomb theory can only explain the crucifixion and the empty tomb; they can't explain the other three facts. The hallucination theory can explain the crucifixion and the disciples' belief that Jesus rose from the dead and appeared to them, but it can't explain the other three facts. The myth theory can only explain Jesus's crucifixion; it can't explain the other four facts. Lastly, the substitution theory explains none of the five facts. Only Jesus's resurrection explains all five of the big facts that we know about Jesus.

Gary Habermas and Michael Licona write the following about these other theories:

> We have seen that, to date, no opposing theories have developed that can adequately account for the collection of facts we have. That leaves us with good reason to hold Jesus rose from the dead and no good reason for rejecting it. Therefore, Jesus' resurrection is more than the most plausible explanation to account for the data. It is the only explanation that accounts adequately for all of the facts.[36]

Because none of the alternative theories can explain all of the five big facts about Jesus, none of them accurately describe what really happened to Jesus after he was crucified.

In addition to not explaining all five facts, the most popular alternative theories suffer from other noteworthy weaknesses. For example, the wrong tomb theory ignores the presence of the women who were at Jesus's crucifixion and observed where Jesus was buried. They knew exactly where he was buried—in Joseph of Arimathea's tomb (see Matthew 27:55–61; Mark 15:40–47; Luke 23:49–56; John 19:25–27). Therefore, the women couldn't have gone to the wrong tomb. Similarly,

The resurrection of Jesus is the only adequate explanation for the five most important facts that we know about him.

the hallucination theory ignores the reality that Jesus's resurrection in a physical body is multiply and independently attested in the Gospels (see Luke 24:36–43; John 20:24–29). It's also impossible to believe that over 500 people could have seen the same hallucination for forty days.[37] Finally, the myth theory fails to consider that there was not enough time for myths or legends about Jesus to develop.

Jesus's death and resurrection were part of the very early creed of 1 Corinthians 15 within several years of Jesus's death.

The myth theory also suffers from another weakness. It doesn't make any sense. Why doesn't it make any sense? There were significant differences between the death and resurrection of Jesus and the death and rising-again myths about Osiris and other mystery religions. The differences between the death and resurrection of Jesus and the dying and rising gods of the mystery religions are the following:

1) Only Jesus died for someone else.
2) Only Jesus died for sin.
3) Only Jesus died once instead of many times.
4) Only Jesus's death was an actual event in history.
5) Only Jesus died voluntarily.
6) Only Jesus's death was a triumph rather than a defeat.[38]

In contrast to the alternative theories, Jesus's resurrection doesn't suffer from any weaknesses as an explanation for the most important historical facts about Jesus of Nazareth. *Jesus's resurrection explains the five big facts about Jesus, and it also explains much more.* These additional explanations of so many facts provide even more evidence that Jesus' resurrection really occurred and that Jesus's resurrection easily passes the all-inclusive test.

Besides explaining the most important facts about him, the resurrection of Jesus explains why the Christian church began and why many early Christians were willing to die for their faith. Why would the early Christians worship a man who was charged with blasphemy by the Jews and with treason and sedition by the Romans? Why would the early Christians worship a man who was crucified as a criminal? Why were the early Christians willing to die for their belief in this man? *The existence of the Christian church and the martyrdom of many early Christians make absolutely no sense unless Jesus did really rise from the dead.* The disciples of Jesus and many other early Christians were only willing to die for their faith because they knew that Jesus had conquered death by rising again. The disciples and other early

Christians weren't lying, mistaken, or hallucinating about Jesus's resurrection; they were telling the truth about it.

Jesus's Remains Would Have Been Found

If Jesus had not risen from the dead, his remains would have been found either immediately or eventually. If Jesus was buried in Joseph of Arimathea's tomb, his body would have been found immediately by the women who went to his tomb on Easter Sunday. Even if Jesus was buried in a different tomb, his remains would have been found eventually. *The fact that Jesus was almost certainly given a proper burial and his remains were never discovered provides indirect evidence that Jesus rose from the dead.*

A modern-day example of human remains that were found in the 1990s makes it clear that if Jesus had not risen from the dead, his remains would also have been found. The remains of a prominent leader who is worshipped as God incarnate—as the one person who is God in the flesh—are going to be found either quickly or eventually!

Have you ever heard of the late Jamaican singer Bob Marley? I used to listen to his music when I was in high school. Marley was not only a famous reggae music star but also a Rastafari icon. As a Rastafari devotee, Marley worshipped Ras Tafari Makonnen, who took the royal name of Haile Selassie I, as God incarnate. [39] Selassie was the emperor of Ethiopia from 1930 to 1974.

Rastafari began to regard Selassie as God incarnate soon after he became the emperor in 1930. They considered Selassie to be God in human flesh because of his powerful royal name (which means "Might of the Trinity" or "Power of the Trinity") and his claim to be a direct descendant of King Solomon of Israel and the Queen of Sheba. [40] Rastafari also regarded Selassie's success in keeping Ethiopia uncolonized by European countries and his powerful speech before the United Nations in 1963 as evidence of his divinity. Selassie's worldly success resulted in his appearing on the cover of *Time* magazine in 1930 as "The King of Kings" [41] and in 1936 as the "Man of the Year." [42] Nevertheless, Selassie couldn't escape being assassinated in 1975. His remains were missing for more than sixteen years until they were found in a secret grave in 1992.[43]

Let's summarize the similarities and differences between Selassie and Jesus. Like Selassie, Jesus was considered to be God incarnate by many people. In addition, Selassie's and Jesus's remains were missing after they died. In contrast to Selassie's remains, Jesus's remains have never been found even though almost 2,000 years have elapsed since Jesus's death. The discovery of Selassie's remains demonstrates that he was a powerful historical figure but not God incarnate. On the other hand, the failure of anyone to ever discover Jesus's remains provides indirect evidence for Jesus being the one and only divine Son of God.

If Jesus didn't rise from the dead, his body would have been found by people who knew him in the first century. If Jesus had not risen from the dead, it's certain that his body would have been found by his disciples, the Jewish religious leaders, or the Roman soldiers. The Jewish leaders and Roman soldiers would have been highly motivated to produce his body and thereby deal a crushing blow to the Christian movement that they greatly despised. The failure of anyone to ever find Jesus's remains despite his being considered God incarnate by his followers offers indirect evidence that Jesus rose from the dead.

Why Does Jesus's Resurrection Still Matter Today?

Why should we care about an event that happened thousands of years ago in the city of Jerusalem? It was so long ago and so far away! Even though Jesus's resurrection occurred almost 2,000 years ago, it still matters to us today. *Jesus's resurrection still matters today for at least six very important reasons.* It shows us the following:

1) God exists.
2) Jesus told the truth about who he was and is as the divine Son of God.
3) Jesus will judge us someday.
4) Like Jesus, we will be resurrected and have immortal resurrected bodies.

5) Jesus enables us to answer life's most important questions.
6) Jesus is the way to God and the one who meets our biggest needs.

The bodily resurrection of Jesus from the dead clearly shows us that God really exists. Jesus's resurrection on Easter Sunday is unquestionably a divine miracle. We all know that when people die, their bodies decompose. Dead people can't and don't rise from the dead unless God intervenes and a miracle occurs. Jesus's resurrection from the dead was a divine miracle in which the laws of nature were suspended. Jesus couldn't have risen from the dead by any natural means. His resurrection must have involved what one writer calls "a direct injection of supernatural power."[44] Since Jesus rose from the dead, God must exist.

Jesus's resurrection also shows that Jesus told the truth about who he was and still is as the divine Son of God. We know that Jesus must have claimed to be God's Son and a King because he never would have been crucified by the Romans if he had not claimed to be divine and a King. Jesus had no army, and thus he posed no military threat to Roman rule. However, his claim to be God's Son and the King of the Jews seemed threatening to the Romans' desire to keep the peace in Palestine. His claims led directly to his crucifixion (see Matthew 26:63–66; John 18:33–37). When Jesus rose from the dead, God demonstrated His approval of Jesus's claim to be the royal and divine Son of God. God would not have raised Jesus from the dead if Jesus had been lying about his identity or anything else that he taught. Gary Habermas, the world's leading expert on Jesus's resurrection, writes, "By raising Jesus from the dead, God placed His stamp of approval on Jesus's entire message, both concerning himself and his other teachings, because God would not have raised a heretic from the dead."[45]

One of Jesus's most important teachings in the Gospels is that he will judge us someday. In John 5:22, Jesus claims that he will judge every one of us someday. Peter and Paul also state that God will have Jesus judge us (see Acts 10:42; Romans 2:16). In his famous words to the atheists and pantheists of his day, Paul states that God has proven that Jesus will judge us by having Jesus rise from the dead (see Acts 17:31). Jesus's judgment of us will be fair because Jesus knows how hard life on earth can be for each of us. Jesus was often tempted to sin, and he suffered a lot during his earthly life, especially when he died on the cross. Moreover, despite his temptations and sufferings, Jesus never sinned (see Matthew 4:1–11; John 8:29, 46; Hebrews 4:15; 1 Peter 2:22). Jesus is the perfect Judge for us. He can fairly judge us, and he will fairly judge us when we die.

In addition to serving as our judge, Jesus shows us that we will also rise from the dead in the future. Jesus says in John 5:28–29 that all of us will be physically resurrected. The prophet Daniel and the apostle Paul say the same thing (see Daniel 12:2; Acts 24:14–15). Those of us who have genuine faith in God will spend eternity with Him, and those of us who haven't really trusted in God will spend eternity away from Him. We will all have our resurrected bodies forever. Jesus's resurrection proves that we also will be resurrected in the future and have resurrected and immortal bodies. Isn't that exhilarating?

Because of his miraculous resurrection, Jesus enables us to answer life's most important questions. Do you remember the five questions that I mentioned at the beginning of chapter 1? The five big questions are the following:

1) Who am I?
2) Where did I come from?
3) Why am I here?
4) What has gone wrong with the world?
5) What solution can solve the problem?

Because we have seen that Jesus rose from the dead, we can now answer all five of these crucial questions. Here are some brief answers for all five of these questions:

1) You are a person with an immortal soul, a conscience, and the ability to think, feel, and choose. As a result, you have physical, emotional, spiritual, social, and financial needs.
2) You were created by God in His image.

3) You are here on earth to live for God and for Jesus. As a result, you have a longing for God and for immortality.

4) Sin has entered into the world, making it broken and making us in need of God's forgiveness.

5) Jesus enables us to be forgiven by God through his perfect life, his death on the cross in our place, and his resurrection from the dead. Everyone who believes in Jesus as our way to God is forgiven by God and given joy, peace, a purpose in life, and eternal life.

The resurrection of Jesus shows that Jesus is the way to God and the one who meets our biggest needs. Jesus is the way to God because he lived a sinless life, died for us, and rose again. No one else in human history has lived a sinless life and risen from the dead in an immortal body. Jesus is only able to offer us peace with God, a joyful life, purpose in life, and forgiveness of our sins because he

Jesus's resurrection makes it possible for us to adequately answer the five big questions.

died for us and rose from the dead. Jesus is the only one capable of offering us eternal life in heaven because he has risen from the dead and because he is still alive today. Could a dead person offer us eternal life in heaven? Of course not! Jesus is ready, willing, and able to meet our biggest needs because he loves us, died for us, and rose again. We all need peace, joy, a purpose in life, hope, and forgiveness. Jesus meets those needs for us if we believe in him.

In John 14:6, Jesus says that he is the way to God, and he says that none of us can come to God without believing in him. Jesus seems to say that not all religions lead to God. Is Jesus really saying that he is the only way to God and that non-Christian religions aren't ways to God?

Does the Christian Faith Pass the Five Big Tests?

Before we address the issue of other religions, let's quickly summarize what we learned in chapters 6 and 7. We have learned that the four Gospels themselves and the Gospel accounts of Jesus's resurrection pass all five big tests and explain all five big facts about Jesus. This fact should make us consider the Gospels trustworthy and the resurrection of Jesus a historical fact. The Christian faith and the Christian worldview pass the five big tests because the four Gospels and their resurrection accounts pass them. Please see table 2 below.

Table 2. Does the Christian Faith Pass the Five Big Tests?

The Five Big Tests	Four Gospels	Resurrection Accounts	Christian Faith
human reason test	✓	✓	✓
contemporary living test	✓	✓	✓
divine glory test	✓	✓	✓
honest reporting test	✓	✓	✓
all-inclusive test	✓	✓	✓

We have learned some very important facts in this chapter and in the previous chapter. Let's list what we have discovered in chapters 6 and 7 from a variety of convincing evidence:

1) The Christian faith and the Christian worldview pass all the five big tests that we can use to determine if our beliefs are true or false.
2) The Gospels tell the truth about what Jesus said and did.
3) Jesus performed miracles, claimed to be divine, died by crucifixion, and rose from the dead.

Robert Bowman and Ed Komoszewski provide a helpful summary of what we know about Jesus based on reliable evidence. They write:

> The evidence shows that the Jesus of history was a real man who performed remarkable healings and exorcisms, who proclaimed that in him the kingdom of God had drawn near, who made various other astonishing claims for himself that his disciples came to understand were claims to deity, who died on a cross by the order of Pontius Pilate, and yes, who rose from the dead.[46]

Perhaps the most important fact that we have learned so far in this book is that Jesus conquered the grave by rising from the dead. *Jesus did really rise from the dead, and our beliefs need to be able to explain the significance of that amazing historical fact.*

Is Jesus the Only Way to God?

Do you believe that Jesus rose from the dead? Do you believe that Jesus is the only way to God? Although many of you reading this book believe in Jesus, many others of you probably think that there are many other ways to God besides Jesus. Aren't all religions ways to God? Many of you think that all religions and worldviews lead to God.

In the next chapter, we will address the issue of whether or not all religions lead to God. With God's help, I will do my best to carefully and adequately handle this sensitive and significant issue. After explaining the main beliefs of the major non-Christian religions, we will use the five big tests to evaluate the major non-Christian religions and worldviews.

8

Aren't All Religions Ways to God?

One of the most memorable experiences of my life was my wife's birthday party in 2009. It was unforgettable because the vast majority of the people who attended the birthday party were Hindus from India. We both enjoyed a wonderful time eating and talking with our Hindu friends. An American friend sang a beautiful song for all of us, and our Hindu friends had a delightful time at our apartment talking about American and Indian culture. We talked about food, sports, clothes, weddings, names, and other interesting topics. I learned a lot about Indian culture that evening! Rosy served a delicious Brazilian meal for all of us, and we ate a yummy cake together. It was a fantastic birthday party filled with learning and laughter!

From 2009 to 2011, Rosy and I lived in an ethnically diverse apartment complex near St. Paul, Minnesota. Most of the people whom we met and talked with in the apartments near us were Hindus from India. We would often go to the apartments of our Hindu neighbors to talk with them, and they frequently offered us delicious Indian food. We sometimes also went out to dinner and a movie with our Hindu friends. They were very kind and friendly toward us, and we always had a great time with them. Rosy and I cherish our memories with our Hindu friends Ravi, Naveena, Prath, Poonam, and many others. We miss seeing them, talking with them, and eating dinner with them. My wife and I feel blessed by God to have had our Hindu friends in our lives.

I would like to believe that all religions lead to God because of my enjoyable personal experiences with people from various religions. God has blessed me with great conversations with Christians, Hindus, Muslims, New Agers, and people from other religious backgrounds. I know from my own personal experience that many Christians, Hindus, Muslims, New Agers, and people from other religious backgrounds are intelligent and friendly people. I want to believe that all religions lead to God and that everyone will spend eternity in heaven with God. However, my desire for this or anything else to be true can be wishful thinking rather than an accurate description of what is really true. I always have to keep in mind that my desire for something to be true doesn't mean that it really is true.

Partly because of our own personal experiences, many of us believe that all religions lead to God. Positive personal experiences with Christians, Muslims, Hindus, Buddhists, and people of other faiths have convinced many of us that all religions are basically the same and that God accepts people of all religions. Many of us want to believe that all religions are equally legitimate ways to find God. Nevertheless, many of us remain unconvinced that all religions lead to God. How do we know whether or not all religions lead to God?

As we seek to evaluate various worldviews, please keep in mind that strong evidence determines what is true. Our personal experiences should influence our beliefs, not determine them. The truth is that some people enjoy killing, stealing, lying, and committing adultery even though these behaviors are wrong. Does someone's enjoyment of such behaviors make them morally acceptable? Of course not! Similarly, our positive or negative experiences with people from different religious backgrounds shouldn't determine our beliefs about the adherents of those religions. *Evidence—not experience—determines what is true in this world as far as our religious and worldview beliefs are concerned.*

In our process of evaluating worldviews, we should also remember another important principle. Here's the principle: *we should base our evaluation of a worldview on the life and beliefs of its founder, not just on the lives and beliefs of its followers.* The lives and beliefs of a worldview's

> **Whether you are a Christian, Jew, Muslim, Hindu, Buddhist, or a New Ager, God loves you. He is ready, willing, and able to meet your most important needs.**

followers can show us that a worldview is livable and attractive and thus possibly true. In contrast, the life and beliefs of a worldview's founder can demonstrate to us whether a worldview is true or false.

In order for a worldview to be true, its founder must have lived a very righteous life and have believed what is true about God.

During our evaluation process, please also remember something else that is very important. *Whether you're a Christian, Jew, Muslim, Hindu, Buddhist, or a New Ager, God loves you. He also loves you if you are an adherent of any other religion or if you are an atheist or an agnostic. God loves you, and He is ready, willing, and able to meet your biggest needs.* He wants you to accept His love, and He wants to meet your emotional and spiritual needs. God wants you to find your joy, peace, and purpose in Him. God wants you to find your hope and forgiveness in Him. He also wants you to have eternal life. Allowing God to meet your biggest needs requires your willingness to honestly and carefully evaluate your own spiritual beliefs so that you know if they are true. God will reveal the truth to you if you sincerely ask Him to do so (see Matthew 7:7–8)!

In chapter 5 of this book, we discovered how each of us can evaluate our spiritual beliefs. We can use the five big tests to determine whether our spiritual beliefs are true or false. Let's review the names of the tests that make up the five big tests. The five big tests include the human reason test, the contemporary living test, the divine glory test, the honest reporting test, and the all-inclusive test. We have already seen that the Christian worldview as presented in the Gospels passes all five of these crucial tests. Will other major world religions also pass all five of the tests? Let's briefly describe and evaluate Judaism, Islam, Hinduism, Buddhism, and the New Age. We will use the five big tests to evaluate each of these non-Christian religions.

Even though I'm a Christian, I would like all the non-Christian religions or worldviews to pass all of the five big tests. But will any of the major non-Christian worldviews pass all five of the tests? We will soon find out!

We can use the five big tests to help us determine if the most common worldviews are true or not.

The five big tests aren't meant to judge any of us, but they are meant to accurately assess our worldviews. Only God can judge us because only He is all-knowing and all-powerful. I can't judge anyone else because I'm not God. However, the five big tests enable us to determine if our worldview provides us with a correct view of God, us as human beings, and the world. Let's begin our description and evaluation of non-Christian worldviews by examining Judaism.

What Is Judaism?

Many Jewish people are smart and successful individuals who are also very well-known. For example, Mayim Bialik is an American actress who has appeared in the NBC sitcom *Blossom* (1991–1995) and the CBS sitcom *The Big Bang Theory* (2010–2019). Since 2021, she has hosted the very popular TV game show *Jeopardy* many times. Bialik is not only an actress and game show host but also an extremely intelligent woman. She was accepted into both Harvard and Yale, but she chose to stay closer to home by earning a bachelor's degree and a PhD in neuroscience from UCLA. Moreover, she was raised Jewish and aspires to be a Modern Orthodox Jew.[1] Bialik is one example of a Jewish person who has made a big impact on American TV.

Since 1973, ABC has aired the Academy Award-winning movie *The Ten Commandments* almost every year at Easter and Passover time. Millions of people watch the movie every year that it's on TV. The classic biblical epic remains one of the most popular films ever made, and it has been one of my favorite movies for over forty years. I have watched the movie so many times that I have memorized many of the actors' and actresses' lines! *The Ten Commandments* was nominated for seven Academy Awards, and it won the Academy Award for Best Special Effects.[2] The parting of the Red Sea and other scenes from the movie are stunning, especially considering that the movie was initially released back in the 1950s. The movie was also a box-office hit and hugely profitable.

Why has *The Ten Commandments* made such a lasting impact on our American culture? Why has the movie remained popular for decades? The movie is based on the true story of Moses, one of the most important people in world history and perhaps the most important man in the Jewish Bible (i.e., the Old Testament). According to some scholars, Moses lived from about 1391–1271 BC.[3] *The Ten Commandments* features Moses's unforgettable story of being rescued from an evil king, becoming a prince of Egypt, and freeing his people from slavery. Moses's parting of the Red Sea is the most remarkable miracle recorded in the Old Testament, and Moses's life is one of the most inspirational and impactful lives that has ever been lived. Moses speaks with God directly, gives his people the Ten Commandments that were inscribed on stone tablets by God, and writes the first five books of the Jewish Bible. Moses is a heroic and courageous man who exhibits tremendous faith in God and reverence for Him. By giving God's laws to Israel, Moses makes a bigger impact on Judaism than any other person has ever made.

Although the enormous impact of Moses can't be denied, he isn't the founder of Judaism. Abraham is the founder of Judaism. Like Moses, Abraham is mentioned frequently in the Old Testament, the New Testament, and the Muslim Quran (Koran). When Abraham is living in Mesopotamia, God promises to bless him with a son and many descendants (see Genesis 12:1–3; 15:5–6). Despite his strong faith in God, Abraham isn't perfect. Abraham asks his wife to lie about who she is while they are in Egypt, and Abraham himself lies about his wife's identity to a king (see Genesis 12:11–13; 20:1–2). He also agrees with his wife Sarah's plan for him to have a son through her Egyptian slave Hagar (see Genesis 16:1–4). Abraham and his wife had grown impatient and had begun to doubt that God would bless them with a son together. Nevertheless, God eventually blesses Abraham with a son named Isaac when he is 100 years old (see Genesis 21:2–5). Abraham, Isaac, and Isaac's son Jacob become the patriarchs of the Old Testament. Each of these three men worships the one God of Israel, whom Moses knew as the LORD, the eternally existing God (see Exodus 3:14–15).

Since the time of Abraham (c. 2150–c. 1975 BC), Judaism has been strictly monotheistic. In other words, Jews worship only one God, the LORD. Devout Jews recite the biblical passage called the Shema every day because it affirms that there is only one God (see Deuteronomy 6:4–5). The existence of only one God is the most important belief in Judaism. Jews believe that they worship the one and only true God. In Deuteronomy 4:39, Moses writes that "the LORD alone is God in heaven above and on earth below; there is no other."[4]

Despite its very ancient origin, Judaism only began to develop its current form as the religion of the rabbis starting in about 200 BC. Its teachings and practices became more well-defined and clearer after the destruction of the temple in AD 70. Since that time, Jews have divided their Jewish Bible into three parts: 1) the Law; 2) the Prophets; and 3) the Writings. Moreover, the Talmud is considered by Jews to offer useful rabbinic interpretations of the Jewish Bible. The Talmud includes the *Mishnah* and the *Gemara*, and it was written between about AD 200 and AD 550.[5]

The most important part of the Jewish Bible is the Law, also known as the Torah. The Torah includes the first five books of the Jewish Bible, which were written by Moses. The Torah includes many commandments, including the famous Ten Commandments. In total, there are 613 commandments in the Torah—248 positive commandments and 365 negative commandments.[6] That's a lot of commandments, isn't it? One of the most important commandments prohibits working on the Sabbath day (i.e., Saturday). Other very important commandments require keeping the dietary laws by eating kosher foods. Other noteworthy commandments require celebrating such holidays or festivals as Passover and Yom Kippur (the Day of Atonement).

In addition to these two holidays, Jews also celebrate such other holidays as Hanukkah and Purim. Hanukkah is a festive holiday that commemorates the victory of the Jewish Maccabees over the Syrian armies of Antiochus Epiphanes (c. 175 BC). Purim is a partylike holiday similar to Marti Gras in the USA or Carnival in South America. It involves dressing in costume, excessive drinking, and making a lot of noise.[7] Purim recounts the story of Esther, the beautiful Jewish woman who becomes queen and helps her people to avoid being destroyed by the evil and anti-Semitic Haman, who was one of the king's advisors.

Besides keeping the Law of Moses and celebrating holidays, Jews also hold key beliefs about human nature and the Messiah. According to Jews, human nature is morally neutral or basically good. Jews reject the doctrine of original sin, which says that humans are born with a tendency to sin. Jews believe that people are born innocent. For that reason, Judaism is a performance-based religion in which people can go to heaven if they do more good deeds than bad deeds.[8] Moreover, Jews contend that the promised Messiah is a human being who isn't divine. They are still waiting for their Messiah to come in the future to establish peace and justice on the earth.

Does Judaism Pass the Five Big Tests?

Judaism passes three of the five big tests. It passes the honest reporting test, the contemporary living test, and the all-inclusive test. However, Judaism seems to fail the human reason test and the divine glory test.

Judaism easily passes the honest reporting test. The number of embarrassing stories in the Jewish Bible is shocking. The Old Testament is full of embarrassing stories about Abraham, Isaac, Jacob, Moses, David, Solomon, and many other important Hebrew figures. The Jewish Bible records stories of Abraham lying, Isaac being deceived by Jacob, Jacob being deceived by his father-in-law, and Moses being prohibited from entering the Promised Land (see Genesis 20:1–2; 27:1–36; 29:15–30; Deuteronomy 32:48–52). The Old Testament also contains stories of King David committing adultery, King Solomon worshipping idols and foreign gods, and other Jewish kings sacrificing their sons in the fire as part of their worship of foreign gods (see 2 Samuel 11:1–4; 1 Kings 11:1–8; 2 Kings 16:1–4; 21:1–6). Furthermore, the Old Testament honestly reports the Jewish kings' evil practices during the time of the divided monarchy. The Jewish Bible describes all twenty of the kings of Israel as being evil, and it describes twelve of the twenty kings of Judah as also being evil.[9]

Because of their evil kings, the people of Israel and the people of Judah became idol worshippers. God punished the people of Israel by allowing them to be taken into exile in Assyria, and He punished the people of Judah by permitting them to be taken into exile in Babylon after the Babylonians destroyed the Jerusalem temple (see 2 Kings 17:7–23; 25:1–21). These embarrassing stories are told in a straightforward manner with no detectable fabricated details.

Judaism also passes the contemporary living test. The Jewish Bible upholds the dignity and value of all human beings, and Judaism presents itself as a livable religion. The Old Testament declares that God made both men and women in His image (see Genesis 1:26–27). The Jewish Bible commands and encourages God's people to be generous toward the poor and foreigners (see Leviticus 19:9–10; Deuteronomy 15:11; Proverbs 19:17). It also commands God's people to defend the rights of the poor and the needy (see Proverbs 31:8–9). The God of the Old Testament clearly cares about men and women of all races and classes. In addition, Judaism is a livable religion even though it does have hundreds of commandments.

Judaism not only passes the contemporary living test but also the all-inclusive test. This test says that a worldview or religion must adequately explain the presence of suffering in the world and receive some support from scientific findings. Judaism adequately explains human suffering, and it receives a lot of support from important scientific findings.

Judaism provides helpful insights about the causes of suffering and how to handle suffering. Judaism correctly points out that some of our suffering results from sin, and some of our suffering results from Satan (see Genesis 6:5–7:24; Job 1–2). God permits us to suffer, but He doesn't cause us to suffer. In addition, the Old Testament correctly asserts that the proper way to handle suffering is to trust in God and to obey Him (see Psalms 13; 42; Ecclesiastes 12:8, 13–14).

Although it's not a science textbook, the Old Testament contains advanced scientific knowledge that provides strong evidence for its divine origin. Due to the COVID-19 pandemic, we all became familiar with quarantines and self-isolation. Both of these concepts originally come from the Old Testament book of Leviticus, which was written about 1400 BC (see Leviticus 13).

Commenting on Leviticus 13, Skip Heitzig writes:

> Leviticus 13:1–8 lays out the law concerning leprosy (a large grouping of infectious skin diseases of varying severity). It consists of a 14-day quarantine, divided by two seven-day examinations to

determine if the disease is a threat to the greater community. If someone tested positive, he or she had to publicly declare themselves unclean. Sounds eerily familiar, doesn't it?[10]

Quarantines weren't practiced in Europe until after the Black Death (bubonic plague) of the 1300s, the most fatal global pandemic in human history. This deadly pandemic killed a mind-boggling 60% of Europe's population[11] because the biblical principles of quarantines and self-isolation weren't followed.

In addition to mentioning quarantines and self-isolation, the Old Testament contains other advanced scientific knowledge showing that the Jewish Bible was ahead of its time and divinely inspired. For example, the idea that blood circulation is the source of life for flesh is clearly stated in Leviticus thousands of years before William Harvey became the first scientist to discover this truth in 1616. Two other examples supply further evidence of the Old Testament's divine origin. The second law of thermodynamics was not discovered by scientists until the 19th century, but it is clearly described in Psalm 102:25–26, which says that the universe will "wear out." Lastly, the expansion of the universe seems to be clearly mentioned in the Old Testament (see Psalm 104:1–2). God's "stretching out the heavens" was not discovered by scientists until Edwin Hubble's famous discovery of the expanding universe in 1929.

Like the Old Testament's advanced scientific knowledge, many archeological finds enable the Old Testament to pass the all-inclusive test. These amazing archeological finds support the accuracy of the Old Testament. For example, a significant archeological find has verified the existence of King David, the most important king in Israel's history. In 1993 and 1994, archeologists digging at Tel Dan in northern Israel found an Aramaic inscription referring to the "house of David" on a stele (an upright stone slab or pillar). The 9th or 8th century BC inscription was made by a king who lived about a hundred years after David. The king claims to have defeated the "king of Israel" and the "king of the House of David." As the first mention of David outside the Bible, this inscription proves that David was a genuine historical figure, not a made-up figure of later Old Testament editors or writers.

Another important archeological discovery is an inscription in King Hezekiah's Tunnel, which was discovered in 1880 by two boys who were swimming. The tunnel was dug through solid bedrock, and it's 1,750 feet long! The inscription verifies the biblical story of King Hezekiah having a tunnel built to divert the waters of the Gihon Spring into Jerusalem so that he and his people could survive an invasion by an enemy's army (see 2 Kings 20:20; 2 Chronicles 32:1–20).[12] Tourists today can walk in knee-high water through Hezekiah's Tunnel, which still carries water from the Gihon Spring to the Pool of Siloam. Doesn't that sound like a fun thing to do?

Although Hezekiah's Tunnel remains an important archeological discovery, the Dead Sea Scrolls are the most important archeological find of all time. Between 1947 and 1956, the Dead Sea Scrolls were found at and near Qumran in eleven different caves by Bedouin shepherds and a team of archeologists. The scrolls were hidden in pots in cliff-top caves. These ancient texts were written in Hebrew, Aramaic, and Greek. They contain Bible verses from all Old Testament books except for Esther, and they date from about 300/250 BC to AD 135.[13] The Dead Sea Scrolls are the oldest known copies of the Old Testament books, and they include a complete copy of the book of Isaiah dated to about 125 BC. Most importantly, the Dead Sea Scrolls are identical to our modern Hebrew Bible in 95% of the text. The 5% variation consists mainly of obvious slips of the pen and spelling alterations.[14] *The Dead Sea Scrolls show that the Old Testament has been accurately copied and preserved.*

While Judaism clearly passes the all-inclusive test, it doesn't seem to pass the human reason test. Judaism seems to fail the human reason test by teaching beliefs that are contrary to the actual teachings of the Jewish Bible. For example, the Old Testament clearly implies in various passages that the one God exists in more than one person. God speaks about "us" creating men and women in His own image (see Genesis 1:26–27). The Old Testament also records God appearing as a man to people several times (e.g., Genesis 18:1–3; 32:24–30; Judges 6:11–23; 13:3–22; Daniel 3:13–30). God even appears to the patriarch Jacob in the form of a man, and he wrestles with Jacob (see Genesis 32:24–30)! In some of these appearances of God (called "theophanies"), the angel of the LORD is described as a divine being who is clearly different from the LORD (see Zechariah 3:1–10; 12:8). Since the angel of the LORD is different from the LORD, the one God must consist of at least two persons. Moreover, unlike modern Judaism, the Old Testament clearly teaches that people are born with the tendency to sin. They aren't born innocent (see Psalm 51:5).

Judaism also seems to fail the divine glory test. This test points out that our spiritual beliefs must portray God as being good and great. Our beliefs shouldn't imply that God currently lacks or has ever lacked any essential divine characteristic, such as love. Our beliefs also shouldn't imply that God needs us. He is self-sufficient. He doesn't need us. However, modern Judaism implies that God is neither completely loving nor self-sufficient. If the one God exists in only one person, then He isn't loving and self-sufficient by nature. Why? If God needs us to be the object of His love and to reciprocate His love, He would only be potentially loving instead of loving by nature. Thus, for God to be loving and self-sufficient by nature, He must have at least one eternal object of His love within the Godhead. The one eternal God must have at least two persons in the Godhead. Furthermore, modern Judaism implies that God isn't completely holy and just. If God never came to earth to live here as a human being, God wouldn't be holy or just. It would be unfair for God to judge us if He never came to earth to directly experience how hard human life can be with its suffering, pain, disappointments, and temptations. Since God is holy and just, He must have come to live on earth as a human being.

Does Messianic Judaism Pass the Five Big Tests?

Have you ever heard of Messianic Judaism? I first heard of it about twenty years ago when I was invited to attend a Passover Seder, which is a ritual feast that marks the beginning of the Jewish holiday of Passover. Although I knew almost nothing about a Passover Seder, I decided to attend it with a friend who invited me. The Seder was held at his local church in a suburb of Minneapolis. It featured kosher food and the beautiful music of Marty Goetz, a Messianic Jew and a modern-day psalmist. I truly enjoyed the food, music, Scripture reading, and conversations that I had that wonderful night. I still remember the words of one of the moving songs I heard that night. After the night was over, I really wanted to attend another Passover Seder in the future.

God gave me the opportunity to participate in another Passover Seder in 2017. The second Passover Seder I attended was held at the home of some friends whom I have known for more than a decade. My wife and I were grateful that our friends invited us to the Seder. God blessed us with stimulating conversations, good food, and the joy of His presence during the meal. It lasted for over six hours, but it was fun and unforgettable. It was also by far the longest meal that I have ever eaten!

In 2016, I had the privilege of meeting a very smart and spiritually mature Messianic Jew named Rabbi Joel Liberman. Rabbi Liberman and I were both students in the same doctoral program, and we were able to have a few good conversations with each other. I always enjoyed responding to his online discussion board posts for the courses we both took in 2015 and 2016. He also responded with encouraging words to many of my online discussion board posts. Rabbi Liberman is the leader of a messianic congregation in San Diego, California, and the current president of the Messianic Jewish Alliance of America. He has been active in the Messianic Judaism movement for over thirty years. Rabbi Liberman is a friendly and intelligent man, and he enjoys a vibrant relationship with God through his faith in Jesus.

Messianic Judaism is a biblically based movement of Jewish people who believe that Jesus is the promised Jewish Messiah predicted in the Old Testament. Messianic Jews believe in Jesus, whom they call *Yeshua* because *Yeshua* is Jesus's name in Hebrew. Messianic Jews believe that Jesus is the Messiah—the Christ.[15] Like Christians, Messianic Jews accept the Old Testament and the New Testament as authoritative Scriptures that are inspired by God. Therefore, Messianic Judaism is considered a form of the Christian faith. Today, there are thousands of Messianic Jews in the USA and in other countries.

Like Christians, Messianic Jews believe in Jesus as the Messiah because he has already fulfilled some important messianic prophecies. Jesus fulfilled the prophecy that the Messiah would be a divine person (see Isaiah 9:6–7; John 1:1, 14). Jesus fulfilled the prophecy that the Messiah would be miraculously born of a virgin (see Isaiah 7:14; Matthew 1:20–25; Luke 1:26–38). He also fulfilled the prophecy that the Messiah would be born in the town of Bethlehem (see Micah 5:2; Matthew 2:1–6; Luke 2:4–7). Jesus fulfilled the prophecies that the Messiah would perform miracles (see Isaiah 29:18; 35:4–6; Matthew 11:2–5). He also fulfilled the prophecy that the Messiah would be crucified (see Psalm 22:1, 16; Mark 15:25, 34). Jesus even fulfilled the prophecy that the Messiah would be killed in the year AD 33 (see Daniel 9:24–27).[16] In addition, Jesus fulfilled the prophecy that the Messiah would die for our sins in our place (see Isaiah 52:13–53:12; 1 Peter 2:21–25). Finally, Jesus fulfilled the prophecy that the Messiah would rise from the dead (see Psalm 16:9–10; Acts 2:24–32; 13:32–35).

> **Jesus has already fulfilled some amazing prophecies found in the Old Testament. There is no possibility that he fulfilled these prophecies by chance.**

There is no possibility that Jesus fulfilled all of these and many other messianic prophecies by chance. God needed to miraculously intervene in Jesus's life in order for Jesus to fulfill these amazing prophecies. The Virgin Mary wouldn't have given birth to Jesus, and Jesus wouldn't have risen from the dead without God's direct involvement in these miraculous events.

Like the Christian faith, Messianic Judaism passes all of the five big tests. Both Judaism and Messianic Judaism pass the honest reporting test, the contemporary living test, and the all-inclusive test. Messianic Judaism also passes the human reason test and the divine glory test. It passes the human reason test by having no contradictions between its teachings and the teachings of the Old Testament. For example, the Old Testament and Messianic Judaism teach that the one God exists in more than one person. Messianic Judaism accepts the divinity of Jesus, which the Old Testament teaches (see Isaiah 9:6–7). The same Hebrew phrase used to describe Jesus as "Mighty God" in Isaiah 9:6 is also used to describe the LORD Himself in Isaiah 10:21. Moreover, Messianic Judaism passes the divine glory test by completely affirming God's greatness and goodness. Only God can tell the future because only He can know and control it (see Isaiah 46:9–10). Only God is completely loving, self-sufficient, merciful, and just. We all depend on God for our existence, and none of us is always loving and fair. God doesn't need us, but we definitely need Him! Messianic Judaism affirms all these essential divine attributes and important differences between us and God. Messianic Judaism and the Christian faith make it clear why we need God and why God deserves our worship and service.

If you would like to know more about Messianic Judaism, I would encourage you to read Eitan Bar's *Refuting Rabbinic Objections to Christianity and Messianic Prophecies.*[17] It's an excellent book!

What Is Islam?

One of the friendliest persons I have ever met is a Muslim from Pakistan. My wife, Rosy, and I met Rida in 2018 when she was a student at a local public university. We had about a dozen conversations with her over the course of a semester. Rida was always very kind and polite to us, and having a conversation with her was always interesting and enjoyable. She told us so many fascinating things about her country and culture, and we were able to share some of our key Christian beliefs with her. Rida always smiled when we spoke with her, and she was always happy to see us and talk with us. She was and still is such a nice person. Rida often made us think of a well-known Pakistani woman who is also currently in her twenties.

One of the most well-known Muslims alive today is Malala Yousafzai. Malala is a Pakistani activist for female education and a Nobel Prize laureate. Malala is famous for being the youngest person to ever win the Nobel Peace Prize. She won this prestigious prize in 2014 at the age of 17. When she was about 10 years old, the Taliban took control of the region of Pakistan where she lived. The Taliban declared that all girls' schools needed to close because they believed that girls and women shouldn't be educated. As a result, many girls were afraid and stopped going to school. However, Malala wasn't afraid of the Taliban. She kept going to school and began a blog about schools being destroyed and violence in the streets. Malala went to school in secret by not wearing her uniform and by hiding her books under her shawl. She often spoke out against the Taliban.

In 2012, when she was 15 years old, Malala was shot in the head by the Taliban on her way back home from school. She was airlifted to a hospital in England, and she survived. The Taliban had failed to silence Malala. Reporters all over the world shared her story, and many people protested in Pakistan against the Taliban. More than two million people signed the Right to Education Petition, which led to education being compulsory for Pakistani children.

After recovering from the murder attempt, Malala and her family moved to England, where she attended a new school and continued her fight for girls' education. Her fight for girls' education included talking in front of the United Nations in New York in 2013. She spoke about peace and girls' right to an education. In 2013, she and her father also started the Malala Fund, which helps girls in various countries to get free, safe, and quality education. Malala's willingness to take a stand for girls' education made her a hero who has changed the world.[18]

I know from my own personal experience that many Muslims are kind, intelligent, and brave like Malala still is today. I have enjoyed friendly and intellectually stimulating conversations with Muslims from Pakistan, Somalia, Egypt, and other countries. I always enjoy talking with Muslims when God gives me the opportunity to speak to them. During my conversations with Muslims, they have sometimes talked to me about their key beliefs.

What do Muslims believe? The main beliefs and practices of Muslims are called the Five Pillars of Islam. These five core beliefs and practices include the following: 1) acknowledging that Allah is the one true God, and Muhammad is his prophet; 2) praying five times a day toward Mecca; 3) donating a fixed portion of one's income to community members in need; 4) fasting during the daylight hours of the month of Ramadan; and 5) taking at least one pilgrimage to Mecca, the holy city in present-day Saudi Arabia. These five core beliefs and practices can be summarized as faith, prayer, charity, fasting, and pilgrimage. The visit to Mecca is only required for those Muslims who are physically healthy enough and financially able to make the journey.

Islamic teachings about the Five Pillars of Islam are found in the Quran and in the Hadith. The Quran is the Muslim sacred book. It consists of 114 chapters, which are called surahs. Muslims believe that Allah revealed the Quran to the prophet Muhammad beginning in around AD 610. They believe that the Quran represents the words of God revealed by the archangel Gabriel to Muhammad. Muhammad lived from c. 570–632, and his prophetic career lasted for 23 years. The Hadith includes the actions and sayings of Muhammad, and it functions as a commentary on the Quran. One of the major and most trusted Hadith collections is the Sahih al-Bukhari, which was published in the first half of the 9th century.[19] In both the Hadith and the Quran, Islam is believed to involve submission to God and His ways.

Both Muslims and even some adherents of other religions have offered arguments for their belief that Islam is a divinely inspired religion. First of all, they contend that the Quran is a literary masterpiece that is unsurpassed in the beauty of its language and poetry. Secondly, they assert that the Quran has great spiritual power that leads many people to convert to Islam after they read or hear its profound words. Thirdly, they maintain that Muhammad was famous for his honesty and always claimed that the Quran was from God. Fourthly, they argue that the speed at which Islam grew in seventh-century Arabia shows that Islam comes from God. Finally, apologists for Islam contend that the Quran contains advanced scientific knowledge of scientific discoveries that were made centuries after Muhammad lived.[20]

Does Islam Pass the Five Big Tests?

Although the arguments for Islam can seem persuasive, we still need to determine if Islam and the Muslim worldview pass the five big tests. Subjective evaluations about the beauty of the Quran don't help us to objectively determine whether Islam is true or false. Similarly, Muhammad's honesty doesn't rule out the possibility that he was sincerely wrong about the Quran coming from God. We can only consider Islam to be true and divinely inspired if it passes all five of the tests. I have carefully read the entire Quran three times, and I have also read some of the Hadith, a few books written by Muslims, and some online articles written by Muslims. What I discovered about Islam may surprise you. It definitely surprised me!

Islam passes at least one of the five big tests, but it doesn't pass three of them. It passes the honest reporting test, and it might also pass the all-inclusive test. However, Islam doesn't pass any of the other three tests.

Like the Christian faith and Judaism, Islam passes the honest reporting test by having some embarrassing stories and verses. For example, in two verses of the Quran, Muhammad is told to ask for forgiveness of his sins (see Quran 40:55; 47:19). Another passage says that Muhammad needed to ask for forgiveness of his sins (see Quran 48:1–2). Similarly, the Hadith records Muhammad as asking God to forgive his past and future sins (see Sahih al-Bukhari 7385). Muhammad's need to confess his sins is embarrassing because most Muslims believe that he never sinned and that all of the prophets were sinless.[21] Neither the Quran nor the Hadith mentions what sins Muhammad committed. Perhaps Muhammad realized that he struggled with such sins as pride, selfishness, worry, and lust. He apparently realized that he wasn't perfect.

It's also possible that Islam passes the all-inclusive test. It's possible that the Quran does contain advanced scientific knowledge. Nevertheless, the passages in the Quran that supposedly contain advanced scientific knowledge aren't easy to understand, and neither are the arguments that are used to support the existence of such knowledge in these passages. These arguments aren't clear and straightforward, unlike the easy-to-understand arguments for advanced scientific knowledge in the Old Testament. If the Quran really contains advanced scientific knowledge, the passages that contain it should be easy to understand instead of baffling and puzzling. We won't discuss any of the so-called advanced scientific knowledge in the Quran because it's more likely to leave you feeling confused than convinced about it as evidence for the Quran's divine inspiration. Arguments from Muslims about this issue can be found online for anyone who wants to read them.

While Islam may pass the all-inclusive test, it doesn't seem to pass the human reason test. Islam fails this test by asserting that Muhammad was sinless even though the Quran and the Hadith point out that he wasn't sinless. Islam also fails this test by claiming that Muhammad was greater than Jesus even though the Quran clearly states that Jesus was born of a virgin and sinless (see Quran 3:45–47; 19:19–27). Moreover, while the Quran points out that Jesus performed miracles (see Quran 3:45, 49; 5:110), it never says that Muhammad performed any miracles. The Quran implies that Jesus is greater than Muhammad despite the fact that Muslims believe that Muhammad is the last and greatest of all the prophets. This inconsistency between what Muslims believe and what their scriptures teach makes these important Muslim beliefs seem unreasonable.

Islam also fails to pass the contemporary living test. Islam is definitely livable, but it doesn't encourage its followers to have a high enough regard for women or for female rights. The Hadith falsely claims that women are less intelligent than men (see Sahih al-Bukhari 304, 1462, 2658). The Hadith also falsely argues that the majority of people in hell are women (see Sahih al-Bukhari 29, 1052, 1462)! In addition, the Hadith contends that females should receive only half of the inheritance that males receive and should have their witness in court count only half as much as the witness of males (see Sahih al-Bukhari 304, 2747). Muslim scholar Ali Dashti writes, "It is because Islamic law regards women as weak that female heirs and witnesses have half the worth of male ones. This lower worth is not a cause, but an effect, of the attribution of inferior status to women."[22] Moreover, the Quran says that a Muslim man may beat his wife if she is disobedient (see Quran 4:34)! Finally, the Quran also states that a Muslim man may have as many as four wives (see Quran 4:3).

The Muslim acceptance of polygamy often results in many Muslim wives not receiving as much love and attention as they need. Because they need more love and attention, many Muslim women who share a husband with another woman experience jealousy. For example, a Muslim man named Qobin lives in Malaysia and has two wives. He has four children with his first wife and two children with his second wife. Qobin tries to be fair. He spends two nights with one wife and then two nights with the other wife. Whatever he buys for one wife, he also buys for the other wife. However, Qobin admits that jealousy is still an issue.[23] It seems likely that jealousy is unavoidable in any polygamous marriage.

Besides being able to have more than one wife, a Muslim man may marry a Christian or a Jewish woman. The Quran clearly states this fact (see Quran 5:5). According to Islamic law (Sharia), a Christian or a Jewish woman married to a Muslim may continue to practice her faith. However, her children must be raised as Muslims. Moreover, the Quran doesn't mention that Muslim women can marry men who aren't Muslims. Only Muslim men have the option to choose an interfaith marriage.[24] Doesn't this seem completely unfair to Muslim women?

The Muslim view of heaven or paradise also seems unfair to women. According to the Quran, paradise features rivers of wine, abundant fruit and meat, and many virgins for men to marry (see Quran 44:51–56; 47:15; 52:17–22; 55:46–76; 56:10–40). The Muslim version of paradise sounds delightful for men, but it doesn't seem to offer nearly as many benefits for women. The Muslim version of heaven seems mainly designed to satisfy the sensual desires of men. The Muslim paradise doesn't seem nearly as enjoyable a place for women to spend eternity as it's described as being for men. Does this seem fair to women? No, it doesn't.

Recent improvements in the lives of women in some Muslim countries are commendable, but they are still not nearly enough for Islam to pass the contemporary living test. In the Muslim country of Saudi Arabia, women finally gained the right to drive a car in 2018.

Loujain al-Hathloul, a Saudi activist who led a campaign for women to gain the right to drive in that country, was released from prison in 2021. This brave woman had spent almost three years in prison just because she wanted Saudi women to have the right to drive![25] Women can now drive in all Muslim countries, but they can't easily vote in all Muslim countries. It's still very difficult for women today to vote in the Muslim countries of Saudi Arabia, Pakistan, Afghanistan, Egypt, Oman, and Qatar.[26] Women couldn't even vote in Saudi Arabia until 2015![27] Isn't that shocking? These shocking facts and the previously mentioned statements in the Quran and Hadith make it clear that Islam still doesn't pass the contemporary living test.

Islam not only fails the contemporary living test, but it also fails the divine glory test. Islam fails to pass the divine glory test by not consistently upholding God's goodness and greatness. Instead of describing God as completely holy, the Quran describes Allah as being deceptive. The Quran actually says that Allah is the best deceiver (see Quran 3:54; 8:30). The Arabic word *makir* is used to describe God in these and other verses. This word comes from the root word *makr*, which means deception.[28] Allah shows his willingness to deceive people by claiming that Jesus didn't really die on the cross; he only appeared to have died on the cross. Instead of dying on the cross, Jesus was taken up to heaven by Allah (see Quran 4:157–158). Muslims believe that Allah would never have permitted one of his prophets to be crucified. Most Muslims believe that someone else (e.g., the traitor Judas Iscariot) was made to have the same appearance as Jesus and then died in Jesus's place.[29] Because the Quran maintains that Allah is deceptive, it contends that God is not completely holy. In addition, the Quran doesn't portray Allah as being truly loving. It says that Allah doesn't love everyone; he doesn't love proud people or those who do wrong (see Quran 2:276; 3:57; 4:36; 5:87; 7:55; 31:18; 42:40). Lastly, unlike the Bible, the Quran contains no detailed prophecies about distant future events. As a result, the Quran doesn't demonstrate that Allah knows and controls the future.

Unlike Christianity, Islam doesn't offer any clear evidence that the Quran (Koran) is divinely inspired. John Ankerberg and John

Weldon write, "Biblical inspiration and accuracy are independently verified by prophecy, archeology, manuscript evidence, and other means... Islam, however, offers no genuine evidence that the Koran is inspired other than Muhammad's own claim he was inspired by Gabriel. But what if Muhammad was wrong?"[30] What if Muhammad was mistaken in his belief that he was submitting to God's will and His ways?

Both the Bible and the historical facts show that Jesus is the ultimate example of someone submitting to God. He humbled himself by becoming a man, living a sinless life, dying on the cross for our sins, and rising again. As a result, we should acknowledge that Jesus is Lord and God's Son (see Philippians 2:5–11).

If you are a Muslim reading this book, I would encourage you to also read Nabeel Qureshi's excellent book *Seeking Allah, Finding Jesus: A Devout Muslim Encounters Christianity.* Qureshi writes, "I knew that the case for Christianity was strong: it had been shown to me that the historical Jesus claimed to be God and then proved it by dying on the cross and rising from the dead."[31] Nabeel asked God to show him the truth about Jesus, and God answered his prayer! God revealed the truth about God and Jesus to Nabeel through the Bible, Christians, and dreams. God will reveal who He is to each of us who sincerely seeks Him and asks Him to reveal Himself.

What Is Hinduism?

As I mentioned at the beginning of this chapter, I have been blessed by being able to enjoy many positive experiences with Hindus. Besides hanging out with Hindu neighbors, I have also been able to talk many times with Hindu students from India. Most of these friendly students that I have known have been students at a local university when I have spoken with them. I like to talk with Hindu students about Indian food and culture, and I have been able to eat some tasty Indian food with them a few times! I have also talked with them about their Hindu beliefs. I don't currently live as close to the local university as I did a few years ago, so I have fewer conversations with Hindu students nowadays than I did a few years back.

One of the most famous Hindus in the world today is Amma, India's "hugging saint." Have you ever heard of her? For more than 30 years, the Hindu guru has spent much of her time traveling the world in order to spread her teachings and to hug as many people as she can. She has taught about such issues as climate change, poverty, and women's rights. It is absolutely remarkable that Amma has hugged more than 40 million people during her travels, and she has sometimes hugged people for more than 22 hours without taking a break.[32] Wow! Amma is obviously full of energy and bubbling over with enthusiasm! She often delivers lectures before hundreds of people line up to receive her embrace. Amma's goal is to alleviate human suffering through loving service and compassion in action. She seeks to hug every person who hears her lectures! Devotees who receive her hug believe that they are receiving a hug from a god in human form. Each person who receives Amma's hug must kneel before her while receiving her embrace. Amma's devotees regard her hug as her blessing, and they believe that her hug can bring such benefits as healing for physical ailments.[33]

If you haven't heard of Amma, you have probably heard of Mahatma Gandhi. He used nonviolent resistance to lead the successful campaign for India's independence from British rule in the 1940s. His nonviolent resistance inspired Martin Luther King Jr. to employ the same method in the United States during the 1960s civil rights movement. Many of us would consider Gandhi to be one of the most important and inspirational persons of the 20th century. In addition to believing in nonviolent resistance, Gandhi was a Hindu who was deeply influenced by the Hindu scripture the *Bhagavad Gita*.[34]

I have read the *Bhagavad Gita* a few times, and I consider it an interesting Hindu scripture and a useful introduction to Hinduism. Like me, many other Westerners find the *Gita* to be interesting, and many Westerners also find it to be inspirational.

What is Hinduism? It's an Eastern religion that is thousands of years older than Islam and Christianity. It began about 4,000 years ago in Central Asia in the Indus Valley, which includes modern-day northern India. The vast majority of Hindus still live in India. There is no founder of Hinduism or date of origin for Hinduism. The

Hindu scriptures called the *Vedas* were written between c. 1500–500 BC, and the scriptures called the *Upanishads* were written between 800–300 BC. The *Bhagavad Gita* is a relatively newer Hindu scripture that was written between 400 BC and AD 200.

The *Bhagavad Gita* is presented as a conversation between a prince named Arjuna and the god Krishna, who serves as Krishna's guide and charioteer. Krishna gives Arjuna advice and encouragement as he hesitates to go to battle against his own relatives. His hesitation is understandable. Wouldn't most people be very reluctant to go to war against their own relatives? The *Gita* provides a helpful introduction to Hinduism for anyone who wants to know more about the religion and about Krishna.

In addition to believing in Krishna, Hindus believe in many others gods and goddesses. Their three main gods are Brahma, Vishnu, and Shiva. Brahma is the creator of the universe, Vishnu is the preserver of the universe, and Shiva is the destroyer of the universe. Krishna is one of the most popular and revered Hindu deities; he is worshipped as one of the incarnations (avatars) of Vishnu. Another popular Hindu god is Ganesha or Ganesh, who has an elephant head and is considered the god of beginnings. Many Hindus keep an idol of Ganesha on the dashboard of their cars.

Besides believing in many gods, Hindus share some other important spiritual beliefs in common. They believe that God is an impersonal oneness that pervades all creation and that everyone is divine. They believe in monism—the essential unity of all existence. Hindus also believe in reincarnation and in karma. Reincarnation (called *samsara*) involves the continuous cycle of life, death, and rebirth. Hindus think that every person lives many different lives here on this earth. A person's karma determines the kind of existence into which he or she will be reincarnated in that person's next lifetime. A person reaps what he or she sows; one gets what one deserves in this life and in his or her future lives. According to Hindus, any individual can be reincarnated as a human, an animal, or an insect. As a result, Hindus revere all living things, and they regard the cow as a sacred animal.

Because of their belief in reincarnation, most Hindus don't eat beef or pork, and many of them are vegetarians. However, many

Hindus—including the ones I have known—do eat chicken and fish. McDonald's restaurants in India serve chicken and fish, but they don't serve beef or pork. Instead of offering a Big Mac with beef, McDonald's restaurants in India offer the Chicken Maharajah Mac.[35] Wouldn't you like to try that big chicken sandwich? I would love to try one!

Hindus believe that we must realize our oneness with God in order to escape from the continuous cycle of life, death, and rebirth. Our problem is that we are ignorant of our divine nature and have forgotten that we are all connected to God, whom Hindus call Brahman. Hindus believe that our apparent separate existence from God and from one another is an illusion. According to Hindus, all living things have a soul, and they are all connected to God and to the supreme soul. The goal of Hinduism is to achieve liberation or salvation (called *moksha*) by realizing that the idea of the individual self is an illusion and that only our oneness with God is real. This realization will bring an end to the cycle of life, death, and rebirth. It will also result in attaining enlightenment by losing one's separate identity and becoming one with the supreme soul.

Hindus regard our purpose in life as recognizing that we are one with God, other people, and all living things. In his article about Hinduism, Joshua Mark writes, "The purpose of life is to recognize the essential oneness of existence, the higher aspect of the individual self, through adherence to one's duty in life."[36] One's duty involves doing good deeds and refraining from sins of commission and omission. Sins of commission refer to doing bad deeds such as stealing and lying, and sins of omission refer to not doing good deeds such as helping one's neighbor.

Does Hinduism Pass the Five Big Tests?

Now that we know what Hindus believe, we must ask the following: Do Hinduism and the Hindu worldview pass the five big tests? Hinduism has no founder, but we can still evaluate it using the five big tests. Hinduism passes the honest reporting test, but it doesn't seem to pass the other four tests.

Hinduism passes the honest reporting test by having some embarrassing stories about its gods in its sacred literature. These stories are also entertaining. For example, there are some embarrassing and entertaining stories about Krishna in Hindu literature. Krishna is the Hindu god of love and compassion who is often depicted as a boy playing a flute. Many Hindus are familiar with these stories about Krishna and enjoy reading them. In one story from the *Bhagavata Purana*, Krishna is a mischievous boy who is caught stealing butter from his mother and then feeding the butter to some monkeys. She runs after her naughty and fearful child, who lets her bind him using a rope so that he can't create any more mischief.[37] Describing Krishna as a butter thief who is bound is embarrassing because he is regarded as divine and all-powerful by Hindus. In another story from the *Bhagavata Purana*, Krishna steals the clothes of some young unmarried ladies while they are bathing in a river. He only gives the clothes back to the women after being able to see them naked. Krishna is explicitly described as being "naughty" in this story,[38] and his behavior seems like it could be motivated by lust.

Although Hinduism passes the honest reporting test, it doesn't seem to pass the other four big tests. It doesn't pass the human reason test because it asserts that our individual existence as persons is an illusion. Hinduism incorrectly argues that we don't really have a separate existence as individuals. The belief that our individual existence as human beings is an illusion contradicts our own personal experience and our knowledge of ourselves gained from our five senses. Our five senses of sight, touch, hearing, smell, and taste correctly tell us that we are individuals with our own names, personalities, talents, experiences, and families. Each and every one of us is a unique person made in God's image. We each have our own conscience and the ability to think, feel, and choose as individuals.

Hinduism also doesn't pass the contemporary living test. The Hindu belief in karma often leads to a lack of empathy and compassion toward the poor, who are viewed as deserving their poverty and suffering. The Hindu beliefs in karma and reincarnation also result in many Hindus regarding poor people as inferior and not deserving to be treated as human beings. The poorest people in India are called "untouchables" or "Dalits," and having physical contact with them is prohibited for all other Indian people. Mistreatment of Dalits by other classes of people is still widespread today even though the category of "untouchables" was legally abolished years ago. Gautham Subramanyam writes, "Untouchability was abolished legally in 1950, when India became a republic. In reality, it remains embedded in India's psyche."[39] Untouchables continue to suffer from a lot of prejudice and discrimination, and karma contributes to what one writer calls "the perpetuation of discrimination" against Dalits.[40] Untouchables must live outside villages, and they are not permitted to enter temples or to come near sources of drinking water used by other classes of people. Dalits are often victims of violence committed by members of other classes. Sujatha Gidla, who was born an untouchable in India, writes, "Every day in an Indian newspaper you can read of an untouchable beaten or killed for wearing sandals, for riding a bicycle."[41] Strong beliefs in karma and reincarnation foster this horrible violence.

Hinduism also fails the all-inclusive test. It fails this test because there is no clear and convincing evidence for reincarnation. The best and most well-known evidence for reincarnation that Hindus have offered is the interesting story of an Indian girl named Shanti Devi (1926–1987). Many Hindus believe that Shanti Devi lived on earth before as Lugdi Devi (1902–1925). Shanti Devi claimed to remember her previous life, and she became the subject of reincarnation research. As a child living in the city of Delhi, Shanti Devi claimed to remember details from one of her past lives. Both Shanti Devi and Ludgi Devi were devotees of the Hindu god Krishna. After reading her official biography,[42] it became clear to me that the evidence for Shanti Devi having lived before as Ludgi Devi is interesting but not compelling. It certainly isn't as compelling as the evidence for Jesus's resurrection. How do we know that Shanti Devi actually remembered details from her previous life? How do we know that she wasn't told details from Ludgi Devi's life by other people, by Krishna, or even by demons? Because we don't know these things, we should regard the best evidence for reincarnation as widespread speculation rather than real proof.

Just as it doesn't pass the all-inclusive test, Hinduism also doesn't pass the divine glory test. Hinduism doesn't completely uphold God's greatness and goodness. For God to be worthy of our worship, He must be great and good. For God to be great, He must be separate from us, and He must be able to predict the future. The Hindu belief in monism regards us as being one with God instead of as having our own individual existence separate from God. In addition, there is no evidence in Hindu scripture or literature that any Hindu gods can foretell future events. There aren't even any prophets in Hinduism! For God to be good, He must be holy. We have already read about Krishna, who is considered to be an incarnation of the supreme God. Because Krishna sometimes stole things, we must conclude that Hinduism doesn't portray God as being completely holy. However, we have to admit that the stories of Krishna also show that Hinduism does describe God as being able to entertain us.

Whether or not we are Hindus, it's helpful for all of us to know that God is holy. Because He is holy, He will judge us after we die. Instead of being reincarnated after we pass away, we will face God's judgment (see Hebrews 9:27). *We can be ready for the day when we die if we embrace the truth about God, ourselves, our world, and Jesus. We don't need to be afraid of dying if we have made our peace with God and truly accepted His love for us.* The last two chapters of this book will clearly explain how we can make our peace with God and truly accept His love.

What Is Buddhism?

I haven't personally known a lot of Buddhists, but I know that one of my former junior high and high school classmates is currently a Buddhist. Cameron and I lived in different parts of the same neighborhood in Minnesota, took the same bus to school, and had several classes together. Cameron was a nice and smart teenage boy who had Christian, Jewish, and Mormon friends. His friends called him "Cam" back then. I was never friends with Cameron, but I did like him as a person. He eventually earned a PhD degree from Harvard in Tibetan and Himalayan Studies. Cameron currently lives in Denmark, where he teaches as an associate professor in the anthropology department at a large public university.

The most famous living Buddhist is the Dalai Lama. Many of us reading this book have heard of him. He is the main leader of one of the schools of Tibetan Buddhism. I have never met him, but I have read one of his books. The Dalia Lama comes across as surprisingly humble in that book. For example, he honestly admits the following: "I am not a God King, as some call me. I am just a Buddhist monk... I fail sometimes. Sometimes I get irritated. Occasionally I use a harsh word."[43] The Dalai Lama also realizes that we all crave meaning and a sense of purpose, and he correctly argues that money and material things don't make us happy. He writes:

> Material advancement alone sometimes solves one problem but creates another. For example, certain people may have acquired wealth, a good education, and high social standing, yet happiness eludes them. They take sleeping pills and drink too much alcohol. Something is missing, something still not satisfied, so these people take refuge in drugs or in a bottle. On the other hand, some people who have less money to worry about enjoy more peace. They sleep well at night. Despite being poor in a material sense, they are content and happy.[44]

The Dalai Lama and other Buddhists believe in the teachings of the Buddha, who founded Buddhism. He lived from about 563 BC to 483 BC. The Buddha was born as a prince named Siddhartha Gautama in northeast India, near the border of Nepal. He felt dissatisfied with his life because he saw that even the wealthiest and the most powerful people struggle with unhappiness and experience sickness and death. Eventually abandoning his life as a prince, the Buddha practiced meditation and achieved enlightenment. He had discovered how to escape the continuous cycle of birth, death, and rebirth. He also became a teacher who sought to instruct his followers in *dharma*, or truth. For about 45 years, the Buddha focused on itinerant preaching in North India. He spoke about the importance of doing good deeds that would result in rebirth in heaven. The Buddha also taught others how to achieve enlightenment through meditative techniques. One meditative technique that he taught was mindfulness, which involves being fully aware of where you are and what you are doing.

The Buddha attracted many followers because he had a magnetic personality and he was a friendly man. He was an eloquent speaker whom others wanted to hear. He was also kind and courteous toward everyone he met. His kindness and politeness impressed even people who rejected his teaching.[45] The Buddha passionately taught what Buddhists believe today.

What do Buddhists believe? Buddhists believe in the Four Noble Truths and the Noble Eightfold Path. The first noble truth says that life includes various forms of suffering such as pain, sickness, unfulfillment, and death. The second noble truth says that we suffer because of our desires and our ignorance. We mistakenly think that we are separate individuals. Barbara O'Brien states, "Suffering and dissatisfaction occur when we cling to desire for an unchanging and permanent self that is impossible and illusory. And release from that suffering requires no longer clinging to the illusion."[46] The third noble truth says that suffering ends when we eliminate our desires and awaken our minds. The fourth noble truth says that we can eliminate our desires and awaken our minds by following the Eightfold Path.

The Eightfold Path involves three parts: developing wisdom, living ethically, and practicing mental discipline. The steps of the Noble Eightfold Path with its three parts are the following:

A) developing wisdom:
1) right understanding;
2) right thought;

B) living ethically:
3) right speech;
4) right action;
5) right livelihood; and

C) practicing mental discipline:
6) right effort;

7)   right mindfulness; and
8)   right concentration.

In his description of the Eightfold Path, Melvin McLeod writes, "By living ethically, practicing meditation, and developing wisdom, we can take exactly the same journey to enlightenment and freedom from suffering that the buddhas do. We too can wake up."[47]
According to Buddhism, waking up or attaining enlightenment involves seeing things as they really are and realizing that the existence of the self as a separate person is an illusion. Achieving enlightenment requires self-reliance, not reliance on God. Many Buddhists don't even believe in God. The Buddha claimed to show the way by which we can escape suffering and attain enlightenment.[48] Buddhists hope to attain the final goal of *nirvana*, a transcendent state in which there is no suffering, desire, or sense of self. In nirvana, the person is freed from the effects of karma and the cycle of death and rebirth. Nirvana is the Buddhist version of heaven or paradise. However, some Buddhists believe that there are *bodhisattvas*—people who refuse to enter nirvana in order to help others on their way to attaining enlightenment.
The most important and well-written book ever written by a Buddhist is probably *Think Like a Monk* by Jay Shetty. In this best-selling book, Shetty explains his Buddhist beliefs in an easy-to-understand way. He points out that we need to live lives characterized by focus, discipline, service, purpose, and meaning. He also writes that we should seek to live lives free of envy, lust, anxiety, and bitterness.[49] Shetty correctly states that forgiveness reduces our stress and brings peace to our minds.[50] He asserts that happiness and fulfillment come from finding our purpose in life, not from pursuing worldly success and earning a lot of money.[51] He also writes that we should spend as much time as possible doing things we are good at and love.[52] Moreover, Shetty contends that we should strive to be humble and grateful because humility and gratitude are good for us. He points out that humility allows us to see our own strengths and weaknesses clearly so that we can work, learn, and grow.[53] Finally, Shetty argues that instead of pursuing pleasure, we should serve others. While liv-

ing for pleasure results in dissatisfaction, serving others makes us happy and gives us meaningful lives.[54]

Although Shetty's book does contain some good advice, it suffers from some weaknesses. First of all, it never directly mentions God. He only indirectly refers to God on one page of his book, when he argues that divinity is present within every person and everything.[55] *Our search for joy, peace, and purpose in life must focus on God. We cannot find lasting peace, real joy, and true purpose in life without pursuing God and enjoying a vibrant relationship with Him.* Secondly, the advice that Shetty offers in his book is very similar to the advice that many secular psychologists frequently give to their clients. Psychologists often tell their clients that focus, forgiveness, gratitude, humility, and serving others are good for us. Shetty's book is essentially a self-help book with some spirituality added to concepts from secular psychology.

Does Buddhism Pass the Five Big Tests?

Now that we know what Buddhists believe, we can use the five big tests to evaluate Buddhism as a religion and as a worldview. Buddhism clearly passes the honest reporting test, and it might also pass the contemporary living test. However, Buddhism doesn't seem to pass the other three tests.

Buddhism passes the honest reporting test. It is embarrassing but true that the Buddha never claimed to be a prophet, a messenger of God, or someone having a special relationship with God. He never claimed to strongly believe in God even though he founded a major world religion! In fact, the Buddha didn't consider the matter of God's existence to be important because it didn't seem relevant to the issue of how to escape suffering.[56] Similarly, Buddhists tend to believe that they can achieve enlightenment without believing in God. Most Buddhists don't find it helpful to discuss whether or not God exists, and Buddhists don't believe in a supreme god or deity. Instead of acknowledging a supreme being, Buddhists focus on achieving enlightenment.

Besides passing the honest reporting test, Buddhism might also pass the contemporary living test. Buddhists successfully live out their beliefs by meditating, seeking to develop wisdom, and serving others. Moreover, the Buddha himself seemed to have high regard for women. He believed that women have the same potential for enlightenment that men have, and he created a parallel nuns' order about five years after the start of the monks' order. Bhikkhu Cintita writes that "the Buddha that shines through the early scriptures is clearly one with complete kindness and compassion toward women, one who was very actively engaged with providing for women equal opportunities for practice."[57] Nevertheless, it's unclear if Buddhism shows as much respect and appreciation for women as it should show them. For example, in the Buddhist scripture called the *Vinaya Pitaka*, there are many more rules for nuns (331) than for monks (227), and this may reveal gender bias against women.

While Buddhism might pass the contemporary living test, it doesn't pass the human reason test. Buddhism falsely claims that the existence of the self as a separate person is an illusion. We know that we are separate individuals who have our own bodies, thoughts, desires, and actions. Every time we look in the mirror, take a shower, make a phone call, eat a meal, or drive a car, we experience our lives as separate individuals. We also each have our own conscience, and we make our own choices. Furthermore, Buddhism incorrectly teaches that none of us even have a soul—a permanent essence of ourselves that survives after our death. We each have our own immortal soul. We are separate individuals, and we have no reason to think that in heaven we will cease to have a sense of ourselves as separate individuals.

Buddhism also doesn't pass the all-inclusive test. There is no proof that the self is an illusion or that there really is a cycle of birth, death, and rebirth from which we need to escape. Just as there is no solid evidence for the Hindu belief in reincarnation, there is no solid evidence for the Buddhist belief that we are reborn and live more than one lifetime.

Buddhism also fails the divine glory test. By regarding God's existence as irrelevant, Buddhism encourages us to doubt or deny His existence. The vast majority of us believe that God exists because of our personal experience of Him in our lives and the persuasive arguments for His existence. We know that God is real, and He is worthy of our worship and service because He is good and great. In addition, serving people and the world without acknowledging God's existence makes our service lack lasting value and eternal purpose.

Regardless of whether or not we are Buddhists, we all need to know that God is real and active in our lives. *God wants us to have victory over our sinful desires and the suffering we experience. He can help us change our desires and overcome our suffering if we believe in Him and have a correct understanding of Him.* In the last two chapters of this book, we will discover what God is really like and how He can transform our desires and our lives.

What Is the New Age?

Have you ever read a daily horoscope? Do you know your zodiac sign? Have you ever practiced meditation or yoga? Have you ever gotten a psychic reading, had your palms read, or played with tarot cards? These are all common New Age practices that you may have tried. If you consider yourself to be spiritual but not religious, you might also regard yourself as a New Ager.

When I was in high school, I occasionally read the daily horoscope in the newspaper for Libra, my zodiac sign. I found the daily horoscope to be interesting, but I doubted that it could tell me what would happen in my life in the future. I have never practiced meditation or yoga, used a psychic's services, had my palms read, or played with tarot cards. However, I have known some New Agers, and I have read several dozen New Age books. I took a lot of notes on what I read.

Because I wanted to correctly understand New Age beliefs, I began looking for New Age books in local libraries several years ago. I have read books by Rhonda Byrne, Deepak Chopra, Eckhart Tolle, Marianne Williamson, Wayne Dyer, Jack Canfield, Sylvia Browne, Esther and Jerry Hicks, Michael Bernard Beckwith, Gary Zukav, Eric Butterworth, Ernest Holmes, Alice Bailey, H. P. Blavatsky, and other New Agers. Some of these authors have written books that have sold millions of copies, and some of these authors have written many books. Rhonda Byrne's book *The Secret* is available in more than 50 languages with over 34 million copies in print.[58] The most prolific New Age author is Deepak Chopra, who has written 86 books, including 14 best sellers.[59]

Most of these New Age authors realize that money and material possessions won't make us happy or bring meaning to our lives. Sylvia Browne writes, "We all need meaning in life. Many of us try identifying ourselves by the amount of money, possessions, business success, or power we have, and ultimately find that it leaves us empty. The simple formula is to live for God."[60]

Many New Agers and authors of New Age books are very intelligent, friendly, and well-educated people. For example, Deepak Chopra is a licensed medical doctor who is very knowledgeable about alternative medicine. Charles Stang, whom I have personally known since the late 1980s, is one of the most brilliant persons I know. Stang is Professor of Early Christian Thought at Harvard University and the director of the Center for the Study of World Religions at Harvard Divinity School. I know from personal experience that Stang is very smart, kind, articulate, and has a good sense of humor. He is also a published author who believes in such common New Age ideas as reincarnation, human divinity, and universal salvation for all human beings.[61]

The most important New Age beliefs are reincarnation and human divinity. Like Hindus, New Agers believe that we all experience the continuous cycle of birth, death, and rebirth many times. What or who we are reincarnated as depends on our karma, the principle of cause and effect that is based on our good and bad deeds and intents. New Agers also believe that we as humans are divine beings with unlimited potential. They argue that there is a spark of divinity in us and that realizing our divinity is the key to unleashing our infinite potential. Deepak Chopra writes, "We have a divine spark inside."[62]

The concept of human divinity is the secret doctrine or secret teaching that all New Age books promote. New Age authors believe that you are God. Ellen Debenport says, "You are God."[63] In *The*

Secret, Rhonda Byrne writes, "You are God in a physical body."[64] Similarly, Deepak Chopra states, "You must keep in mind that the real you is love, is truth, is God."[65] New Agers contend that you are a creator who can have whatever you think about and whatever you want. In the New Age view, God is like the Genie from the movie *Aladdin* who will give you whatever you ask for. Have you ever seen *Aladdin*? The Genie in *Aladdin* says, "Your wish is my command!" The genie or god of the New Age is the law of attraction, which works through people, circumstances, and events to give you whatever you think about and desire the most.[66] The law of attraction argues that you are like a magnet that attracts what you most frequently think about and most strongly desire.

According to New Agers, God is an impersonal force that you can use to get what you want. Have you watched any of the *Star Wars* movies? In this very popular series of nine movies, the phrase "May the force be with you" is used many times to refer to an impersonal force or energy. The "force" is also mentioned in other ways in the nine movies. In *Star Wars: A New Hope*, the spirit of Obi-Wan Kenobi says to Luke Skywalker, "Use the force, Luke!" Luke hears these powerful words from his mentor as he flies his X-wing into the trenches of the massive space station in order to fire a missile into a very small hole. Luke uses the force to fire a direct hit that obliterates the Death Star. The force of the *Star Wars* movies is similar to the God of the New Age. God is frequently referred to as an impersonal force in New Age books and online articles. This impersonal force of the New Age has also been called the Universe, Awareness, the Universal Self, the Universal Mind, and some other similar names.

The vast majority of New Agers and New Age authors believe in monism and pantheism. Monism is the belief that God is One—a force or energy that can be called the Universe, Awareness, the Universal Self, the Universal Mind, or something similar. Monism contends that all reality consists of one substance, which is the divine force that permeates all things. It also asserts that our separate existence as individual persons is an illusion. For example, Rhonda Byrne directly says that each of us is "not really a person at all."[67] Similarly, pantheism is the belief that all is God. Pantheism argues that everything is divine and is connected to the divine Oneness that pervades through all things. Pantheism identifies God with the universe instead of regarding God as a personal Being who is distinct from the universe.

In addition to believing that God is impersonal, New Agers believe that everyone is saved. They contend that God is so loving and merciful that He would never condemn anyone to an eternity of suffering in hell.[68] They believe that everyone is a child of God. According to New Agers, God is so tolerant and nonjudgmental that even Satan will not spend eternity in hell! New Agers either deny Satan's existence or argue that he will also be saved from God's punishment.

Satan is sometimes described in the Bible as being a serpent or taking the form of a serpent (see Genesis 3; Revelation 12:9; 20:2). Some New Agers actually have a positive view of the serpent of Genesis 3 as a being who brings knowledge to human beings! For example, in his comments on the temptation of Adam and Eve by the serpent, Deepak Chopra writes, "The only character in the episode of Eve and the apple who seems to tell the truth is the serpent... The serpent is holding out a world of awareness, independence, and decision making. All these things follow when you have knowledge."[69] Elaine Pagels, an author and a professor at Princeton University, also argues that the serpent told Adam and Eve the truth—that they would gain knowledge and become like divine beings if they ate the forbidden fruit.[70]

Like Deepak Chopra and Elaine Pagels, the founder of the New Age movement also had a positive view of the serpent that appears in Genesis 3 of the Bible. The New Age movement began in 1875 when Helena Blavatsky founded the Theosophical Society. Both Christian writers[71] and Deepak Chopra[72] acknowledge this important fact. Blavatsky was a Russian author who wrote the highly influential and important book *The Secret Doctrine* (1888). In this monumental two-volume book, Blavatsky asserts that Satan enables people to be divine by freeing them from their ignorance.[73] In her comments on Genesis 3, Blavatsky claims that the serpent helped Adam to discover his way to immortality.[74] She also points out that the serpent is Satan himself.[75] Finally, Blavatsky argues that Satan is Lucifer the Light-Bearer and Life-Bringer who is described as a fallen angel[76] (see Isaiah 14:12–15 and Ezekiel 28:12–17 in the New King James Version). While Christians regard Satan as the prince of darkness and father of lies (see John 8:44; 2 Corinthians 4:4), Blavatsky considers Satan to be Lucifer the Light-Bearer who told the truth that humans are divine beings. As a result, she founded *Lucifer Magazine*, which was a monthly publication of the Theosophical Society from 1887 to 1897.[77]

Does the New Age Pass the Five Big Tests?

We have seen that the New Age movement is quite similar to Hinduism. Both of these worldviews promote the beliefs of reincarnation and human divinity. Both of them also assert that God is an impersonal force and that our existence as separate persons is an illusion. Will the New Age fare any better than Hinduism as far as passing the five big tests is concerned?

Like Hinduism, the New Age movement doesn't pass all of the five big tests. Nevertheless, it does pass two of the tests instead of just one of them. The New Age movement fares better than Hinduism by passing both the honest reporting test and the contemporary living test. However, the New Age fails to pass the other three tests.

The New Age movement passes the honest reporting test by arguing that the serpent told the truth to Adam and Eve in the Garden of Eden (see Genesis 3). While Christians argue that the serpent was lying to them, New Agers contend that he was telling them how to know that they are divine beings like God. This story and the New Age interpretation of the story can be considered very embarrassing to New Agers because Christians believe that the serpent is Satan, the father of lies (see John 8:44; Revelation 12:9; 20:2). As we have seen, Helena Blavatsky, the founder of the New Age movement, says that the serpent of Genesis 3 is Satan. Moreover, she also claims that Satan brings helpful truth, light, and knowledge to Adam and Eve. Blavatsky's beliefs about Satan should be shocking and disturbing to everyone who identifies themselves as New Agers.

The New Age movement also passes the contemporary living test. The New Age seems livable and emotionally appealing to many of us. The New Age correctly acknowledges that money, material possessions, and other worldly things won't satisfy our souls. Eknath Easwaran states, "Wealth, possessions, power, and pleasure have never brought lasting satisfaction to any human being. Our needs go too deep to be satisfied by anything that comes and goes. Nothing but spiritual fulfillment can fill the void in our hearts."[78] The New Age also correctly points out that we must find our purpose outside of these worldly things. Our purpose runs deeper than seeking such superficial things as money, possessions, status, and comfort.[79] In addition, some New Age authors attempt to address such contemporary issues as climate change, recycling, LGBT rights, and other current issues. They offer emotionally appealing arguments for their positions on these issues, and many people find their positions persuasive. Regardless of whether one agrees or disagrees with their positions on these issues, the New Age can't be accused of being silent on them or of being misogynist, homophobic, or outdated. Since the New Age movement only began in 1875, we would expect it to address relevant and contemporary issues. Some New Age authors do write about these issues.[80] Lastly, the New Age movement correctly argues that we are all equally important and valuable as human beings. Deepak Chopra writes, "The equality of souls banishes the differences between rich and poor, men and women, the weak and the powerful."[81]

Although the New Age movement passes the contemporary living test, it doesn't pass the human reason test. New Agers wrongly contend that we aren't really separate individuals even though we know from our own experiences that we are separate persons. We can't read one another's minds, and each of us has our own thoughts, feelings, conscience, and actions. We are individual persons, not just one person. We are responsible for our own behavior because we make our own choices.

The New Age also doesn't pass the all-inclusive test. Some New Agers have incorrectly argued that Jesus was a New Age guru who visited India, believed in reincarnation, and believed that we as humans are divine beings. For example, Elizabeth Clare Prophet wrote an entire book maintaining that Jesus spent 17 years in India and other countries in the east.[82] Similarly, Deepak Chopra has written two books claiming that Jesus was like a guru who had attained enlightenment by realizing that he and every one of us are divine.[83] The truth is that Jesus never visited India. There is no evidence that he went there. From about age 12 to age 30, Jesus was learning to be a carpenter and then became a carpenter like his father Joseph, and that is why Jesus was known as a carpenter and a carpenter's son (see Matthew 13:55; Mark 6:3). The false belief that Jesus went to India is largely based on Nicholas Notovitch's book *The Unknown Life of Jesus Christ*, which all recognized scholars regard as a modern forgery.[84] Jesus also never believed in reincarnation or taught about it. Instead of teaching about reincarnation, Jesus taught that there will be a general resurrection at the end of time (see Matthew 22:23–33; John 5:28–29; 6:40; 11:25–26). *Rather than teaching that we as human beings are divine, Jesus taught that he is the only divine Son of God and the only way to God (see Matthew 11:27; John 5:18; 8:58; 10:30; 14:6).*

Many New Age books also fail the all-inclusive test by asserting that Satan doesn't exist. For example, Deepak Chopra denies that Satan exists.[85] If Satan doesn't exist, we can't adequately explain why there are so many school shootings, mass murders, and other killings in the world. If he doesn't exist, we can't sufficiently explain why the Holocaust or other genocides have taken place and resulted in the murder of millions of human beings. If Satan isn't real, we are unable to provide a believable explanation for gruesome murders involving decapitation and dismemberment. *Any credible explanation for the existence of evil and suffering must acknowledge the existence of Satan and his active involvement in the world.*

The New Age fails not only the all-inclusive test but also the divine glory test. It fails this test by not upholding God's holiness and His greatness. Because God is holy, He must be separate from us as sinful human beings. We all have told lies, and we have all looked with lust at someone who is not our spouse. We have all assassinated someone else's character by calling him or her "stupid," an "idiot," or a "jerk." We all disobeyed our parents at least once when we were kids. None of us is perfect. Only God is perfect. Since we aren't perfect and God is perfect, we can't be one with God. We are separate persons who aren't divine. God is both an immanent being who is near to us due to His omnipresence and a transcendent being who is separate from us due to His holiness. The New Age also fails to uphold God's greatness; it diminishes God's greatness by calling us divine beings. Unlike God, none of us is omnipresent, all-knowing, or all-powerful. Unlike God, none of us can predict the future with a 100% accuracy. We can't know or control the future. We can only guess what might happen in the future, and most of what we guess will occur in the future doesn't actually occur!

The New Age also fails the divine glory test by denying that some people go to hell. Because God is holy and just, He must punish our sins. Those of us who freely choose to rebel against God will experience eternal punishment. Those of us who freely choose to reject God's love will experience eternal banishment from His loving presence. God respects our choices; He won't force us to accept Him and to love Him. True love is a choice that can't be forced upon anyone. In addition, God can't let everyone into heaven without violating our free will and His own goodness, holiness, and justice. Tim Challies writes, "God's goodness doesn't negate eternal punishment in hell; it demands it."[86]

The Jesus of the Bible has a very different view of hell than the Jesus of the New Age. Instead of denying that some people go to hell, the biblical Jesus clearly states that some people do go there. Some people choose to go to hell; God doesn't send them there. Jesus makes it very clear in the Gospels that God loves all of us, and God will punish those who reject His love (see Matthew 25:41–46; John 3:14–18). However, everyone who accepts God's love by believing in Jesus receives eternal life in heaven and the eternal enjoyment of God's loving presence (see John 1:12; 3:36; 5:24; 14:1–6; Revelation 21:1–4).

What We Have Discovered about Major Worldviews

Let's summarize what we have discovered about various religions or worldviews in this chapter and in the previous two chapters. A table will help us to quickly summarize how many of the five big tests each worldview passes. Each of the six religions or worldviews is listed in the order that they were discussed in this book. Please see table 3 and my comments on it below.

Table 3. Do The Major Religions Pass the Five Big Tests?

The Five Big Tests	Christianity	Judaism	Islam	Hinduism	Buddhism	New Age
human reason test	✓					
contemporary living test	✓	✓			?	✓
divine glory test	✓					
honest reporting test	✓	✓	✓	✓	✓	✓
all-inclusive test	✓	✓	?			

Let's sum up what the table tells us. First of all, we can see in the table above that only the Christian faith passes the human reason test and the divine glory test. All the other five worldviews fail these two tests. Secondly, we can also see in the table above that at least half of the worldviews pass the contemporary living test. The Christian faith, Judaism, and the New Age pass this test. It's possible but not clear from the evidence that Buddhism also passes the contemporary living test. Thirdly, we can see in the table above that all the worldviews pass the honest reporting test. All the worldviews have some embarrassing stories about their founders or have some beliefs that can be considered embarrassing to their adherents. Finally, only the Christian faith and Judaism clearly pass the all-inclusive test. It's possible but not clear from the evidence that Islam also passes the all-inclusive test.

Now that we know the results of using the five big tests, what do these results mean? The results of using the five big tests are very encouraging for the Christian faith and for the Bible. *Only the Christian faith passes all of the five big tests.* By being the only worldview to pass the human reason test, the Christian faith is the only worldview that is truly intellectually satisfying. By being the only worldview to pass the divine glory test, the Christian faith is the only worldview that is truly theologically sound. By passing the all-inclusive test, the Christian faith shows that the Old and New Testaments of the Bible are trustworthy. By passing the contemporary living test, the Christian faith demonstrates that it still is emotionally appealing in the 21st century. By passing the honest reporting test, the Christian faith provides further evidence of its being intellectually satisfying and emotionally appealing.

The results of using the five big tests are mixed for all of the non-Christian worldviews. By passing the honest reporting test, all the non-Christian worldviews are at least somewhat intellectually and emotionally appealing. By passing the contemporary living test, some worldviews are more emotionally appealing in today's world than other worldviews are in the 21st century. By passing the all-inclusive test, Judaism passes more tests than the other non-Christian worldviews. *By not passing a majority of the tests, most of the worldviews are much more emotionally appealing than they are intellectually satisfying and theologically sound.*

What about atheism, agnosticism, and relativism? We examined these worldviews before we discussed the five big tests. We saw in the first part of this book that these three worldviews are false because they aren't intellectually satisfying. However, let's quickly see how many of the five big tests each of these three worldviews pass. Please see table 4 and my explanation of this table below.

Table 4. Do The Major Nontheistic Worldviews Pass the Five Big Tests?

The Five Big Tests	Atheism	Agnosticism	Relativism
human reason test			
contemporary living test	?	?	
divine glory test			
honest reporting test	✓	✓	
all-inclusive test			

Atheism only clearly passes one of the five big tests. It passes the honest reporting test because Darwin admitted that the theory of evolution has some weaknesses. Atheism could be considered to also pass the contemporary living test if more atheists would openly acknowledge that absolute moral values exist. Atheism fails the human reason test and the all-inclusive test by lacking any real evidence showing that God doesn't exist. Obviously, atheism fails the divine glory test by denying that God exists even though the arguments for His existence are persuasive.

Like atheism, agnosticism only clearly passes one of the five big tests. It passes the honest reporting test by claiming not to know whether or not God exists. Agnosticism could also be considered to pass the contemporary living test if more agnostics would acknowledge that moral absolutes exist. Agnosticism fails the human reason test and the all-inclusive test by lacking any strong evidence demonstrating that God may not exist. Lastly, agnosticism fails the divine glory test by doubting that God exists. The vast majority of us regard God's existence as an obvious fact and a necessary explanation for the universe's existence.

Unlike agnosticism, relativism doesn't seem to pass any of the five big tests. Relativism doesn't seem to pass the honest reporting test because it argues that there are no moral absolutes even though everyone knows that there really are moral absolutes. We all know that murder, stealing, lying, and committing adultery are wrong. Relativism fails to pass the contemporary living test because it is impossible to live as if there are no moral absolutes. Relativism isn't livable. Relativism fails the human reason test by claiming that there are no moral absolutes; this claim itself is an absolute statement about morality. Moreover, relativism fails the all-inclusive test by offering insufficient evidence for moral values being relative instead of absolute. Finally, relativism doesn't pass the divine glory test because it doesn't clearly affirm God's existence.

Only the Christian worldview passes all five big tests that we can use to know if our main beliefs are true or false. The Christian faith is the only worldview that is intellectually satisfying, emotionally appealing, and theologically sound. None of the other five theistic worldviews or three nontheistic worldviews passes all five big tests. These non-Christian views are somewhat intellectually and emotionally appealing, but they aren't theologically sound. As a result, we must conclude that the Christian worldview offers the most accurate view of reality—the most accurate view of God, people, the world, and Jesus. Moreover, Jesus is the only founder of a world religion or worldview who both lived a righteous life and believed what is true about God.

I would like to believe that all religions lead to God, but that desire is just wishful thinking. I wish that everyone could spend eternity with God in heaven, but that wish isn't going to be fulfilled. The results of using the five big tests have helped me to know beyond a shadow of a doubt that

Only the Christian worldview passes all of the five big tests.

not all religions or worldviews teach us what is true about us, God, and the world. Not all religions lead to God. Not all worldviews tell us the truth about where we come from, why we are here, and where we are going when we die.

The different worldviews feature mutually exclusive claims about us, God, the world, and Jesus. We as humans can't be both born good and born with a tendency to sin. We can't be both divine and also not divine. God can't be both one God in one person and one God in three persons. God can't be both one God and many gods. The world can't be both God and also separate from God. Jesus can't be both divine and not divine. These competing claims about us, God, the world, and Jesus clearly contradict one another.

The death and resurrection of Jesus show that he is the Christ and a divine person. In other words, he is the promised divine Messiah and Savior who was predicted in the Old Testament. His death and resurrection show that he is the Son of God and his words in the Gospels are the words of God Himself.[87]

The resurrection of Jesus clearly demonstrates that he is the only way to God. Jesus is the only person in human history who has ever lived a sinless life and risen from the dead in an immortal body. Jesus is the only way to a vibrant relationship with God and to an eternity of enjoying God's loving presence. Jesus is the only one who can save you from an eternity away from God's loving presence. Steven Davis writes:

> The resurrection of Jesus, then, is God's decisive proof that Jesus is not just a great religious teacher among all the great religious teachers in history... The resurrection is God's way of pointing to Jesus and saying that he is the one in whom you are to believe. He is your Savior. He alone is Lord.[88]

After rising from the dead, Jesus is recorded in the Gospels as claiming that God has given him all authority in heaven and on earth. The risen Jesus makes this powerful statement to his disciples in Matthew 28:18–20. In her comments on this extraordinary statement, Rebecca McLaughlin writes, "Jesus claims rule over all of heaven and earth. He presents himself not as one possible path to God, but as God himself. We may choose to disbelieve him. But he cannot be one truth among many. He has not left us that option."[89]

If you are a Christian, the results of using the five big tests to evaluate your beliefs should greatly encourage you. You should thank God that He has shown you the truth that sets you free and makes it possible for you to live for Him. You shouldn't feel superior to those who aren't Christians. Christians aren't better or smarter than adherents of other faiths. God is the only One who is superior, and He is far greater than all of us! Christians should feel genuine love and compassion for those who haven't trusted in Jesus as the way to God and to eternal life in heaven.

The results of using the five big tests should cause all of us to consider Jesus's claims.

God loves Christians, Jews, Muslims, Hindus, Buddhists, New Agers, atheists, agnostics, and relativists, and so do I. True followers of Jesus love people of all the different worldviews.

If you aren't a follower of Jesus, the results of using the five big tests should concern you. They should cause you to consider changing your beliefs and to consider the claims of Jesus. The results should motivate you to find your joy, peace, purpose, hope, and forgiveness in Jesus. Accepting God's love involves asking Jesus to meet your most important needs. Accepting His love also requires allowing the Bible and Jesus to provide you with the answers to life's biggest questions.

Since we know the results of using the five big tests, we have further confirmation about the correct answers to life's biggest questions. The five big questions that we all need to have answers for are as follows:

1) Who am I?
2) Where did I come from?
3) Why am I here?
4) What has gone wrong with the world?
5) What solution can solve the problem?

Question 1 is about our identity. Question 2 is about our origin. Question 3 asks about our purpose—our reason for being alive on earth. Question 4 asks about why there is evil and suffering in the world. Question 5 seeks the best solution to the problem of evil and suffering in the world.

The Bible and Jesus provide the correct answers to the five big questions. We mentioned these answers at the end of chapter 7, but let's review them quickly right now. The answers are the following:

1) You are a person with an immortal soul, a conscience, and the ability to think, feel, and choose. As a result, you have physical, emotional, spiritual, social, and financial needs.
2) You were created by God in His image.
3) You are here on earth to live for God and for Jesus. As a result, you have a longing for God and for immortality.
4) Sin has entered into the world, making it broken and making us in need of God's forgiveness.

5) Jesus enables us to be forgiven by God through his perfect life, death on the cross, and resurrection from the dead. Everyone who believes in Jesus as our way to God is forgiven by God and given joy, peace, a purpose in life, and eternal life.

Answering Objections: Is Jesus Really *the* Way to God?

The three most important people in the New Testament all clearly say that Jesus is the only way to God. Jesus himself claims to be the only way to God (see John 14:6). Peter, the leader and spokesperson of Jesus's disciples, contends that Jesus is the only way to God (see Acts 4:12). Paul, the church persecutor whose life was completely changed by Jesus, argues that Jesus is the only mediator between people and God (see 1 Timothy 2:5–6). Both Peter and Paul died for their belief that Jesus is the only way to have peace with God and eternal life in heaven.

> **The Bible and Jesus provide the correct answers to life's most important questions.**

Some of us reading this book may have some objections to the belief that Jesus is our only way to God. Some of us think that this belief is narrow-minded, and some of us have more questions about the Christian worldview. Please read below for my answers to four objections about Jesus being the only way to God and the Christian worldview being the most accurate worldview. I will wait until the next chapter to address a fifth objection to the Christian worldview.

Objection 1: Can't We Earn Our Way to Heaven?

Many of us think that we can earn our way to heaven by trying to be good people. The majority of people believe that if someone does more good deeds than bad deeds, he or she will probably go to heaven. All non-Christian religions teach that heaven is like a prize or reward for good behavior. This perspective that good people go to heaven by doing more good deeds than bad deeds is most clearly taught in Islam, where a person's good deeds are placed on a scale to see if he or she has done enough good works (see Quran 7:8–9; 21:47; 23:102–103; 101:6–11). The idea that we can earn or deserve our way to heaven appeals to our pride and our desire to feel like we are good people. It seems doable and reasonable to us. But it's not true.

Unlike other religions and worldviews, the Christian faith teaches that if we trust in Jesus as the only way to God, we can be 100% sure that we will go to heaven. *The Christian faith teaches that eternal life in heaven is a gift that we can't earn or deserve* (see Romans 6:23). Eternal life is a gift of God's grace—His unmerited favor—to everyone who believes in Jesus (see Romans 3:28; Galatians 2:16; Ephesians 2:8–9; Titus 3:5). Jesus says that we all try to be good, but we all fail to be good because none of us is perfect. Only God is truly good because He is perfect (see Matthew 5:48; Luke 18:18–19). It's not good people that go to heaven; it's forgiven people who go there. Jesus and the Bible say that forgiven people go to heaven (see Matthew 6:14–15; 1 John 1:9). If we have truly trusted in Jesus as the way to God, we will do good works out of our gratitude for God's forgiveness and salvation and out of our love for Him (see Ephesians 2:10; James 2:14, 26). We won't do good works in order to try to earn our way to heaven because eternal life is a gift that we receive at the moment that we trust in Jesus.

We all love to receive gifts for our birthday, Christmas, or some other occasion. It's awesome to feel loved and appreciated! Eternal life is like a Christmas gift or a birthday gift that we received from our parents each year even if we weren't very obedient children. However, eternal life is even better than any gift we could ever receive during this lifetime. Eternal life is the best gift we could ever receive because it lasts forever. Toy cars, dolls, money, and all other gifts we receive don't last long. The toys and other gifts that we receive will get old and become worn out, and we can't take them with us to heaven. The happiness that we get from them also disappears after a short time.

Has anyone ever tried to bribe you? A few years ago, I bought a sleep-aid product on Amazon. The product only slightly improved the quality of my sleep, so I didn't think it deserved a four or five-star rating. I may have been willing to give it a three-star rating. Nevertheless, the product came in the mail with an offer for a free bottle of the same product if I would take a photo of the product that I had purchased and write a five-star rating for it on Amazon. The company selling the sleep-aid product was trying to bribe me! They were bribing people to write five-star reviews of their product. I didn't want more of the mediocre product, and I didn't feel comfortable accepting a bribe. As a result, I decided to say "No, thank you!" to the company's offer for a free bottle. This personal experience helped me to realize that just as I didn't want to accept a bribe, God wouldn't and couldn't accept a bribe. I knew that I couldn't get into heaven by bribing God with my good works.

Why can't we earn our way to heaven by doing good works? There are three reasons why we can't earn our way to heaven:

1) Heaven is for the humble, not for the proud.
2) Our good deeds done in order to earn our way to heaven have selfish motives.
3) God is holy and can't accept bribes.

Let me briefly explain these three reasons. First of all, if we are trying to earn our way to heaven, we will be proud instead of humble. Heaven is for those of us who humbly admit to God that we can't earn our way there (see Isaiah 57:15; 66:2; Ephesians 2:8–9; James 4:6). Secondly, if we are attempting to earn our way to heaven, our good deeds will be done with selfish motives. We will do them in order to try to gain the approval of God and other people. We will use people out of our selfish desire to feel good about ourselves. Finally, if we are trying to earn our way to heaven, we are trying to bribe God with our good deeds. Because God is holy, He can't accept any bribes. It's inconceivable that a holy God would allow us to bribe Him. Nevertheless, we can be accepted by God and spend eternity with Him if we trust in Jesus's work on the cross instead of in our good works as our way to heaven.

Objection 2: Isn't There a Wideness in God's Mercy?

Many Christians believe that God is merciful toward those who are unable to understand the good news about Jesus's death and resurrection. The Bible seems to teach that all aborted babies and all young children will go to heaven (see Deuteronomy 1:39; 2 Samuel 12:22–23; Isaiah 7:15–16; Matthew 19:14). Aborted babies and young children haven't reached the age of accountability, which is the time when they adequately understand the difference between right and wrong. Young children also can't fully understand what it means to trust in Jesus as the only way to God. God has mercy on young children because they can't understand how we can get right with God through faith in Jesus. Yes, there is a wideness in God's mercy.

A few years ago, a Latina friend whom my wife and I know decided to have an abortion. We tried to encourage this Latina friend to keep the baby, but she decided to terminate the pregnancy. We felt so sad about our friend's decision! However, my wife and I believe that we will be able to meet that aborted baby someday in heaven. God is merciful toward the unborn and toward children. He loves them so much!

Unlike young children, all of us reading this book know the difference between right and wrong, and we can understand what it means to trust in Jesus. We don't have any excuses that God will accept. We need to believe in Jesus in order to be forgiven by God and to spend eternity with Him. God is ready, willing, and able to forgive us and give us eternal life when we trust in Jesus as the way to heaven. Jesus is always standing with his arms wide open, ready to forgive us and give us a place in heaven if we trust in him as the way to get there. Because He loves us, God is also ready to give us joy, peace, and a purpose in life. God loves us more than we can imagine or comprehend, and many of us have experienced His love through our faith in Jesus.

Objection 3: Isn't it Too Hard to Believe in the Trinity?

Many of us reading this book have heard of the Christian belief in the Trinity and also regard this belief as too difficult to understand. Our concerns about the Trinity are legitimate because it seems like a paradox. Fully understanding the Trinity is impossible, but we can understand enough about it to believe in it. The Trinity is a rational belief even though it's also a mystery. God will help us to understand His triune nature if we are open to believing in it.

The Trinity is the belief that God exists as one God in three Persons: God the Father, God the Son, and God the Holy Spirit. God the Father is our heavenly Father who loves us, created the world, and controls everything that happens in the world. Jesus is God the Son, who came to earth as the man Jesus of Nazareth over 2,000 years ago. God the Holy Spirit is whom Jesus sent to be with us after his own death, resurrection, and ascension into heaven. Like God the Son, the Holy Spirit participated in the world's creation, and He lives in us forever if we trust in Jesus as our way to heaven. One helpful illustration of the Trinity is sound: God the Father is the Speaker or Source, Jesus is the Word spoken, and the Holy Spirit is the way that God continues to speak to us today.[90] This illustration is based on the Bible and enables us to see how God can be one God in three Persons (see Genesis 1; John 1, 14–16; Hebrews 1).

We can't completely understand the Trinity, but our inability to completely comprehend it doesn't mean that the Christian faith should be rejected as irrational or as demeaning to God. We can understand the basic concept that God eternally exists as one God in three Persons. However, we can't fully understand or explain God's triune nature. If we could fully understand the triune nature of God, He wouldn't be worthy of our worship. For God to be worthy of our worship, He must be greater than us. While God is infinite, we are finite. We aren't all-knowing; we are limited in our knowledge and understanding. The Trinity shows us that God is greater than we are and thus worthy of our worship. In other words, the Trinity passes both the human reason test and the divine glory test. It's rational, God-honoring, believable, and true.

Objection 4: Isn't Reincarnation True?

Some of us reading this book believe in reincarnation and think that it accurately describes what happens to us when we die. It's interesting for some of us to speculate about what we might have been doing in a past life. We can choose to believe in reincarnation if we want to believe in it, but there is no convincing evidence for it. In contrast, we have discovered that there is convincing evidence for Jesus's resurrection. Because Jesus rose from the dead, we know that we will also be raised from the dead in the future (see Daniel 12:2; John 5:29; Acts 24:15; 1 Corinthians 6:14; 15:20–22, 42–53). Resurrection and reincarnation are mutually exclusive concepts; we can't be both resurrected and reincarnated after we die. In addition, the Bible clearly teaches that we won't be reincarnated by saying that each of us only dies once and then faces judgment (see Hebrews 9:27). After we pass away, we will spend eternity in heaven with Jesus if we trust in him as the only way to God. The resurrection of our bodies will occur in the future when Jesus returns to earth, and we will spend eternity with God if we believe in Jesus (see 1 Corinthians 15:51–53; 1 Thessalonians 4:16; Revelation 19–21).

Objection 5: Is the Christian Faith Really Livable Today?

Many of you reading this book may still not be sure that the Christian faith is livable today. You may think it's no big deal that Christianity passes all five big tests. You may think that the Christian faith isn't really relevant or livable in the 21st century. In other words, you aren't fully convinced that the Christian faith really passes the contemporary living test. You may not even consider Jesus's claims until you are more confident that it's still possible to live the Christian faith. Is it still possible to live the Christian faith in today's world? Is Jesus still the Life Changer who is transforming the lives of many people? In the next chapter, we will answer those questions and discuss five big truths as we discover how we can experience life-changing truth.

Part 3

Experiencing Life-Changing Truth

9

The Life Changer Is Still Transforming Lives!

Do you like movies based on true stories? I do. Some of my favorite movies are based on true stories. I love the movies *The Ten Commandments, Luther, Schindler's List, Amazing Grace, Hoosiers,* and *Rudy* partly because they are based on true stories. These movies based on real people and real stories show how God has been actively working in people's lives throughout history and in recent times.

One of my favorite movies is *Woodlawn*, a 2015 film based on the true story of a high school football team in Alabama in the 1970s. In this powerful movie, a spiritual revival captures the hearts of almost all the players on the Woodlawn High School football team. After a riot at the school, the Woodlawn football coach allows a traveling sports chaplain to speak to the team as a motivational speaker. The chaplain speaks about Jesus and the football players' need for change and forgiveness. When the chaplain finishes his speech, almost the entire team chooses to trust in Jesus, and the new believers join together in prayer. The spiritual revival results in significantly reducing racial tensions and hate at a newly desegregated high school and in the surrounding community. Jesus changes the lives of the Black superstar Tony Nathan, other football players, the football coach, and football players on another team. Jesus also transforms the lives of many students and many parents. Jesus enables the football players and the community to overcome racial tensions so that they can play football together, go to school together, and live together in harmony. At the end of the movie, Tony Nathan goes on to play college football for the University of Alabama, and he and his teammates win the national title. *Woodlawn* is a great movie based on various emotional and encouraging events.

Many of you might be thinking something like this: "The movie *Woodlawn* is based on events in the 1970s, not events in the

21st century. The 1970s were decades ago, and the last time Jesus walked on this earth was almost 2,000 years ago. Are Jesus and the Christian faith still relevant to us in today's world?"

Are Jesus and the Christian Faith Still Relevant Today?

It's understandable that many of you reading this book wonder if Jesus and the Christian faith are still relevant today. The world has changed so much since Jesus lived on earth and since the Gospels were written about 2,000 years ago. Changes in society and technology have greatly altered how people live since Jesus walked on this earth. Women today can vote, work outside their homes, and earn a good amount of money. Cell phones, computers, cars, microwaves, emails, and the internet make the pace of life move much faster today than the pace of life in Jesus's time. In Jesus's time, there wasn't even a printing press to print books, and there was no electricity! Life is so different now than it was back then.

The major changes in the world since Jesus lived on earth make many of us have doubts about whether or not the Christian faith can still work for us today. Do the huge differences between life in today's world and life in Jesus's time make the Christian faith outdated and unlivable today? Or is it still possible for us to live the Christian faith in today's world?

The Christian faith is still relevant today because it's not racist, misogynist, homophobic, or unlivable. Jesus and the Bible strongly oppose racism, sexism, and any other type of prejudice and discrimination. In addition, the Christian faith is still livable in the 21st century. These facts are clearly described below.

The Christian faith isn't racist, sexist, homophobic, or unlivable.

Just as racism is still a relevant issue today, Jesus is still relevant today. The Christian faith that Jesus founded is also still relevant today. Jesus and the New Testament clearly address racism and express strong opposition to it (see Luke 10:25–37; John 4:1–42; Acts 10:34–35; Galatians 3:28).

Racism is wrong, and the Bible acknowledges this important and timeless truth.

The greatest president in U.S. history apparently noticed the Bible's stand against racism. Abraham Lincoln freed the slaves in the USA when his Emancipation Proclamation went into effect in 1863. Lincoln either became a Christian during the last several years of his life, or he was interested in knowing more about Jesus and becoming a Christian. Lincoln expressed his belief in Jesus or at least a strong interest in Jesus in the moments before his assassination at the Ford's Theatre. Lincoln was assassinated on Good Friday in 1865, just two days before Easter. He spoke his last dramatic words to his wife about his desire to visit the Holy Land in Jerusalem in order to see where Jesus lived. Lincoln leaned forward toward his wife, Mary, and said, "We will visit the Holy Land and see those places hallowed by the footsteps of the Savior. There is no place I so much desire to see as Jerusalem."[1] Lincoln would never have spoken those words if he thought that Jesus or the Bible approved of racism and the brutal treatment of slaves in America. Lincoln regarded the barbaric treatment of slaves as evil, and he must have thought that Jesus and the Bible's authors also opposed it.

Whether or not Lincoln was a Christian, it was the followers of Jesus who led the abolition movement and the civil rights movement in the USA. Frederick Douglass, Harriet Beacher Stowe, Sojourner Truth, and Harriet Tubman were Christians who led the abolition movement in the USA. In England, the most prominent abolitionist was William Wilberforce. For twenty years, Wilberforce served as the leader of the successful parliamentary campaign to stop the British slave trade. Wilberforce then worked twenty-five more years to free the slaves in the British territories. He was also an evangelical Christian.[2] Lastly, Martin Luther King Jr. was not only the most prominent leader of the civil rights movement but also a Christian minister. We celebrate Martin Luther King Jr. Day every January in the USA because he led marches for Blacks' right to vote, desegregation, labor rights, and other basic civil rights. King and all of these abolitionists were brave heroes and also strong Christians.

Besides regarding racism as wrong, the Bible also acknowledges that sexism is wrong. Many of Jesus's followers in the Gospels are women, and the first people to see the risen Jesus are women. In the book of Acts, women are described as being essential to the early Christian movement. There are many women who are filled with the Holy Spirit (see Acts 1:14; 2:4, 18), believe in Jesus (see Acts 5:14), and get baptized (see Acts 8:12). A woman named Tabitha is raised from the dead (see Acts 9:36–41), and a woman named Mary hosts a prayer meeting for men and women (see Acts 12:12). A woman named Lydia and the other members of her household trust in Jesus and are baptized (see Acts 16:14–15). A woman named Priscilla and her husband, Aquila, correct a man named Apollos's understanding of Christian doctrine; Apollos soon becomes a great defender of the Christian faith (see Acts 18:24–26). Furthermore, the New Testament epistles also regard women and men as equally deserving of respect and appreciation (see Romans 16:3; Galatians 3:28; Philippians 4:2–3).

Because the Bible is opposed to sexism, Christians in the USA led the movement for women to win the right to vote. American women gained the right to vote in 1920 mainly due to the efforts of Christians to help them gain that right. Wendy Alsup writes, "In 1920, women finally won the right to vote in the United States, due in large part to the efforts of Christians… Based in part on their understanding of Jesus and the Bible, men and women of faith fought together for women to have the right to vote."[3] This movement for women's rights in the USA resulted in women being able to vote, inherit land, and gain a voice in legislation.[4]

In addition to considering sexism as wrong, the New Testament doesn't promote homophobia. Christians are to love everyone, including people who consider themselves lesbian, gay, bisexual, or transgender (LGBT). Some of the early Christians entered the church while struggling with same-sex attraction (see 1 Corinthians 6:9–11). LGBT people weren't prohibited from attending the early Christians' gatherings. There was no sign at the door saying, "LGBT people aren't welcome here!" However, the Bible clearly states that sexual intimacy is designed by God only for heterosexual marriages (see Genesis 2:24; Leviticus 18:22; Romans 1:26–27; 1 Timothy 1:9–10). Jesus himself points out that God's design for sex is sexual intimacy within the context of heterosexual marriage (see Matthew 19:4–6). He also clearly states that adultery and lust are wrong (see Matthew 5:27–28). People who struggle with same-sex attraction can choose not to be sexually intimate with someone of the same sex, and married heterosexual people can choose to not commit adultery. Everyone can and should practice sexual restraint so that they can please God. Joy and peace are the results of having godly desires and making God-honoring choices.

If you want to read more about what the Bible says about homosexuality, please see Rebecca McLaughlin's excellent book *Confronting Christianity*.[5] Her book answers some of the most difficult questions that the Christian faith must answer, including questions about homosexuality and racism. McLaughlin also honestly shares how she has sought to please God while struggling with and overcoming same-sex attraction.

The Unparalleled Impact of Jesus

Before we discuss if the Christian life is still livable today, let's keep in mind the unparalleled impact Jesus has made. Everyone who wants to live the Christian life seeks to imitate the example of Jesus, history's most important and impactful person. No one else in human history has made such a positive and global impact. The years of history are divided into BC and AD because of Jesus's immense impact on the world. Despite his relatively short public ministry, Jesus Christ has influenced history, education, literacy, hospitals, art, music, and movies more than any other person. Countless schools have been built and numerous hospitals have been founded because of the unparalleled positive impact of Jesus's life and teachings. The Buddha had a 45-year itinerant ministry, and Muhammad had a 23-year prophetic ministry. The Buddha, Muhammad, and other religious founders and great philosophers have made a lasting mark on the world. But none of these men have influenced the world as much as Jesus. Henry Bosch writes:

> *Socrates taught for 40 years, Plato for 50, Aristotle for 40, and Jesus for only 3. Yet the influence of Christ's three-year ministry infinitely transcends the impact left by the combined 130 years of teaching from these men who are among the greatest philosophers of all antiquity. Jesus painted no pictures, yet some of the finest paintings of Raphael, Michelangelo, and Leonardo de Vinci received their inspiration from Him. Jesus wrote no poetry, but Dante, Milton, and scores of the world's greatest poets were inspired by Him. Jesus composed no music, still Haydn, Handel, Beethoven, Bach, and Mendelssohn reached their highest perfection of melody in their hymns, symphonies, and oratories they composed in His praise. Every sphere of human greatness has been enriched by this humble carpenter of Nazareth.*[6]

The Christian Faith Is Still Livable Today

Millions of people during the last 2,000 years have followed Jesus and had their lives completely changed by him. The church persecutor Paul, the skeptic James, the early Christians, and many other people since the time of the early Christians have experienced life transformation due to Jesus's impact on their lives. Many people today continue to follow Jesus because the Christian faith is still livable today. The followers of Jesus in today's world know that the Christian life is livable and meaningful.

Finding peace with God, experiencing lasting joy, and having a life of true purpose and meaning require knowing Jesus, the Life Changer.

Like other followers of Jesus, I know from personal experience that it's still possible to live the Christian faith in today's postmodern world. I have discovered that finding peace with God, experiencing lasting joy, and having a life of true purpose and meaning require knowing Jesus, the Life Changer. Jesus is the one who fills our lives with joy, peace, and a sense of purpose. By giving us a sense of purpose, Jesus also provides us with meaning and hope as we experience God's love and forgiveness. Jesus is the true path to peace and joy and the only one who enables us to enjoy the abundant life we were meant to live on this earth.

Countless Christians living in today's world have experienced life transformation due to their belief in Jesus and their commitment to live for him. Many people who used to be atheists, agnostics, relativists, and adherents of non-Christian religions have found their peace, joy, and purpose in Jesus. They have also found their hope and forgiveness in him. Praise God!

Jesus Is the Life Changer: He Is Still Changing Lives!

Jesus is the Life Changer. Jesus has changed the lives of millions of people throughout the world. Former atheists, skeptics, addicts, and abuse victims have found their fulfillment and purpose in Jesus. Jesus has changed the lives of people of all ages, classes, races, and religious backgrounds. He has changed the lives of famous people and ordinary people like me. Jesus has changed my life, my wife's life, the lives of many of our friends and relatives, and the lives of so many other people whom I know. Jesus has enabled millions of us to find our joy, peace, and purpose by trusting him and living for him. Jesus has also provided forgiveness, love, grace, mercy, and eternal life to all of us who believe in him. He has made it possible for me and all his other followers to become more humble, loving, kind, gentle, patient, and self-controlled as we depend on him to change us. No Christians are perfect people, but Jesus is still doing amazing and marvelous things in the lives of every one of us who has decided to live for him. *Jesus makes a huge difference in our lives by turning our mess into his message and enabling us to conquer our fears through our faith. Jesus is awesome!*

The fifteen people listed and described below are some of the countless lives whom Jesus has transformed. These followers of Jesus have experienced various benefits and blessings as a result of their commitment to live for him. Their changed lives show that following Jesus isn't easy, but it's definitely worth it. Jesus has given them peace and joy even during their most challenging times. The best decision that these fifteen people ever made was their decision to trust in Jesus and to follow him. He has changed them from the inside out so that they can share their encouraging stories of life transformation with us. Have you ever heard of any of the people on this list?

Table 5. Fifteen People Whom Jesus Has Changed

Their Names	Their Occupations	How Jesus Has Changed Them
1. Josh McDowell	author and speaker	former agnostic, abuse victim
2. Lee Strobel	author and speaker	former atheist
3. J. Warner Wallace	homicide detective	former atheist
4. Sarah Irving-Stonebreaker	university professor	former atheist
5. Doreen Virtue	author	former New Ager
6. Steven Bancarz	author	former New Ager
7. Kirk Cameron	actor and evangelist	former atheist
8. Stephen Baldwin	actor, producer, etc.	former drug addict
9. Yami Fernandez	business owner	former porn addict, abuse victim
10. Bethany Hamilton	professional surfer	shark attack survivor
11. Ally Yarid	Instagram evangelist	survivor of a suicide attempt
12. Cheryl Broyles	author	brain cancer survivor
13. Jeff Lowery	missions mobilizer	legally blind but still serves Jesus
14. Vaneetha Riser	author	suffers from polio but serves Jesus
15. Sydney McLaughlin	Olympic hurdler	boldly sharing her faith

Jesus has completely changed the life of Josh McDowell. Before he was a Christian, Josh was a college student and an agnostic who wanted to write a book proving that the Christian faith was a sham. While researching Jesus's claims, he was shocked by what he discovered. Josh became convinced that Jesus's claims were true! The evidence for Jesus's claims was overwhelming. He realized that Jesus was God's Son who had died for him and rose again. He decided to trust in Jesus as the way to God. His new faith enabled him to forgive the family's hired cook and housekeeper who had sexually abused him for several years. Josh stopped hating his abuser and even told him about Jesus![7] Since he decided to live for Jesus, Josh has been involved in youth ministry for over 50 years. He has spoken to more than 46 million people, giving over 27,000 talks in 139 countries. Josh has also written or coauthored 151 books.[8] Wow! God has given Josh a passion for sharing and defending his faith in Jesus!

Like Josh McDowell, Lee Strobel was a skeptic who didn't believe in Jesus or in the Bible. Strobel considered himself an atheist who thought that belief in God was wishful thinking. He was an award-winning journalist who thought Jesus was just an unusually wise and kind man. Lee wasn't interested in considering the claims of Jesus until his wife, Leslie, stunned him by telling him that she had become a Christian. Lee began to notice the positive changes Jesus was making in her life. As a result, he began to read books and interview experts so that he could consider the evidence for the Christian faith. His spiritual journey led him to not only consider the claims of Jesus but to be convinced by them based on the evidence that he found. Lee's rigorous search for truth led him to believe in Jesus.[9] Since his decision to trust in Jesus, Lee has been enthusiastically sharing with others the reasons why he believes in Jesus. He has written more than forty books, and his spiritual journey was depicted in an award-winning movie called *The Case for Christ* (2017).[10]

Like Lee Strobel, J. Warner Wallace was an atheist before he believed in Jesus. As a cold-case homicide detective, he realized that the Gospels could be examined much like the murder cases he solved. After carefully examining the evidence for Jesus, he was persuaded that the Gospels were true. As a result, he became a Christian at the age of 35.[11] Since he decided to trust in Jesus, Wallace has written the excellent book *Cold-Case Christianity* (2013). Wallace has written other Christian books and served as a professor at a Christian university. He enjoys telling other people why he believes in Jesus.

Sarah Irving-Stonebreaker is also a former atheist who now believes in Jesus. While growing up in Australia, she thought that Christians were anti-intellectual and self-righteous. However, she eventually realized that atheism doesn't provide a sufficient ethical foundation for her beliefs in human equality and human value. After she moved to Florida, she became interested in Jesus because she saw Christians there feeding the homeless and housing migrant farmworkers. She then read a Christian book, and she decided to trust in Jesus and live for him. Sarah realized that eternal life in heaven is a gift that she couldn't earn or deserve. She also understood that we are all broken people who need to be fixed by trusting in Jesus, who died in our place and rose again. Lastly, she realized that God wants us to carefully examine our beliefs so that we can determine if they are true. Sarah writes, "God wants us to wrestle with Him, to struggle through doubt and faith, sorrow and hope. Moreover, God wants broken people, not self-righteous ones. And salvation is not about us earning our way to some place in the clouds through good works."[12] Sarah is currently a history professor at Western Sydney University, and she seeks to live for Jesus every day.

Besides changing the lives of former atheists, Jesus is also changing the lives of former New Agers. Doreen Virtue and Steven Bancarz were New Agers before they believed in Jesus. Doreen was a top-selling New Age author who meditated and did yoga daily for 20 years. At the age of 58, she decided to trust in Jesus and live for him after she realized that New Age beliefs were against the Bible's teachings.[13] Doreen came to understand that only Jesus can quench our thirst for true love. She writes, "Jesus quenches our thirst for love, because He offers a love that fills our hearts in a way that no mortal relationship can."[14] Similarly, in his early twenties, Steven realized that his New Age beliefs and meditation practices weren't helping him spiritually. He had built a website that was earning over $40,000 a month in ad revenue alone, but he felt empty inside. Steven determined that his New Age beliefs were false, and he chose to trust in Jesus and live for him. He immediately felt a profound sense of God's love, peace, and forgiveness.[15] Since he trusted in Jesus, Steven has coauthored a book and founded an apologetics website that he uses to defend his faith in Jesus. You can check out his website at www.reasonsforjesus.com.

Jesus is also changing the lives of actors who have decided to live for him. Kirk Cameron and Stephen Baldwin are two American actors whose lives have been changed by Jesus. Have you ever heard of Kirk Cameron or Steve Baldwin? Have you heard their stories of how Jesus changed their lives? You'll enjoy reading their powerful and unforgettable stories!

Kirk Cameron used to believe that God was just a fairy tale like Santa Claus and the Easter Bunny. He was an atheist who believed in evolution and was earning a lot of money as an actor. Kirk is best known for his role as teen Mike Seaver in the American television sitcom *Growing Pains* (1985–1992). He won two People's Choice awards and was nominated for two Golden Globe awards while playing that role. Kirk began considering the claims of Jesus in high school because he sensed that there was more to life than making money and having fun. After searching for more meaning in his life, Kirk realized that atheism is illogical and that many intelligent people are Christians. He decided to follow Jesus. Since he became a Christian, Kirk has been an actor in faith-based films such as the *Left Behind* series (2000–2005) and *Fireproof* (2008). He has also become an outspoken evangelist and apologist for his Christian beliefs.[16] Kirk has been married to actress Chelsea Noble for over 30 years, and they have six kids together.

Stephen Baldwin is another well-known actor whose life has been dramatically changed by Jesus. He is the youngest member of the Baldwin acting family, which also includes Alec, Daniel, and William. They are the most famous brother dynasty in Hollywood history. As a young actor, Stephen had a reputation of being one of Hollywood's bad boys. He was addicted to cocaine, did sex scenes in movies, and sometimes hung out at the Playboy mansion. He also hung out with billionaires and flew around on their private jets. Yet he never felt really comfortable in the world of a Hollywood celebrity. Stephen came to realize that drugs, alcohol, and sex were meaningless instead of fulfilling. He knew that there had to be more to life than pleasure and money.[17]

Stephen's life would soon change after he and his wife Kennya hired a Brazilian nanny named Augusta. Due to Augusta's singing about Jesus, his wife became interested in Jesus and decided to live for him. After the terrorist events of September 11, 2001, Stephen himself also chose to believe in Jesus and live for him. Since he trusted in Jesus, Stephen has been reading the Bible every day,[18] and he has become involved in extreme sports ministry. Stephen no longer cares about how much money he makes or what kind of car he drives. He is living for God instead of trying to impress people with expensive cars and fancy shoes. Stephen says, "I've been around the world, hung out with movie stars, and the experience I am having now…is so much more awesome and powerful and satisfying than anything I've ever experienced in Hollywood. And that's the truth."[19] Stephen has appeared as an actor in Christian movies such as *Six: The Mark Unleashed* (2006) and *God's Club* (2015). He is the father-in-law of singer Justin Bieber, who often posts on Instagram about how his life has also been changed by Jesus.

Like Stephen Baldwin, Yami Fernandez is a former addict whose life has been radically changed by Jesus. Yami is a young Latina woman in her twenties who was born in Cuba but was raised in Florida. After becoming addicted to porn as a child, she suffered from that addiction for 16 years. Yami endured so much pain and trauma as a victim of sexual abuse. She also struggled with hate, drugs, anxiety, and depression, and she even attempted suicide. But God has changed her life and enabled her to overcome her addiction and struggles! Since she trusted in Jesus in 2017, Yami has become a totally new person who is shining the light of Jesus to everyone she meets. She is a child of God who is filled with joy and peace, and her purpose is to live for God so that

Jesus is still changing millions of lives all over the world. He turns our mess into his message and enables us to conquer our fears through our faith.

other people come to know and follow Jesus. Yami shares her story and encourages thousands of women who follow her on Instagram, YouTube, and TikTok. She currently has over 100,000 followers on TikTok. Yami also has her own Christian clothing company.[20] Jesus is doing great things in Yami's life!

Another young woman with a powerful story is Bethany Hamilton. At age 13, Bethany was a rising surfing star when a 14-foot tiger shark bit off her left arm while she was surfing in Hawaii. She almost died from blood loss due to the attack! It was a scary attack that would have caused many surfers to give up on the sport. However, because of her strong faith in Jesus, she began surfing again only a month later, and she won her first national surfing title within two years of the shark attack. Jesus has enabled Bethany to never give up and to keep pursuing her dreams. She is a fearless female athlete who has become one of the best professional female surfers of all time, and she is also an author and motivational speaker.[21] Bethany's inspirational and courageous story is featured in the movie *Soul Surfer* (2011). *Soul Surfer* is an excellent movie that everyone should see!

Like Bethany Hamilton, Ally Yarid is a courageous young woman who is a survivor. Ally lives in Texas. She suffered from depression, anxiety, bitterness, and self-centeredness before she knew Jesus. She became so depressed that she attempted to take her life at age 14 while she was riding in the back of an ambulance. After surviving her suicide attempt, Ally realized her need for Jesus's forgiveness and grace. She knew that she deserved God's punishment, and she decided to trust in Jesus and to live for him. Since she trusted in Jesus, she has enjoyed a new life of joy and contentment even though she suffers from hypothyroidism and Hashimoto's disease (an autoimmune disease). Her suffering from a disease hasn't diminished her joy or her trust in Jesus because she is a new person in Jesus! Ally has discovered God's unconditional love and wonderful purpose through her faith in Jesus. She knows from personal experience that Jesus is better than anything this world has to offer. God has blessed Ally with the boldness to share her faith in Jesus on Instagram, where she has over 100,000 followers. She is truly living for God's kingdom and glory instead of for herself![22]

Another survivor with an encouraging story is Cheryl Broyles. Cheryl is a brain cancer survivor and an author who has inspired many people with her courageous battle against cancer. God has enabled her to live more than 20 years since she was diagnosed with glioblastoma multiforme, the most aggressive and deadly type of brain cancer. At the time of her diagnosis, doctors told Cheryl that she had less than a year to live. Cheryl's fight against brain cancer has included six brain surgeries, radiation treatments, and boosting her immune system by eating healthy and taking many herbal supplements and vitamins. She is a wildlife biologist in Oregon who continues to enjoy outdoor activities such as fishing, camping, backpacking, and mountain bike riding. Although her brain cancer has recurred eight times, Cheryl continues to trust in Jesus to give her the strength to fight it. She thanks Jesus for enabling her to not give up and to keep going.[23] Jesus has given Cheryl a life of joy, peace, and hope that inspires countless people. Cheryl's advice to other people who have been diagnosed with cancer is to remain hopeful and to depend on God for strength and peace because He will always be there.[24] Cheryl has written an inspirational book titled *Life's Mountains* (2012) about her battle against brain cancer and her experience of climbing Mount Shasta in Northern California.[25]

Just as Jesus is helping Cheryl to endure difficult life circumstances, Jesus is also enabling Jeff Lowery to handle challenging life circumstances. Jeff is a Christian missions mobilizer in Florida who was declared legally blind several years ago. After being stabbed and deeply cut by an attacker, Jeff was nearly killed more than 20 years ago. The attack eventually resulted in his completely losing his vision in his right eye and having 20/400 vision with a corrective lens in his left eye. Despite his legal blindness and brain injury from the attack, Jeff has served Jesus in youth ministry and in missions. He trusts that God is in control of his life, and God has given him lasting hope. He is also excited about his learning to read braille because he loves to read. Jeff continues to live for Jesus because He knows that God is still good and worthy of his service and worship. God is still working in Jeff's life in a powerful way![26]

Like Jeff, Vaneetha Riser has endured some difficult life circumstances while following Jesus. Vaneetha suffers from polio, which she initially contracted as an infant before receiving the polio vaccine. She grew up angry at God because she endured many surgeries as a child, and she couldn't walk until she was 7 years old. Due to her walking with a limp, kids made fun of Vaneetha and bullied her. Her stressful childhood experiences frustrated and discouraged her. She eventually tried to imitate Tiny Tim from Charles Dickens' *A Christmas Carol* by being kind and cheerful to everyone, but she was mean to her sister and teased her. Soon after attending some Fellowship of Christian Athletes meetings, Vaneetha wondered if God is real or not. While wondering why God allowed her to have polio, she read in the Bible about the blind man in John 9 who was healed by Jesus. Vaneetha realized that the blind man's blindness and her own polio were a privilege with a purpose, not a punishment from God. His blindness and her polio gave God the opportunity to display His goodness and greatness. Because reading John 9–13 made Vaneetha feel understood and loved, she decided to commit her life to Jesus at age 16. Jesus has enabled Vaneetha to be genuinely kind toward her sister, to endure the death of her infant son, and to keep living for God when her husband left her for someone else. In addition, God has blessed Vaneetha with His constant presence in her life and the strength to keep serving Him for His glory.[27] Vaneetha shares her inspiring story in her book *Walking Through Fire* (2021).[28] Her encouraging book shows that God can turn tragedies into triumphs!

Do you usually watch some of the Olympics on TV? If you do, you may have heard of Sydney McLaughlin. She is an American Olympic hurdler and a world record holder in the 400-meter hurdles. In August 2021, Sydney broke her own world record on her way to winning a gold medal at the Tokyo Olympic Games. She ran an electrifying race in which she dethroned her teammate and the defending Olympic and world champion Dalilah Muhammad, who ran the second-fastest time in the history of women's 400-meter hurdles. After the thrilling race, Sydney didn't boast, scream, dance, or cry. She calmly smiled,[29] knowing that God had given her the most important victory of her career. She humbly said that she was giving all the glory to God and was grateful to be able to represent the USA in the Olympics. She also shared Jesus's words from Matthew 23:12 about the benefits of humility: "But those who exalt themselves will be humbled, and those who humble themselves will be exalted."[30]

Jesus has made Sydney a humble, joyful, and grateful person who seeks to live for God every day. The day after winning her gold medal in the 400-meter hurdles, she posted on Instagram: "What I have in Christ is far greater than what I have or don't have in life. I pray my journey may be a clear depiction of submission and obedience to God... I have never seen God fail in my life."[31] Sydney knows that God is in control of her life, and she thanks Jesus for her salvation. God has given Sydney a million Instagram followers with whom she is sharing her life experiences and her strong faith in Jesus.

Jesus Is More Than a Man

The Gospels, the resurrection accounts, and the changed lives of Christians tell us something significant about Jesus. They tell us that Jesus is not just another prophet like the prophets of many other religions and worldviews. Jesus is unique because only he lived a sinless life, rose from the dead in an immortal body, and is active in the world today.

Jesus is not just an ordinary man who lived on the earth a long time ago. Jesus was a man who was also a carpenter, a prophet, and a healer on the earth 2,000 years ago. However, Jesus lived a perfect life, rose from the dead, and is alive today and active in our world in the 21st century. *Jesus's sinless life, his resurrection, and his continued activity in the lives of people today show that Jesus is much more than a man, a carpenter, a prophet, and a healer. He is the Life Changer who is transforming millions of lives all over the world. He is the way to God, the revealer of truth about God, and the key to abundant life on earth.* Jesus is the divine Son of God who gives us peace with God, joy in all circumstances, and a new purpose in life. Jesus is the Light of the world who makes it possible for us to know the truth about ourselves, God, and the world. He enables us to know the truth that sets us free from false beliefs, negative feelings, and bad habits. Jesus says

> Jesus's sinless life, his resurrection, and his activity in the world today show that Jesus is much more than a man, a teacher, a prophet, and a healer. He is the divine Son of God and the only way to God.

that if we believe in him, we can know the truth that sets us free (see John 8:31–32, 36). Moreover, Jesus forgives us and gives us eternal life in heaven at the moment that we trust in him as our only way to get right with God. Jesus is the main proof that God loves us, and he is our only way to spend eternity with God.

None of us are perfect people who deserve to spend eternity with God, but God loves us anyway. We have all lied, lusted, and struggled with pride and selfishness. Jesus took the punishment that we deserve. Jesus died in our place for all our sins, and he conquered sin, death, and Satan by rising again. Jesus is ready, willing, and able to forgive us and to give us abundant life here on earth and eternal life in heaven. Many of us have already trusted in Jesus and are experiencing the abundant life that God promises to give us. The abundant life is full of joy, peace, and purpose because it is given to us by a God who loves us.

The Five Big Truths

The Gospels, the resurrection accounts, and the changed lives of Christians make it clear that the Christian worldview passes all of the five big tests. This chapter has provided additional support for the Christian faith, demonstrating that it certainly passes the contemporary living test. The Christian worldview is still relevant, livable, and true.

Let's summarize the most important truths that we have discovered in this book. Because we have discovered that the Christian faith is true, we can state the following five big truths:

1. God is real, and His truth is absolute.
2. The four Gospels tell us the truth about what Jesus said and did.
3. Jesus lived a sinless life, died on the cross for our sins, rose from the dead, and appeared alive again to many people in his physical body.
4. The changed lives of millions of people show that Jesus is still active in the world today.

5. Jesus's sinless life, resurrection in an immortal body, and continued activity in the world today prove that he is divine and the only way to God.

God Loves You and Wants You to Live for Him!

God loves you. He wants you to live for Him and to spend eternity with Him in heaven. Jesus showed that he loves you by living a perfect life, dying on the cross for your sin, and rising again. He lived the perfect life that you couldn't live, took God's punishment for you on the cross, and rose again. Jesus wants to meet your spiritual and emotional needs because he loves you more than you can even imagine. If you haven't already trusted in Jesus, I have two questions for you:

May I share with you how you can find your joy, peace, and purpose in life? May I share with you how you can be 100% sure about spending eternity with God in heaven?

In the next chapter, I will share the life-changing message about Jesus (i.e., the gospel) with all of us reading this book. This crucial message will clearly explain why we need Jesus, why we should want Jesus, and how we can trust in Jesus as the way to God.

If you are already a follower of Jesus, you are familiar with the gospel and the good news it contains. However, reading the next chapter will still be encouraging to you because it will give you good tips about how you can share your faith with others in a clear way.

If you aren't a Christian, the next chapter is the most important chapter of this book. Please read it carefully so that you can understand it and reap the amazing benefits of the life-changing message.

10

The Life-Changing Message

Jesus is the true path to a life full of peace and purpose, and he is the one who enables us to enjoy the abundant life that we were meant to live on this earth. Jesus says that he wants to give us an abundant life filled with joy (see John 10:10; 15:11). It's Jesus who brings us joy, peace, and purpose in life. It's Jesus who shines the light of his truth in this world filled with darkness and deception. It's he who changes our lives by enabling us to see the truth and to live it out in our lives. Jesus says that knowing the truth will set us free (see John 8:31–32, 36). Jesus is the Life Changer who is the focus of the life-changing message. Every one of us who trusts in Jesus as the way to God is a completely new person who is empowered by God to live for Him (see 2 Corinthians 5:17; Galatians 2:20).

If we believe in it, the life-changing message infuses our lives with peace, promise, and purpose. It enables us to find peace with God and God's plan for our lives. The life-changing message satisfies the mind, heart, and soul. It's rational, relevant, exciting, and spiritual. It's intellectually satisfying, emotionally appealing, and theologically sound. *The life-changing message is the best news ever because it appeals to every part of us, provides satisfying answers to life's most important questions, and reveals life's most essential truths.* It shows us how to find our joy, peace, and purpose in a healthy and vibrant relationship with God. It's provided by a worldview that acknowledges Jesus as not only history's most influential person but also our only way to God.

The life-changing message is summarized in the gospel that is found in the teachings of Jesus and in the Bible. The gospel is the most important and exciting message that we can hear! Jerry Bridges says, "The gospel is not only the most important message in all of history; it is the only essential message in all of history."[1]

Are you ready to hear the life-changing message of the gospel? The gospel is the good news about Jesus, and it's the best news ever! Before we read the good news about Jesus, we need to know why all of us in this broken world need Jesus.

Why Do We Need Jesus?

Are you 100% sure that if you died today, you would go to heaven? Would you like to be 100% sure about going to heaven? Would you like to be 100% sure that you can find God's joy, peace, and purpose for your life? May I share with you what Jesus and the Bible say about having this assurance? The truth is that we can be 100% sure about going to heaven and spending eternity with God, who loves us more than we can imagine. Jesus can give us this assurance of spending eternity in God's loving presence, where there is no suffering, sickness, or sin. Jesus also assures us that we can find our joy, peace, and purpose in him.

> The gospel is the good news about Jesus. It's the life-changing message and the best news ever!

God created us and everything in the world. He created us to live for Him, not for ourselves. He created the first human beings named Adam and Eve, who lived in a perfect place called the Garden of Eden. Despite their perfect environment, Adam and Eve chose to disobey God. They rebelled against Him. As a result, we all inherit the tendency to disobey God and to live for ourselves (see Psalm 51:5; Romans 5:12). We can't blame Adam and Eve for our tendency to be rebellious because if we had been in the Garden of Eden, we also would have disobeyed God. After Adam and Eve's disobedience, God predicted that Jesus would take the punishment for Adam and Eve's sins and our sins by dying for us (see Genesis 3:15; Psalm 22; Isaiah 53).

Whether we realize it or not, we all need Jesus. We need Jesus because all of us try to be good persons, but none of us is perfect. We have all lied, lusted, and struggled with pride and selfishness. We have called people such things as "jerks," "idiots," and "morons." We all disobeyed our parents at least once when we were kids, and we tend to love money and material possessions more than we love God. Unlike God, we're not perfect. Because God is holy and sinless, His standard is perfection (see Romans 3:23). We all fall short of the standard of perfection God has set for entrance into heaven. Jesus tells us that God's standard is perfection, not doing more good works than bad works (see Matthew 5:48). We all need God's forgiveness.

Do you ever play any sports? If you do, you know that it's impossible to play them perfectly. Basketball players sometimes miss shots, baseball players sometimes strike out, soccer players sometimes make bad passes, and football players sometimes drop passes that they should have caught. Everyone who plays a sport loses at least some games even if he or she plays well.

If you are a student, do you always get 100% on all your exams and quizzes? Of course not! You may be an excellent student, but no one is a perfect student.

If you have a job, do you always do everything right at your job? Do you never make any mistakes at work? Of course not! You may be very hardworking and great at what you do, but no one is a perfect employee. Everyone makes a mistake at work at least once in a while.

You may be more athletic, intelligent, or hardworking than I am, but you still make mistakes. Neither you, nor I, nor anyone else lives a perfect life. Isn't that the truth?

Just as none of us is a perfect athlete, student, or employee, none of us is a perfect person. We all fail to please God sometimes, and we must be willing to admit that we need God's forgiveness. God wants us to be humble and honest with Him.

In the Gospels, Jesus tells a story called the parable of the Pharisee and the tax collector (see Luke 18:9–14). In this parable, a Pharisee and a tax collector go to the temple to pray. The Pharisee proudly prays, thanking God that he is more righteous than the tax collector and other sinful people. The tax collector humbly prays, "God, have mercy on me, a sinner." Jesus says that the proud Pharisee was rejected by God, but the humble tax collector was accepted by God. Jesus says that God rejects proud people who don't see their need for forgiveness, but God accepts humble people who see their need for it.

Jesus also tells a Gospel story called the parable of the lost son (see Luke 15:11–32). In this parable, a man has two sons. The younger son asks his father for his share of the inheritance so that he can take a trip to a faraway country. He spends all of his money, wasting it on wild living. He is starving due to his foolish living and a famine in the land, so he takes a job feeding pigs. The younger son feels hungry, dirty, and dissatisfied while working the job, so he decides to return home to his dad. When his dad sees him returning home, his dad is filled with love and compassion. His dad runs to his son and hugs him. The younger son tells his dad, "I have sinned against God and you, and I don't even deserve to be called your son." Instead of being angry with his son, the father throws a welcome home party for his son to celebrate his return. The father forgives his rebellious son, who clearly deserves to be punished! The oldest son hears the music and dancing from the party, and he becomes angry at his dad and jealous of his younger brother. The older brother protests his brother's party by saying that his dad never threw a party for him and his friends even though he has been such a good worker for his dad.

God is like the father in the parable. God is ready, willing, and able to forgive us if we will confess our sins to Him. Each of us is like the rebellious younger brother or the religious older brother. Like the rebellious younger brother, many of us tend to rebel against God by doing things that don't please Him. Like the religious older brother, many of us try to earn our way to heaven by doing good works.

We sin against God in three different ways: 1) when we do bad things; 2) when we don't do as many good works as we should do; and 3) when we do good works with selfish and proud motives. Our sins show that we don't love God and people as much as we should love Him and them. We aren't perfect people. We often feel guilty, afraid, and ashamed because of our sins.

Have you ever told a lie? Have you ever looked with lust at someone who is not your spouse? Have you ever stolen anything, even something small? Have you ever called someone a "jerk," an "idiot," or a "moron"? Did you ever disobey your parents when you were a child? Have you ever loved your job, your money, or your possessions more than you love God?

Our sins are serious errors that offend God. Jesus says that lust is like adultery, and calling someone "stupid" or a "jerk" is like killing him or her with our words (see Matthew 5:21–22, 27–28). Loving anything or anyone more than we love God is idolatry, and we all struggle with idolatry. We all struggle with putting our priorities in the right order. We tend to put our jobs first, family second, and God third. We know that God should be first, our family should be second, and our jobs or career should be third. When we don't put God first in our lives, we fail to please Him, and we miss out on having the joy, peace, and purpose in life that He wants to give us.

Many of us are so busy that we don't take the time to help others in need. We don't get to know our neighbors or spend as much time with our kids as we should.

Some of us are more religious than we are too busy or rebellious. We try to earn God's approval and the approval of other people. We want people to like us. We are nice to others, but sometimes we are being nice so that we feel good about ourselves. We sometimes use others for our own benefit instead of loving them for their benefit. Our motives for helping others can be tainted by selfishness and pride instead of focused on a desire to love and serve them.

Have you always done as many good deeds as you should do? Have you ever done any good deeds with selfish motives? If you are being honest, you will answer "no" to the first question and "yes" to the second question. It's great that you are willing to be honest about your sins and shortcomings.

We all need God's forgiveness. We have all done bad things, we have all failed to do as many good things as we should do, and we have all done some good deeds with selfish motives. None of us is perfect; only God is perfect. God has existed forever, but He has never sinned. We have all sinned many times. Because of our sins, there is a separation between us and God. Due to our sinful choices, we deserve God's punishment. We deserve to die and spend eternity away from God's loving presence. When we work, we deserve to be paid. Because we all sin, we deserve to die and to be banished from God's loving presence forever (see Romans 6:23).

Why Should We Want to Believe in Jesus?

We've read the bad news that we have sinned and deserve God's punishment. Now let's discuss the good news of the gospel, the life-changing message. The gospel is the best news ever! We don't have to spend eternity away from God! We can choose to believe the good news about Jesus and spend eternity with God, who loves us perfectly and will love us forever. We can enjoy a life full of joy, peace, and purpose by trusting in Jesus. He helps us overcome our guilt, fear, and shame.

The good news is that Jesus took the punishment for our sins when he died on the cross. Jesus died in our place, as our substitute, taking the punishment that we deserve for our sins. Jesus's death in our place shows that God loves us even though we have sinned many times against Him (see Romans 5:8). Jesus suffered so much as he bore our sins on the cross. He could die in our place and serve as our substitute because he never sinned—not even once (see 2 Corinthians 5:21; 1 Peter 2:22; 1 John 3:5). He came to earth as a baby, he was tempted like we are tempted, but he never sinned. Jesus lived the perfect life we couldn't live, and he died for us in our place.

After his death, Jesus was buried by his followers. He was buried in a rich man's new tomb, and a huge and heavy round stone was rolled in front of the tomb. Roman soldiers guarded the tomb so that no one could steal Jesus's body. It seemed like Jesus's life on earth was over!

Three days after his crucifixion, something miraculous occurred. Jesus rose from the dead! An earthquake occurred, and an angel rolled the heavy stone away from the tomb's entrance. When some female disciples came to the tomb, they found it empty. The risen Jesus soon appeared to the women, his male disciples, and over 500 people at one time (see 1 Corinthians 15:2–6). Jesus was alive! He had conquered the grave! Jesus rose from the dead in a physical immortal body. He proved that his resurrected body was physical by eating broiled fish with his disciples and by letting them touch him (see Luke 24:36–43; John 20:26–29).

Jesus's resurrection proves that what Jesus says in the Gospels is true. Jesus says that he is the divine Son of God and the only way to God (see John 14:6). Jesus says that if we believe in him, we have peace and joy on this earth and eternal life in heaven (see John 5:24; 15:10–11; 16:33). Jesus says that we have a new purpose in life—living for God and for him—if we choose to believe in him (see John 15:5–8, 16; 2 Corinthians 5:15). Jesus also says that he is preparing a place in heaven for all of us who believe in him (see John 14:1–2).

We have discovered that Jesus is the only way to God. Other religious leaders were very successful on earth, but they didn't rise from the dead, and they aren't able to offer us eternal life. They can't give us what they don't have. *Jesus is alive, and he is ready, willing, and able to offer us peace with God, joy, a new purpose in life, the forgiveness of our sins, and eternal life in heaven.* Because of Jesus, we don't need to fear death. He wants to give us eternal life in heaven.

Do you know what heaven and hell are like? The Bible describes heaven as being a beautiful and perfect place. There is no suffering, pain, sickness, disease, or disappointment in heaven. Everyone is happy in heaven all of the time, enjoying God's presence and serving Him (see Revelation 21:1–22:5). Everyone in heaven gets the opportunity to talk with Jesus, his disciples,

> **Jesus died for our sins in our place. He is alive, and he is ready, willing, and able to offer us peace with God, joy, a new purpose in life, the forgiveness of our sins, and eternal life in heaven.**

and all of the other people there. People in heaven learn a lot about God, bask in the radiance of God's glory, participate in a variety of fun activities, and walk on streets of gold. Every day in heaven, everyone feels like they have won a championship in sports or a house as a grand prize in a raffle. Being in heaven is an exhilarating experience that lasts forever! Doesn't heaven sound wonderful?

While heaven is much better than earth, hell is much worse than earth. Jesus says that hell is a horrible place of suffering in which the people there are always sad and angry (see Matthew 13:40–42, 49–50). Jesus says hell is a place of eternal punishment and spiritual suffering in which people are forever banished from God's presence (see Matthew 25:41, 46; Luke 16:19–31). The authors of the Bible also depict hell as a place of punishment and banishment from God's loving presence (see 2 Thessalonians 1:9; Revelation 21:8). Hell is like a prison that holds people in solitary confinement as they suffer from permanent depression. Being in hell is an excruciating experience that many people choose. Everyone who rejects God's love chooses to go to hell; God doesn't send anyone there.

God wants us to go to heaven, not to hell. He gives us the choice of where we will spend eternity. The gospel tells us that we can choose to spend eternity with God in heaven or away from God in hell. We can choose to experience God's loving presence forever by believing in Jesus, who loves us so much that he suffered an infinite amount when he died for us. Isn't it awesome to have that choice?

Jesus is the Life Changer! He meets all of our most important emotional and spiritual needs, and he gives us the abundant life on earth and the eternal life in heaven that we earnestly desire. Jesus saves us from God's punishment, and he gives us God's peace and purpose for our lives. He enables us to love our family, friends, and other people much better than we can love them without his help. Jesus gives us the opportunity to have vertical access—access to God's love, peace, purpose, and forgiveness. Jesus changes our lives at the moment that we choose to trust in him as the way to God.

At the moment that we trust in Jesus, we are able to have peace with God, joy in our hearts, a new purpose of living for Him, and forgiveness of our sins. We become a child of God, a friend of God, and an ambassador of God (see John 1:12; 15:13–15; 2 Corinthians 5:20). We are also able to really understand the Bible and apply it to our lives. The Bible is God's love letter to us, and Jesus's death on the cross is the ultimate demonstration of God's love for us. God loves us so much, and He wants us to trust in Jesus!

How Can We Trust in Jesus?

We can all experience the amazing blessings and benefits of trusting in Jesus as our way to God. I trusted in Jesus alone as my way to heaven about 20 years ago. Trusting in Jesus involves truly believing in him by having genuine faith in him.

Let me give you an illustration. Trusting in Jesus is like trusting in a chair when you sit on it. If you trust a chair to hold you up, you don't sit partly in the chair and put some of your weight on your own legs. If you trust the chair, you sit on the chair comfortably, relaxing on it and having full confidence in it. Just as you don't have to help the chair to support you, you don't have to help Jesus give you a new life on this earth or eternal life in heaven. You need to trust in Jesus alone to meet your biggest needs.

If we are trying to earn our way to heaven by doing good works, we aren't trusting in Jesus alone as our way to heaven. Jesus's perfect life, death, and resurrection are sufficient to save us from God's punishment. As a result, Jesus doesn't need our good works or our help for us to go to heaven. All he needs is for us to stop trusting in our good works as our way to heaven and to put all of our trust in him

> **Trusting in Jesus alone as the only way to God is the best decision you can make!**

as our only way to heaven. Eternal life in heaven is a gift that we can't earn or deserve. It's like a Christmas gift or a birthday gift that kids receive from their parents even if they don't behave well (see Ephesians 2:8–9). Eternal life in heaven is a gift, not a prize for good behavior. In order to trust in Jesus and receive the gift of eternal life, we must tell God that we are trusting in Jesus alone and no longer in our good works as our way to heaven.

Because God is holy, He can't accept us into heaven on the basis of our good works. Trying to earn our way to heaven by doing good works is like trying to bribe God with our good works. Because God is holy, He can't accept bribes. His standard is perfection, not doing more good deeds than bad deeds. We must be humble and honest with God and admit that we can't earn our way to heaven.

In order to trust in Jesus and receive the benefits of trusting in him, we need to talk with God and tell Him that we are deciding to trust in Jesus alone as the way to God. We must tell God that we are no longer trusting in our goods works as the way to eternal life in heaven with Him. It's not easy to live for Jesus, but it's definitely worth it! *Trusting in Jesus will enable you to become the person that God wants you to be and to live the life that God wants you to live. Deciding to trust in Jesus and to live for him is the best decision that you could ever make! Jesus is the Life Changer, and He will transform your life!*

Below is a suggested prayer for you to tell God that you have decided to trust in Jesus and live for him. You don't need to say the prayer exactly as it's written, but the prayer contains the main things you need to tell God if you want to live for Him on earth and spend eternity with Him in heaven. You may have different sins to confess to God than the sins that the prayer includes. The prayer emphasizes that you: 1) see your need for Jesus; 2) want to trust in Jesus alone for eternal life; and 3) are deciding to trust in Jesus alone for eternal life.

The Choice Is Yours!

God loves you, and He is working in your life. He wants you to find your peace, joy, and purpose by trusting in Jesus. He also wants to forgive you and to give you lasting hope and eternal life. He wants you to experience His amazing love. You can choose to trust in Jesus right now if you want to do so! You can begin the exciting new life that God wants to give you!

You can accept God's love for you by choosing to trust in Jesus!

The choice is yours! Here is a suggested prayer if you want to tell God that you are trusting in Jesus:

> Dear God, please forgive me. I'm not perfect. Only You are perfect. I have sinned against You. I haven't loved You as much as I should love You, and I haven't loved other people as much as I should love them. I have disobeyed You. I have lied, lusted, and put other people down. I didn't always obey my parents when I was a child. I struggle with pride, selfishness, and worry. I deserve Your punishment. I deserve to spend eternity away from Your loving presence, but I don't want to be away from You. I believe that Jesus

is Your Son and that He never sinned. I believe that Jesus died for me in my place on the cross, as my substitute, taking the punishment for my sins. I believe that Jesus rose again and wants to give me eternal life, forgiveness, joy, peace, hope, and a new purpose in life. I have decided to trust in Jesus alone as my way to heaven. I'm not trusting anymore in my good works as my way to heaven. I receive the gift of eternal life by trusting in Jesus. Thank You for forgiving me and for giving me eternal life, hope, joy, peace, and a new purpose. Help me to live for You instead of for myself. Free me from my sinful choices, and help me to break my bad habits. Help me to love You and other people by putting You first in my life. Help me to read the Bible and to pray every day so that I can live for You. Help me to spend time with others who believe in Jesus so that I can grow in my faith. In Jesus's name, amen.

If you trusted in Jesus alone for eternal life, congratulations! You are a new person in Jesus! You are God's child, friend, and ambassador. God will enable you to live for Him from now on. If you aren't yet sure about trusting in Jesus, just ask God to help you see the truth about Jesus. God will show you the truth about Jesus, and the truth will set you free!

Help Us Share the Truth!

If my book was a blessing to you, please bless others by telling them about it, or make a post about it on your social media profile. If you bought this book on Amazon or on another website where you can rate it, please leave a positive rating. Thank you!

Notes

Introduction

[1] Harper Lee, *To Kill a Mockingbird* (New York: Warner Books, Inc., 1960), 34.
[2] Ibid.

Chapter 1: My Story and Nicole's Story

[1] Caroline Cole, "Meet Hope Warrior Nicole Inman," *Hurricane Lake Living*, August 2019, 13.

Chapter 2: How Can We Find Joy, Peace, and Our Purpose?

[1] Rhonda Byrne, *The Greatest Secret* (San Francisco, CA: HarperOne, 2020), 11.
[2] Deepak Chopra, *The Book of Secrets: Unlocking the Hidden Dimensions of Your Life* (New York: Harmony Books, 2004), 1.
[3] Harold Kushner, *When All You've Ever Wanted Isn't Enough: The Search for a Life that Matters* (New York: Simon and Schuster, 2002), 20–21.
[4] Jonathan Haidt, *The Happiness Hypothesis: Finding Modern Truth in Ancient Wisdom* (New York: Basic Books, 2006), 239.
[5] Kushner, *When All You've Ever Wanted Isn't Enough*, 18.
[6] Matthew Kelly, *Resisting Happiness* (North Palm Beach, FL: Beacon Publishing, 2016), 11–12.
[7] Ibid., 13.
[8] Gary Thomas, *Sacred Marriage: What if God Designed Marriage to Make Us Holy More Than to Make Us Happy?* (Grand Rapids, MI: Zondervan, 2015), 26.
[9] Jay Shetty, *Think Like a Monk: Train Your Mind for Peace and Purpose Every Day* (New York: Simon & Schuster, 2020), xvi.
[10] Louie Giglio, *The Comeback: It's Not Too Late and You're Never Too Far* (Nashville, TN: Thomas Nelson, 2015), 6–7.
[11] Philip E. Johnson, *Defeating Darwinism by Opening Minds* (Downers Grove, IL: InterVarsity Press, 1997), 45.
[12] Jessica Toomer, "It's Time We Recognize The Prince of Egypt as the Greatest Animated Movie of All Time," SyFy Wire, March 9, 2019, accessed August 14, 2021, https://www.syfy.com/syfywire/its-time-we-recognize-the-prince-of-egypt-as-the-greatest-animated-movie-of-all-time.

Chapter 3: Aren't Your Beliefs True for You But Not for Me?

1 Ashlin, "Mini Adventures," TikTok post, June 29, 2021, accessed September 24, 2021, https://www.tiktok.com/@miniadvantures?

2 Adriana Diaz, "TikToker's Alleged Travel Hack for Sneaking an Extra Bag on Flight Goes Viral," *New York Post*, July 9, 2021, accessed July 10, 2021, https://nypost.com/2021/07/09/tiktokers-travel-hack-for-sneaking-extra-bag-on-flight/.

3 Barna Group, "The End of Absolutes: America's New Moral Code," Barna Group, May 25, 2016, accessed July 10, 2021, https://www.barna.com/research/the-end-of-absolutes-americas-new-moral-code/.

4 George Barna, "Survey Finds Americans See Many Sources of Truth—and Reject Moral Absolutes," The Cultural Research Center at Arizona Christian University, May 19, 2020, accessed July 10, 2021, https://www.arizonachristian.edu/wp-content/uploads/2020/05/AWVI-2020-Release-05-Perceptions-of-Truth.pdf.

5 Brendan Cole, "Serial Rapist Jailed for 1,088 Years After Four-Year Crime Spree," *Newsweek*, May 28, 2021, accessed May 28, 2021, https://www.newsweek.com/sello-abram-mapunya-south-africa-rape-1088-years-pretoria-1595712.

6 Majd Arbil, "Ten Commandments from the Bible and Koran," Islamicity, May 12, 2007, accessed November 4, 2021, https://www.islamicity.org/3096/ten-commandments-from-the-bible-and-quran/. Arbil quotes Quran 5:32, 38; 17:32; 24:7.

7 Subhamoy Das, "The 5 Principles and 10 Disciplines of Hinduism," Learn Religions, March 22, 2017, accessed November 4, 2021, https://www.learnreligions.com/principles-and-disciplines-of-hinduism-1770057.

8 Marcus Borg, ed., *Jesus and Buddha: The Parallel Sayings* (Berkley, CA: Seastone, 1999), 31, 49, 191. Borg quotes Khuddakaptha 2 and Sutta Nipata 242, 396.

9 Greg M. Epstein, *Good Without God: What a Billion Nonreligious People Do Believe* (New York: William Morrow, 2009), 119.

10 Kim Willsher, "Samuel Paty Murder: How a Teenager's Lie Sparked a Tragic Chain of Events," *The Guardian*, March 8, 2021, accessed March 10, 2021, https://www.theguardian.com/world/2021/mar/08/samuel-paty-how-a-teenagers-lie-sparked-a-tragic-chain-of-events.

11 Gallup Editors, "Marriage," Gallup, May 3–18, 2021, accessed July 11, 2021, https://news.gallup.com/poll/117328/marriage.aspx.

12 Norman L. Geisler, *Systematic Theology in One Volume* (Minneapolis, MN: Bethany House, 2011), 84.

Chapter 4: Did God Create Us, or Did We Create God?

1 Emma Goldberg, "The New Chief Chaplain at Harvard? An Atheist," *The New York Times*, August 26, 2021, accessed September 1, 2021, https://www.nytimes.com/2021/08/26/us/harvard-chaplain-greg-epstein.html.

2   Tré Goins-Philipps, "Harvard's New Lead Chaplain is Atheist," Faithwire, August 27, 2021, accessed September 1, 2021, https://www.faithwire.com/2021/08/27/harvards-new-lead-chaplain-is-atheist/.

3   Jon Wertheim, "Q & A with Rafael Nadal," *Sports Illustrated*, July 16, 2010, accessed October 24, 2021, https://www.si.com/more-sports/2010/07/16/nadal-interview.

4   James Buddell, "Rafael Nadal: The Humble Champion," ATP Tour, August 21, 2017, accessed October 30, 2021, https://www.atptour.com/en/news/nadal-no-1-emirates-atp-rankings-2017-tribute.

5   Amelia Meyer, "Iguazu Falls," Brazil.org.za, 2010, accessed August 7, 2021, https://www.brazil.org.za/iguazu-falls.html.

6   Ibid.

7   Jeffrey M. Jones, "Belief in God in U.S. Dips to 81%, a New Low," Gallup, June 17, 2022, accessed June 17, 2022, https://news.gallup.com/poll/393737/belief-god-dips-new-low.aspx.

8   Georgia Purdom, "De-Nyeing Science," *Answers Magazine*, July-September 2013, 44.

9   Ian Sample, "Massive Human Head in Chinese Well Forces Scientists to Rethink Evolution," *The Guardian*, June 25, 2021, accessed July 12, 2021, https://www.theguardian.com/science/2021/jun/25/massive-human-head-in-chinese-well-forces-scientists-to-rethink-evolution.

10 Ann Gibbons, "Stunning 'Dragon Man' Skull May be an Elusive Denisovan—or a New Species of Human," Science, June 25, 2021, accessed July 12, 2021, https://www.sciencemag.org/news/2021/06/stunning-dragon-man-skull-may-be-elusive-denisovan-or-new-species-human.

11 Maya Wei-Haas, "Mysterious Ancient Human Found on the 'Roof of the World,'" *National Geographic*, May 1, 2019, accessed August 18, 2021, https://www.nationalgeographic.com/science/article/mysterious-ancient-human-denisovan-found-roof-world.

12 Katie Hunt, "New Clue to Human Evolution's Biggest Mystery Emerges in Philippines," CNN, August 16, 2021, accessed August 17, 2021, https://www.cnn.com/2021/08/16/world/denisovan-dna-philippines-scn/index.html.

13 Stephen J. Gould, *The Richness of Life: The Essential Stephen J. Gould*, ed. Steven Rose (New York: W.W. Norton & Company, 2007), 263.

14 Vincent Bugliosi, *Divinity of Doubt: God and Atheism on Trial* (New York: Vanguard Press, 2012), 73. He also comments that he is not comfortable with evolution because of "the paucity of supporting evidence that evolutionists bring to the table from the vast museum of the earth's surface" (p. 72). He points out that the theory of evolution is "a theory so lacking in empirical evidence" (p. 74).

15 Karla K. Johnson, "COVID-19's Global Death Toll Tops 5 Million in Under 2 Years," AP News, November 1, 2021, accessed November 4, 2021. The global

COVID-19 pandemic has contributed to and caused the hospitalizations and deaths of millions of people throughout the USA and the world.

16 Ryan Severino, "COVID-19 Job Losses Continue to Mount," JLL, May 12, 2020, accessed July 20, 2021, https://www.us.jll.com/en/trends-and-insights/research/COVID-19-related-job-losses-continue-to-mount.

17 Chris Stein, "Pandemic Caused Worst Year for U.S. Economy Since 1946," International Business Times, January 28, 2021, accessed July 20, 2021, https://www.ibtimes.com/pandemic-caused-worst-year-us-economy-1946-3132677.

18 Mark E. Czeisler, Rashon I. Lane, Emiko Petrosky, et. al, "Mental Health, Substance Use, and Suicidal Ideation During the COVID-19 Pandemic—United States, June 24–30, 2020," Center for Disease Control and Prevention, August 14, 2020, accessed July 20, 2021, https://www.cdc.gov/mmwr/volumes/69/wr/mm6932a1.htm?s_cid=mm6932a1_w.

19 Julie Steenhuysen and Daniel Trotta, "U.S. Drug Overdose Deaths Rise 30% to Record During Pandemic," Reuters, July 14, 2021, accessed July 20, 2021, https://www.reuters.com/world/us/us-drug-overdose-deaths-rise-30-record-during-pandemic-2021-07-14/.

20 The Old Testament is also called the Jewish Bible, the Hebrew Bible, the Hebrew Scriptures, and the Tanakh.

21 Tommy Mitchell, *Why Does God's Creation Include Death and Suffering?* (Hebron, KY: Answers in Genesis, 2006), 8.

22 Ken Ham, *The Purpose and Meaning of Life from Creation to the Cross* (Hebron, KY: Answers in Genesis, 2007), 7.

23 R. K. Rowling, *Very Good Lives: The Fringe Benefits of Failure and the Importance of Imagination* (New York: Little, Brown and Company, 2008), 34.

24 There are hundreds of millions of Protestant Christians in the world today. Luther was an amazing man, but he was not perfect. He became anti-Semitic at some point during his life. Like many other Christians today, I strongly oppose anti-Semitism.

25 In chapter 7, we will discuss arguments for and against Jesus's resurrection. In my opinion, the arguments for his resurrection are much more compelling than the arguments against it.

26 Gary R. Habermas and Michael R. Licona, *The Case for the Resurrection of Jesus* (Grand Rapids, MI: Kregel Publications, 2004), 73–74.

27 Alexander Kacala, "Pregnant Influencer Emily Mitchell's Cause of Death Revealed by Family," NBC Today, January 14, 2021, accessed July 20, 2021, https://www.today.com/parents/pregnant-influencer-emily-mitchell-s-cause-death-revealed-t205864.

28 Emily Mitchell, "The Hidden Way," Instagram, accessed October 18, 2021, https://www.instagram.com/the.hidden.way/.

29 Allyson Speake, "Support the Mitchell Family," Go Fund Me, December 23, 2020, accessed July 20, 2021. https://www.gofundme.com/f/6n4vy-support-the-mitchell-family.

30 Ibid.

31 Jessica Schladebeck, "Wisconsin Nurse Donates Part of Her Liver So Third-Grader Can Receive Life-Saving Transplant," *New York Daily News*, September 14, 2019, accessed July 21, 2021, https://www.nydailynews.com/news/national/ny-wisconsin-nurse-donates-liver-third-grader-life-saving-20190914-i3bgbo7on5gn7e2do35egnm264-story.html.

32 Ibid.

33 Jeff Alexander, "Wrightstown Boy Receives 'Miracle' Gift," WBAY, September 2, 2019, accessed July 21, 2021, https://www.wbay.com/content/news/Wrightstown-Boy-Receives-Miracle-Gift-559180231.html.

34 Allen Kim, "A Boy's Condition Quickly Worsened, As His Family Desperately Sought a Donor. Then a Transplant Nurse Stepped Forward," CNN, September 14, 2019, accessed July 21, 2021, https://www.cnn.com/2019/09/14/us/brayden-nurse-cami-transplant-trnd/index.html.

35 Frank Turek, *Stealing from God: Why Atheists Need God to Make Their Case* (Colorado Springs, CO: NavPress, 2014), 137.

36 Joe Binder, "Two Illegal Alien MS-13 Gang Members Get 40 Years in Prison for Murdering Girl in Satanic Ritual," Breitbart, May 29, 2021, accessed August 30, 2021, https://www.breitbart.com/politics/2021/05/29/two-illegal-alien-ms-13-gang-members-get-40-years-in-prison-for-murdering-girl-in-satanic-ritual/.

37 Associated Press, "Two Gang Members in U.S. Illegally are Accused of Kidnapping 3 Girls, Killing 1 in a Satanic Ritual," *Los Angeles Times*, March 3, 2017, accessed August 30, 2021, https://www.latimes.com/nation/nationnow/la-na-texas-kidnap-killing-20170303-story.html.

38 Avi Selk, "MS-13 Gang Members Accused of Killing Teen Claimed Satan 'Wanted a Soul,' Police Say," *The Washington Post*, March 5, 2017, accessed August 30, 2021, https://www.washingtonpost.com/news/true-crime/wp/2017/03/05/ms-13-gang-members-accused-of-killing-teen-claimed-satan-wanted-a-soul-police-say/.

39 Eileen AJ Connelly, "Prison Guards 'Didn't Notice' that Satanist Tortured, Beheaded Cellmate," *New York Post*, May 29, 2021, accessed August 30, 2021, https://nypost.com/2021/05/29/prison-guards-didnt-notice-satanist-tortured-beheaded-cellmate/.

40 I didn't watch the miniseries for two reasons: (1) I don't have Netflix at home; and (2) I heard that the miniseries featured graphic imagery. I would recommend that you read about Ramirez instead of watching the miniseries.

41 Maura Hohman, "Netflix's 'Night Stalker' Shocks Viewers with Graphic Scenes," Today, January 17, 2021, accessed August 31, 2021, https://www.today.com/popculture/netflix-s-night-stalker-shocks-viewers-graphic-scenes-t205846.

42 Sam Baker, "How Rotting Teeth and an AC/DC Hat Finally Led Los Angeles Police to Night Stalker Richard Ramirez who Killed 13 People in 1985 and is the Focus of Netflix's New Gruesome Documentary Night Stalker,"

Daily Mail, January 14, 2021, accessed August 31, 2021, https://www.dailymail.co.uk/news/article-9147521/How-rotting-teeth-AC-DC-hat-finally-led-Los-Angeles-police-Night-Stalker-Richard-Ramirez.html.

43 David A. Rausch, *A Legacy of Hatred: Why Christians Must Not Forget the Holocaust* (Chicago: Moody Press, 1984), 176.

44 History.com editors, "The Holocaust," History, January 25, 2021, accessed September 3, 2021, https://www.history.com/topics/world-war-ii/the-holocaust.

45 Richard Weikart, *Hitler's Religion: The Twisted Beliefs that Drove the Third Reich* (Washington, DC: Regnery History, 2016), 277.

46 William L. Shirer, *The Rise and Fall of the Third Reich: A History of Nazi Germany*. Fiftieth Anniversary Edition (New York: Simon and Schuster, 2011), 240.

47 Ray Comfort, *Hitler, God, and the Bible* (Washington, DC: WND Books, 2012), 129–130.

48 Weikart, 278, 280.

49 Matthew White, *Atrocities: The 100 Deadliest Episodes in Human History* (New York: W. W. Norton & Company, 2013), 455–456. For similar statistics, see Ian Johnson, "Who Killed More: Hitler, Stalin, or Mao?" *The New York Review*, February 5, 2018, accessed September 3, 2021, https://www.nybooks.com/daily/2018/02/05/who-killed-more-hitler-stalin-or-mao/.

50 Stephen Kotkin, "Communism's Bloody Century," *The Wall Street Journal*, November 3, 2017, accessed September 3, 2021, https://www.wsj.com/articles/the-communist-century-1509726265.

51 R. J. Rummel, "The Killing Machine That is Marxism," The Schwartz Report, December 15, 2004, accessed September 3, 2021, https://www.schwarzreport.org/resources/essays/the-killing-machine-that-is-marxism.

52 Fyodor Dostoevsky, *The Karamazov Brothers*, trans. Ignat Avsey (New York: Oxford University Press, 2008), 330.

53 Richard Lewontin, "Billions and Billions of Demons," *The New York Review of Books*, January 9, 1997, 31. See also Richard Lewontin, "Billions and Billions of Demons," *The New York Review*, January 9, 1997, accessed September 1, 2021, https://www.nybooks.com/articles/1997/01/09/billions-and-billions-of-demons/.

54 Epstein, 119, 137. Epstein makes it clear that humanists believe that murder, stealing, lying, and committing adultery are wrong.

55 Katherine Dahlsgaard, Christopher Peterson, and Martin E. P. Seligman, "Shared Virtue: The Convergence of Valued Human Strengths Across Cultures and History," *Review of General Psychology 9*, no. 3 (2005): 203–213, accessed October 31, 2021, https://doi.org/10.1037/1089-2680.9.3.203.

56 Alex Rosenberg, *The Atheist's Guide to Reality: Enjoying Life without Illusions* (New York: W.W. Norton & Company, 2011), 102. He also writes, "There is

good reason to think that there is a moral core that is almost universal to almost all humans" (p. 108).

57 United Nations General Assembly, "Universal Declaration of Human Rights," United Nations, December 10, 1948, accessed September 4, 2021, https://www.un.org/en/about-us/universal-declaration-of-human-rights.

58 This version of the moral argument has been adapted from William Lane Craig, *Reasonable Faith: Christian Truth and Apologetics* 3rd ed. (Wheaton, IL: Crossway, 2008), 172.

59 To read what the Bible says about us being made in God's image, see Genesis 1:26–27, 5:1, 9:6; James 3:9.

60 Richard Dawkins, *The God Delusion* (New York: Mariner Books, 2008), 266.

61 Martin A. Nowak and Sarah Coakley, eds., *Evolution, Games, and God: The Principle of Cooperation* (Cambridge, MA: Harvard University Press, 2013).

62 Martin A. Nowak and Roger Highfield, *Super-Cooperators: Altruism, Evolution, and Why We Need Each Other to Succeed* (New York: Free Press, 2012), 10, 14.

63 Rosenberg, 330.

64 Ibid, 95.

65 Rosenberg writes, "What is the purpose of the universe? There is none. What is the meaning of life? Ditto. Why am I here? Just dumb luck" (p. 2). Rosenberg understands that if God doesn't exist, life has no purpose or meaning. But life does have purpose and meaning because God does exist.

66 If God doesn't exist, then suicide isn't wrong; it's morally acceptable. However, God exists, and we are made in His image, and thus suicide is wrong. We should all be grateful that God exists and that He loves us.

67 Craig, *Reasonable Faith*, 111. He and other writers call this version of the cosmological argument the kalam cosmological argument. Kalam is an Arabic term meaning "word/speech."

68 Fred Heeren, *Show Me God: What the Message from Space Is Telling Us About God* (Wheeling, IL: Searchlight Publications, 1995), 119–120.

69 Jim Lucas, "What is the Second Law of Thermodynamics?" Live Science, May 22, 2015, accessed September 4, 2021, https://www.livescience.com/50941-second-law-thermodynamics.html.

70 Robert Jastrow, *God and the Astronomers.* 2nd ed. (New York: W.W. Norton & Company, Inc., 1992), 9.

71 Ibid., 14.

72 Robert Jastrow, "A Scientist Caught Between Two Faiths," interview by Bill Durban, *Christianity Today*, August 6, 1982, 18. This interview can also be found at: https://www.christianitytoday.com/ct/1982/august-6/scientist-caught-between-two-faiths.html.

73 David J. Eicher, "How Many Galaxies are There? Astronomers are Revealing the Enormity of the Universe," *Discover*, May 19, 2020, accessed September 4, 2021, https://www.discovermagazine.com/the-sciences/how-many-galaxies-are-there-astronomers-are-revealing-the-enormity-of-the.

74 Atheist Stephen Hawking incorrectly argued that "the universe can and will create itself from nothing." See Stephen Hawking and Leonard Mlodinow, *The Grand Design* (New York: Bantam Books, 2010), 180.

75 Heeren, 69.

76 Bertrand Russell, an agnostic, asked, "Who made God?" After asking that question, he incorrectly argued, "If everything must have a cause, then God must have a cause." See Bertrand Russell, *Why I Am Not a Christian* (New York: Simon & Schuster, Inc., 1957), 6.

77 The teleological argument gets its name from the Greek word *telos*, which means the "end, purpose, aim, or goal" of something.

78 Craig, *Reasonable Faith*, 161.

79 Hugh Ross, "A Fine-Tuned Universe," World, August 24, 2019, accessed September 5, 2021, https://wng.org/roundups/a-fine-tuned-universe-1617224984.

80 ———, *The Creator and the Cosmos: How the Latest Scientific Discoveries Reveal God.* 4th ed. (Covina, CA: Ready to Believe Press, 2018), "Appendix A: Evidence for the Fine-Tuning of the Universe," 233–241.

81 Ibid., "Appendix B: Evidence for the Fine-Tuning of the Milky Way Galaxy, Solar System, and Earth," 243–266.

82 Josh McDowell and Sean McDowell, *Evidence that Demands a Verdict: Life-Changing Truth for a Skeptical World* (Nashville, TN: Thomas Nelson, 2017), xlvii.

83 Isaac Newton believed in God, but he did not believe in Jesus's divinity or in the Christian doctrine of the Trinity. For more information on Newton's beliefs about God, please see Danny R. Faulkner, "The Misplaced Faith of Isaac Newton," Answers in Genesis, February 25, 2018, accessed September 5, 2021, https://answersingenesis.org/creation-scientists/misplaced-faith-isaac-newton/.

84 René Descartes clearly believed in God and considered himself a Roman Catholic. However, his view of God may not have been orthodox. For more information on Descartes' beliefs about God, please see: Troy Lacey, "René Descartes on Science, Philosophy, and God," Answers in Genesis, March 31, 2020, accessed September 6, 2021, https://answersingenesis.org/presuppositions/presuppositions/rene-descartes-on-science-philosophy-god/.

85 Francis S. Collins, *The Language of God: A Scientist Presents Evidence for Belief* (New York: Free Press, 2006), 11–31.

86 Ibid., 225. Collins makes a case for God-directed evolution in his book. I definitely disagree with his belief in theistic evolution (evolutionary creation). However, his conversion to Christianity seems genuine.

87 Chris Wilson, "Early COVID-19 Vaccine Results Look 'Really Encouraging,' Says NIH Boss Dr. Francis Collins," *Time*, July 16, 2020, accessed September 6, 2021, https://time.com/5867272/francis-collins-covid-vaccine/.

88 Collins, 231.

89 Edward Feser, *The Last Superstition: A Refutation of the New Atheism* (South Bend, IN: St. Augustine's Press, 2008), 10.

90 Rick Warren, *The Purpose Driven Life: What on Earth Am I Here For?* (Grand Rapids, MI: Zondervan, 2012), 22.

Chapter 5: How Can We Know if Our Beliefs Are True?

1 Minyvonne Burke, "Woman Who Drove into 2 Children Because of Their Race Gets 25 Years in Federal Prison," NBC News, August 20, 2021, accessed September 9, 2021, https://www.nbcnews.com/news/us-news/woman-who-drove-2-children-because-their-race-gets-25-n1277303.

2 Ibid.

3 Postmodernism began to be the most prevalent worldview in American culture in about 1990.

4 The consistency test is based on the "test of consistency" found in Paul D. Feinberg, "Cumulative Case Apologetics," in *Five Views on Apologetics*, ed. Steven B. Cowan (Grand Rapids, MI: Zondervan, 2000), 153–154.

5 The correspondence test is based on the "test of correspondence" found in Feinberg, 154.

6 The livability test is based on the "test of livability" found in Feinberg, 155.

7 The cover-up test is based on what scholars commonly call the "criterion of embarrassment," which has been used for the last thirty years to evaluate the sayings and acts of Jesus reported in the New Testament. For a definition and description of the criterion of embarrassment, please see John P. Meier, *A Marginal Jew: Rethinking the Historical Jesus, Vol. I: The Roots of the Problem and the Person* (New York: Doubleday: 1991), 168–171. For more information about the original cover-up test, see Craig Blomberg's interview with Lee Strobel in Lee Strobel, *The Case for Christ: A Journalist's Personal Investigation of the Evidence for Jesus* (Grand Rapids, MI: Zondervan, 1998), 49–50.

8 The simplicity test is similar to the "test of simplicity" found in Feinberg, 155.

9 J. Warner Wallace, *Cold-Case Christianity: A Homicide Detective Investigates the Claims of the Gospels* (Colorado Springs, CO: David C Cook, 2013), 41.

10 The comprehensiveness test is based on the "test of comprehensiveness" found in Feinberg, 154–155.

11 The corroboration test is based partly on the test of the same name found in Strobel, 50–51.

12 Charles Darwin, *The Origin of Species: 150th Anniversary Edition* (New York: Signet Classics, 2003), 314–315. See also his comments on pages 160–161.

13 Ibid., 172.

14 Charles Darwin, *The Descent of Man, and Selection in Relation to Sex.* 2nd edition (New York: D. Appleton and Company, 1889), 93.

15 Richard Dawkins, *The Blind Watchmaker: Why the Evidence of Evolution Reveals a Universe Without Design* (New York: W.W. Norton and Company, 1996), 4.

16 Darwin, *The Descent of Man*, 93–95, 156.

17 Ibid., 557, 563–564, 605.

18 Some evolutionists have contended that the theory of evolution isn't inherently racist. However, scientists believe based on fossil evidence that humanity had its origins in Africa. See: Smithsonian National Museum of Natural History, "Introduction to Human Evolution," Smithsonian National Museum of Natural History, October 27, 2020, accessed September 10, 2021, https://humanorigins.si.edu/education/introduction-human-evolution. If humans originated in Africa and the theory of evolution is true, Black people are more like apes than White people are like apes. The racist implications of evolution are appalling and repugnant. No one should believe the lie that we evolved from apelike ancestors! We were created by God!

19 Nicholas Bogel-Burroughs and Will Wright, "Little Has Been Said About the $20 Bill that Brought Officers to the Scene," *The New York Times*, April 19, 2021, accessed September 10, 2021, https://www.nytimes.com/2021/04/19/us/george-floyd-bill-counterfeit.html.

20 Jeff Truesdell, "George Floyd Told Officers 'I Can't Breathe' More than 20 Times Before He Died, Transcript Reveals," *People*, June 9, 2020, accessed September 10, 2021, https://people.com/crime/george-floyd-transcript-i-cant-breathe-20-times/.

21 Amy Forliti, Steve Karnowski, and Tami Webber, "Expert: Lack of Oxygen Killed George Floyd, Not Drugs," *AP News*, April 8, 2021, accessed September 10, 2021, https://apnews.com/article/derek-chauvin-trial-expert-lack-of-oxygen-killed-floyd-b1092d8b70ea934776161355fdf171a4.

22 Janelle Griffith, "Derek Chauvin Sentenced to 22.5 Years for the Murder of George Floyd," NBC News, June 25, 2021, accessed September 11, 2021, https://www.nbcnews.com/news/us-news/derek-chauvin-be-sentenced-murder-death-george-floyd-n1272332.

23 Ariel Zibler, "Revealed: Widespread Vandalism and Looting During BLM Protests Will Cost the Insurance $2 BILLION after Violence Erupted in 140 Cities in the Wake of George Floyd's Death," *Daily Mail*, September 16, 2020, accessed September 10, 2021, https://www.dailymail.co.uk/news/article-8740609/Rioting-140-cities-George-Floyds-death-cost-insurance-industry-2-BILLION.html.

24 Ibid.

25 Michael Sainato, "'They Set Us Up': US Police Arrested Over 10,000 Protesters, Many of Them Nonviolent," *The Guardian*, June 8, 2020, accessed September 10, 2021, https://www.theguardian.com/us-news/2020/jun/08/george-floyd-killing-police-arrest-non-violent-protesters.

26 Craig J. Hazen, "Christianity in a World of Religions," in *Passionate Conviction: Contemporary Discourses on Christian Apologetics,* eds. Paul Copan and William Lane Craig (Nashville, TN: B & H Academic, 2007), 145.

Chapter 6: Can We Trust the Story of Jesus in the Gospels?

1   Josh McDowell and Sean McDowell, *Evidence for the Resurrection: What It Means for Your Relationship with God* (Ventura, CA: Regal, 2009), 83.
2   The majority of scholars recognize that this passage is authentic with the exception of three brief sections that were added by Christian editors, probably in the third or fourth centuries. See Meier, 61–64.
3   Gary Habermas, "Why I Believe the New Testament Is Historically Reliable," in *Why I am a Christian: Leading Thinkers Explain Why They Believe.* 2nd ed., eds. Norman L. Geisler and Paul K. Hoffman (Grand Rapids, MI: Baker Books, 2006), 164.
4   Andreas J. Köstenberger, *The Jesus of the Gospels: An Introduction* (Grand Rapids, MI: Kregel Academic, 2020), 248.
5   Andreas J. Köstenberger and Alexander E. Stewart, *The First Days of Jesus: The Story of the Incarnation* (Wheaton, IL: Crossway, 2015), 19.
6   Colin J. Hemer, *The Book of Acts in the Setting of Hellenistic History*, ed. Conrad H. Gempf (Winona Lake, IN: Eisenbrauns, 1990), 108–158. For a full list of the eighty-four facts, see Norman L. Geisler and Frank Turek, *I Don't Have Enough Faith to Be an Atheist* (Wheaton, IL: Crossway Books, 2004), 256–259.
7   A. N. Sherwin-White, *Roman Society and Roman Law in the New Testament* (Oxford: Oxford University Press, 1963), 189.
8   Sir William Mitchell Ramsay, *The Bearing of Recent Discovery on the Trustworthiness of the New Testament* (New York: Hodder and Stoughton, 1915), 81.
9   Ibid, 222.
10 Norman L. Geisler, *Baker Encyclopedia of Christian Apologetics* (Grand Rapids, MI: Baker Books, 1999), 430. Geisler also adequately answers the other concerns that some scholars have about the historical accuracy of the census in Luke 2.
11 Craig S. Keener, "Acts: History or Fiction?" in *Jesus, Skepticism and the Problem of History: Criteria and Context in the Study of Christian Origins*, eds. Darrell L. Bock and J. Ed Komoszewski (Grand Rapids, MI: Zondervan Academic, 2019), 338.
12 Geisler and Turek, 262.
13 Evidence of Luke's being Paul's travel companion is found in the so-called "we passages" of Acts in which Luke describes Paul's journeys (see Acts 16:10–17; 20:5–15; 21:1–18; 27:1–28:16). Paul knew Jesus's disciples Peter and John, and he also knew Jesus's brother James (Galatians 1:18–19; 2:1–9).
14 Keener, 324.
15 Papias of Hierapolis (c. AD 60–130) is quoted by Eusebius in *Church History*, 3.39.15 as saying that Mark was Peter's interpreter (translator). Irenaeus of Lyons (c. AD 130–c. 202) is also cited in Eusebius in *Church History*, 5.8.3 as saying the same thing. Finally, Clement of Alexandria (c. AD 150–c. 215) is

quoted by Eusebius in *Church History*, 2.15.1–2 as saying that Mark wrote his Gospel as Peter's disciple. Eusebius wrote his *Church History* about AD 324. For more about this and about Mark's relationship to Peter, see Brant Pitre, *The Case for Jesus: The Biblical and Historical Evidence for Christ* (New York: Image, 2016), 43–44.

[16] See Acts 12:1–19, especially verse 12. Early Christians sometimes gathered at the house of Mark's mother, whose name was Mary.

[17] Mark 2:14; Luke 5:27.

[18] Irenaeus, *Against Heresies* 3.1.1. He wrote this work about the year AD 180.

[19] Tertullian, *Against Marcion* 4.2. He wrote his work about the year AD 210.

[20] John's brother James was closely associated with Peter and John in the four Gospels. However, James was martyred in the year AD 42 (Acts 12:2), which was many years before the Gospel of John was written.

[21] For example, see James R. Rochford, "Who Wrote the Four Gospels?" Evidence Unseen, accessed September 17, 2021, https://www.evidenceunseen.com/theology/scripture/historicity-of-the-nt/who-wrote-the-four-gospels/.

[22] Louis Markos, *Atheism on Trial: Refuting the Modern Arguments Against God* (Eugene, OR: Harvest House Publishers, 2018), 83.

[23] Matthew, Mark, and Luke are called the "Synoptic Gospels" from a Latin word that means "seen together." These three Gospels tell many of the same stories, often using the same words and frequently following the same order.

[24] Jesus predicts the temple's destruction in Matthew 24:1–2, Mark 13:1–2, and Luke 21:5–6.

[25] David A. Fiensy, *The College Press NIV Commentary: New Testament Introduction* (Joplin, MO: College Press Publishing Company, 1997), 41–42.

[26] Craig A. Evans, *Fabricating Jesus: How Modern Scholars Distort the Gospels* (Downers Grove, IL: IVP Books, 2006), 126.

[27] Craig Keener, *The Gospel of John: A Commentary* (Grand Rapids, MI: Baker Academic, 2003), 58.

[28] Richard Bauckham, *Jesus and the Eyewitnesses: The Gospels as Eyewitness Testimony*. 2nd ed. (William B. Eerdmans Publishing Company, 2017), 346.

[29] Robert McIver, "Collective Memory and the Reliability of the Gospel Traditions," in *Jesus, Skepticism and the Problem of History: Criteria and Context in the Study of Christian Origins*, eds. Darrell L. Bock and J. Ed Komoszewski (Grand Rapids, MI: Zondervan Academic, 2019), 138–139. There were also at least one thousand to four thousand eyewitnesses still alive when John wrote his Gospel (p. 138).

[30] Paul Rhodes Eddy, "The Historicity of the Early Oral Tradition: Reflections on the 'Reliability Wars,'" in *Jesus, Skepticism and the Problem of History: Criteria and Context in the Study of Christian Origins*, eds. Darrell L. Bock and J. Ed Komoszewski (Grand Rapids, MI: Zondervan Academic, 2019), 163.

[31] Louis Fischer, *Gandhi: His Life and Message for the World* (New York: Signet Classics, 2010).

[32] Pitre, 77.

[33] Michael Licona, *Why are There Differences in the Gospels? What We Can Learn from Ancient Biography* (New York: Oxford University Press, 2017), 3–4.

[34] Thucydides, *History of the Peloponnesian War* 1.22. Thucydides (c. 460–c. 400 BC) was a Greek historian.

[35] Josephus, The *Life of Flavius Josephus*, 336–339.

[36] Evans, *Fabricating Jesus*, 234.

[37] Fiensy, 145.

[38] Matthew 24:36; Mark 13:32. Before God came to earth as a man, the three Persons of the Trinity decided that Jesus's knowledge during his earthly life would include knowing everything except the date and hour of his second coming to earth. Jesus is portrayed as omniscient in the Gospels.

[39] Matthew 26:14–16, 47–50; Mark 14:43–46; Luke 22:1–6, 47–48; John 18:2–12.

[40] Matthew 27:35; Mark 15:24; Luke 23:33; John 19:18.

[41] Dwight Longenecker, "Was Jesus Really Born in a Stable?" The Stream, December 17, 2020, accessed September 19, 2021, https://stream.org/was-jesus-really-born-in-a-stable/.

[42] Randy Alcorn, "Shepherd Status," in *Come, Thou Long-Expected Jesus: Experiencing the Peace and Promise of Christmas*, ed. Nancy Guthrie (Wheaton, IL: Crossway Books, 2008), 87–88.

[43] *Babylonian Talmud* Sanhedrin 107b and *Babylonian Talmud* Sanhedrin 43a admit that Jesus did miracles. However, they assert that Jesus performed magic/sorcery and "led Israel astray."

[44] The Word in this passage is Jesus as the second Person of the Trinity (the Triune God). See also Matthew 1:18–23.

[45] In these passages, Jesus was referring to Daniel 7:13–14 and claiming to be the divine figure called the Son of Man. He was also referring to Psalm 110:1 and implying that he would share in God's presence and glory. In other Old Testament passages, the image of riding on clouds was used only for divine figures (see Exodus 14:20; 34:5; Numbers 10:34; Psalm 104:3; Isaiah 19:1). See J. Ed Komoszewski, M. James Sawyer, and Daniel B. Wallace, *Reinventing Jesus: How Contemporary Skeptics Miss the Real Jesus and Mislead Popular Culture* (Grand Rapids, MI: Kregel Publications, 2006), 177.

[46] Various passages in the Gospels teach the triune nature of God. For example, it is taught in such passages as the accounts of Jesus's baptism and in Jesus's words found in Matthew 28:18–20.

[47] Ron Rhodes, *What Did Jesus Mean?* (Eugene, OR: Harvest House, 1999), 82.

[48] Millard J. Erickson, *Christian Theology*. 3rd ed. (Grand Rapids, MI: Baker Academic, 2013), 401.

[49] For more information about this famous archeological finding, see Titus Kennedy, *Unearthing the Bible: 101 Archeological Discoveries that Bring the Bible to Life* (Eugene, OR: Harvest House Publishers, 2020), 190–193.

50 Jodi Magness, "What Did Jesus' Tomb Look Like?" *Biblical Archaeology Review* 32, no. 1 (2006): 46–49.

51 Craig A. Evans and Greg Monette, "Jesus's Burial: Archeology, Authenticity, and History," in *Jesus, Skepticism and the Problem of History: Criteria and Context in the Study of Christian Origins*, eds. Darrell L. Bock and J. Ed Komoszewski (Grand Rapids, MI: Zondervan Academic, 2019), 280–281.

52 Kristen Romney, "Exclusive: Age of Jesus Christ's Purported Tomb Revealed," *National Geographic*, November 28, 2017, accessed September 20, 2021, https://www.nationalgeographic.com/history/article/jesus-tomb-archaeology-jerusalem-christianity-rome. See also Kristen Romney, "Unsealing of Christ's Reputed Tomb Turns Up New Revelations," National Geographic, October 21, 2016, accessed September 20, 2021, https://www.nationalgeographic.com/culture/article/jesus-christ-tomb-burial-church-holy-sepulchre.

53 Dan Bahat, "The Church of the Holy Sepulchre—Jesus' Tomb," in *Where Christianity was Born: A Collection from the Biblical Archeological Society*, ed. Hershel Shanks (Washington, DC: Biblical Archeological Society, 2006), 184. The online version can be found at https://www.baslibrary.org/biblical-archaeology-review/12/3/1. Most scholars reject the Garden Tomb found in the 1800s as the location for Jesus's tomb because the Garden Tomb was built in the eighth to seventh centuries BC. Jesus's tomb was new, not a previously used tomb (Matthew 27:57–61; Luke 23:50–53; John 19:41–42). See Gabriel Barkay, "The Garden Tomb—It Isn't," in *Where Christianity was Born: A Collection from the Biblical Archeological Society*, ed. Hershel Shanks (Washington, DC: Biblical Archeological Society, 2006), 196–211. The online version of this article can be found at https://www.baslibrary.org/biblical-archaeology-review/12/2/2.

54 Jesus's burial and resurrection are described in all four Gospels (see Matthew 27:57–28:8; Mark 15:42–16:8; Luke 23:50–24:8; John 19:38–20:10).

55 Kennedy, 199.

56 Zvi Greenhut, "Where the High Priest Caiaphas Was Buried," in *Where Christianity was Born: A Collection from the Biblical Archeological Society*, ed. Hershel Shanks (Washington, DC: Biblical Archeological Society, 2006), 148, 150–152.

57 Hershel Shanks, "The Siloam Pool—Where Jesus Cured the Blind Man," in *Where Christianity was Born: A Collection from the Biblical Archeological Society*, ed. Hershel Shanks (Washington, DC: Biblical Archeological Society, 2006), 108, 110–112, 115.

58 Randall Price, *The Stones Cry Out: What Archeology Reveals about the Truth of the Bible* (Eugene, OR: Harvest House Publishers, 1997), 316.

59 Josh McDowell and Sean McDowell, *Evidence for the Resurrection*, 143–144. See also Gleason Archer Jr., *A Survey of Old Testament Introduction*. Updated and Revised Edition (Chicago: Moody Publishers, 2007), 25.

60 There are 36,289 quotes from the New Testament (including 19,368 quotes from the Gospels) by the early Church Fathers, who wrote between AD 150

and 325. See H. Wayne House, *Chronological and Background Charts of the New Testament*. 2nd ed. (Grand Rapids, MI: Zondervan, 2009), 23.

[61] Komoszewski, Sawyer, and Wallace, 55–60.

[62] Craig L. Blomberg, *Can We Still Believe the Bible? An Evangelical Engagement with Contemporary Questions* (Grand Rapids, MI: Brazos Press, 2014), 27.

[63] "Revelation Song" is based on Revelation 4–5. Another popular song based on Revelation 4–5 is "Angus Dei" ("Worthy is the Lamb") (1990). A violinist played this second song at my wedding ceremony in 2006.

[64] Jesus's feeding of the five thousand men and many women and children is particularly noteworthy because it is multiply attested in all four Gospels (see Matthew 14:13–21; Mark 6:31–44; Luke 9:12–17; John 6:1–14).

[65] Jesus's first prediction of his own death and resurrection is found in Matthew 16:21–23, Mark 8:31–32, and Luke 9:21–22. His second prediction is found in Matthew 17:22–23, Mark 9:30–32, and Luke 9:43–45. Jesus's third prediction of his death is found in Matthew 20:17–19, Mark 10:32–34, and Luke 18:31–34. He also predicts his death in the parable of the wicked tenants (see Matthew 21:33–46; Mark 12:1–12; Luke 20:9–19).

Chapter 7: Did Jesus Really Rise from the Dead?

[1] J. P. Moreland, *Scaling the Secular City: A Defense of Christianity* (Grand Rapids, MI: Baker Book House, 1987), 160.

[2] Hank Hanegraaff, "Part II: But What is Truth," in Paul L. Maier and Hank Hanegraaff, *The Da Vinci Code: Fact or Fiction?* (Carol Stream, IL: Tyndale House Publishers, Inc., 2004), 60.

[3] Sylvia Browne, *End of Days: Predictions and Prophecies about the End of the World* (New York: Dutton, 2008), 210.

[4] Ibid., 204–218.

[5] Sylvia Browne, *The Mystical Life of Jesus: An Uncommon Perspective of the Life of Christ* (New York: Dutton, 2006), 157–158, 174–190.

[6] Browne falsely claims that Jesus was married to Mary Magdalene. In his book *Truth and Fiction in the Da Vinci Code: A Historian Reveals What We Really Know about Jesus, Mary Magdalene, and Constantine* (New York: Oxford University Press, 2004), Bart Ehrman writes, "Not a single one of our ancient sources indicates that Jesus was married, let alone married to Mary Magdalene" (p. 144).

[7] Alok Jha, "How Did Crucifixion Kill?" *The Guardian*, April 8, 2004, accessed October 29, 2021, https://www.theguardian.com/science/2004/apr/08/thisweekssciencequestions.

[8] John Ankerberg and John Weldon, *Knowing the Truth about the Resurrection* (Eugene, OR: Harvest House, 1996), 12.

[9] Robert W. Funk and the Jesus Seminar, *The Acts of Jesus: What Did Jesus Really Do?* (New York: Polebridge Press, 1998), 133.

10 John Dominic Crossan, *Who Killed Jesus: Exposing the Roots of Anti-Semitism in the Gospel Story of the Death of Jesus* (San Francisco, CA: HarperSanFrancisco, 1995), 5.

11 John Dominic Crossan, *Jesus: A Revolutionary Biography* (San Francisco, CA: HarperSanFrancisco, 1994), 153–154.

12 Bart D. Ehrman, *Jesus: Apocalyptic Prophet of the New Millennium* (New York: Oxford University Press, 1999), 225.

13 *Digesta* 48.24.1, 48.24.3.

14 Craig A. Evans, "Getting the Burial Traditions and Evidences Right," in *How God Became Jesus: The Real Origins of Belief in Jesus' Divine Nature*, ed. Michael F. Bird (Grand Rapids, MI: Zondervan, 2014), 78.

15 Evans and Monette, 281.

16 See *Mishnah Sanhedrin* 6:5.

17 William Lane Craig, "Closing Response," in *Jesus' Resurrection: Fact or Figment? A Debate Between William Lane Craig and Gerd Lüdemann*, eds. Paul Copan and Ronald K. Tacelli (Downers Grove, IL: InterVarsity Press, 2000), 172.

18 Moreland, 167.

19 Habermas and Licona, 52–53.

20 Gary R. Habermas, *The Risen Jesus and Future Hope* (Lanham, MD: Rowman and Littlefield, 2003), endnotes 75–102, pp. 40–43.

21 Gary R. Habermas, "The Resurrection of Jesus Time Line," in *Contending with Christianity's Critics: Answering New Atheists and Other Objectors*, eds. Paul Copan and William Lane Craig (Nashville, TN: B & H Academic, 2009), 124–125.

22 Josephus, *Antiquities* 4.219; Mishnah, *Rosh Hashanah* 1:8; Mishnah, *Yevamot* 16:7; Mishnah, *Ketubot* 2:5; Mishnah, *Eduyot* 3:6. The male disciples didn't initially believe the female disciples when the women told them that the tomb was empty (see Luke 24:9–11).

23 Craig, *Reasonable Faith*, 368.

24 See Justin Martyr, *Dialogue with Trypho* 108, written about AD 160; Tertullian, *The Shows* 30, written about AD 200. See also Habermas and Licona, 70–71.

25 For a detailed chart about all twelve of Jesus's resurrection appearances, see Köstenberger, 356–357.

26 The *Gospel of Peter* 10:39–42. This Gospel was a forgery that was written in the middle of the second century. It wasn't written by Peter, the disciple of Jesus mentioned in the New Testament.

27 John Chrysostom, *Homilies on Matthew* 1.6.

28 Simon Greenleaf, *The Testimony of the Evangelists: The Gospels Examined by the Rules of Evidence* (Grand Rapids, MI: Kregel Classics, 1995), 34–35.

29 For example, see N. T. Wright, "The Transforming Reality of the Bodily Resurrection," in *The Meaning of Jesus: Two Visions*, eds. Marcus J. Borg and N.T. Wright (San Francisco, CA: HarperSanFrancisco, 2000), 122.

30 Craig, *Reasonable Faith*, 381.

31 Ken Curtis, "What Ever Happened to the Twelve Apostles?" Christianity.com, April 28, 2010, accessed September 26, 2021, https://www.christianity.com/church/church-history/timeline/1-300/whatever-happened-to-the-twelve-apostles-11629558.html.

32 Josh McDowell and Sean McDowell, *More Than a Carpenter* (Carol Stream, IL: Tyndale Momentum, 2009), 97.

33 Habermas and Licona, 59.

34 Based partly on the five facts found in Habermas and Licona, 48–69.

35 Gary R. Habermas, "Experiences of the Risen Jesus: The Foundational Historical Issue in the Early Proclamation of the Resurrection," *Dialog: A Journal of Theology* 45, No. 3 (Fall 2006): 292.

36 Habermas and Licona, 149. They don't discuss the substitution theory.

37 Josh McDowell and Sean McDowell, *More Than a Carpenter*, 131.

38 Ronald H. Nash, *The Gospel and the Greeks: Did the New Testament Borrow from Pagan Thought?* 2nd ed. (Phillipsburg, NJ: P & R Publishing, 2003), 160–161.

39 Timothy White, *Catch a Fire: The Life of Bob Marley* (New York: Henry Holt and Company, 2006), 3.

40 Nathaniel Samuel Murrell, William David Spencer, and Adrian Anthony McFarlane, eds., *Chanting Down Babylon: The Rastafari Reader* (Philadelphia, PA: Temple University Press, 1998), 6, 159–160.

41 Time Magazine Editors, "Haile Selassie," *Time*, November 3, 1930, accessed October 27, 2021, content.time.com/time/covers/0,16641,19301103,00.html.

42 Time Magazine Editors, "Haile Selassie, Man of the Year," *Time*, January 6, 1936, accessed October 27, 2021, content.time.com/time/covers/0,16641,19360106,00.html.

43 Jane Perlez, "Ethiopia Finds Remains of Emperor," *The New York Times*, February 18, 1992, accessed October 27, 2021, https://www.nytimes.com/1992/02/18/world/ethiopia-finds-remains-of-emperor.html.

44 Ard Louis, "Miracles, Science, and the Laws of Nature," Biologos, March 12, 2018, accessed September 27, 2021, https://biologos.org/articles/miracles-science-and-the-laws-of-nature.

45 Habermas, *The Risen Jesus and Future Hope*, 110.

46 Robert M. Bowman and J. Ed Komoszewski, "The Historical Jesus and the Biblical Church: Why the Quest Matters," in *Jesus, Skepticism and the Problem of History: Criteria and Context in the Study of Christian Origins*, eds. Darrell L. Bock and J. Ed Komoszewski (Grand Rapids, MI: Zondervan Academic, 2019), 42.

Chapter 8: Aren't All Religions Ways to God?

1 Biography.com Editors, "Mayim Bialik," Biography.com, June 30, 2020, accessed October 22, 2021, https://www.biography.com/actor/mayim-bialik.

2   Imdb.com Editors, "The Ten Commandments," IMDb, accessed October 27, 2021, https://www.imdb.com/title/tt0049833/.

3   However, according to Christian scholar H. L. Wilmington, Moses lived from 1525–1405 BC. See H. L. Wilmington, *The Complete Book of Bible Lists* (Wheaton, IL: Tyndale House Publishers, Inc., 1987), 135.

4   Adele Berlin and Marc Zvi Brettler, eds., *The Jewish Study Bible* 2nd ed. (New York: Oxford University Press), 354–355.

5   Dean C. Halverson, ed., *The Compact Guide to World Religions* (Minneapolis, MN: Bethany House Publishers, 1996), 122, 130.

6   For a full list of the 613 commandments, see George Robinson, *Essential Judaism: A Complete Guide to Beliefs, Customs, and Rituals* (New York: Atria Paperback, 2016), 205–222.

7   Ibid., 119.

8   Harold S. Kushner, *How Good Do We Have to Be? A New Understanding of Guilt and Forgiveness* (Boston: Little, Brown, and Company, 1996), 161.

9   Andrew H. Hill, *Baker's Handbook of Bible Lists* (Grand Rapids, MI: Baker Books), 183–185.

10 Skip Hetzig, "The Biblically Quarantined Life," Christianity Today, May 1, 2020, accessed October 4, 2021, https://www.christianitytoday.com/pastors/2020/may-web-exclusives/biblically-quarantined-life.html.

11 From 1346–1353, the Black Death killed about fifty million of the approximately eighty million people living in Europe. Ole Benedictow, "The Black Death: The Greatest Catastrophe Ever," History Today, March 3, 2005, accessed October 4, 2021, https://www.historytoday.com/archive/black-death-greatest-catastrophe-ever.

12 Bill T. Arnold and Bryan E. Beyer, eds., *Readings from the Ancient Near East: Primary Sources for Old Testament Study* (Grand Rapids, MI: Baker Academic, 2002), 171.

13 Peter W. Flint, *The Dead Sea Scrolls* (Nashville, TN: Abingdon Press, 2013), xxi.

14 Randall Price and H. Wayne House, *Zondervan Handbook of Biblical Archeology* (Grand Rapids, MI: Zondervan Academic, 2017), 222.

15 *Christ* is the Greek word for *Messiah*. Both *Christ* and *Messiah* mean "anointed one" (one chosen by God).

16 Daniel 9:24–27 is about 70 "weeks" of 7 years each—a total of 490 years. The 490 years began in 445 BC with the decree by King Artaxerxes to rebuild the city of Jerusalem and its walls in keeping with the request of his Jewish cupbearer Nehemiah (Nehemiah 1:3, 2:4–8).

In his book *Major Bible Prophecies: 37 Crucial Prophecies That Affect You Today* (HaperPaperbacks, New York, 1994), prophecy expert John Walvoord writes the following about Daniel 9:24–27:

If the 490 years begin in 445 B.C., it would provide fulfillment for the 483 years by A.D. 33. In the computation, the prophetic year of 360 days must be understood in keeping with scriptural prophecy where this is consistently used.

The Jewish calendar consisted of 12 months of 30 days each, with provision that after enough days had accumulated a thirteenth month would be added to correct the calendar. In prophecy, however, this thirteenth month is not considered. In Revelation 11:3 and 12:6, for instance, the 3 ½ years of 360 days is confirmed by the use of 1,260 days. Also, 42 months cover the same period (Rev. 11:2; 13:5). The expression, 'a time, times, and half a time' is also considered as 3 ½ years: a 'time' equals 1 year, 'times' equals 2 years, and 'half a time' equals 6 months, for a total of 3 ½ years in keeping with other prophecy (Dan. 7:25; 12:7; Rev. 12:14). Until recently it was assumed that the death of Christ occurred several years earlier, but modern scholarship has given credence to the conclusion that the death of Christ occurred in 33 A.D., which would fit precisely into the pattern of 483 years, leaving the last 7 years to be fulfilled sometime after the death of Christ. (p. 197)

The last seven years refer to the future seven-year period called the Tribulation. Christian and secular scholars believe that Jesus was crucified in either AD 30 or AD 33.

17 Eitan Bar, *Refuting Rabbinic Objections to Christianity and Messianic Prophecies* (Colleyville, TX: One for Israel Ministry, 2019).

18 Malala's story is told here based on information found in a short book. See Shana Corey, *Malala: Hero for All* (New York: Random House, 2016).

19 Muhammad Al-Bukhari, *The Translation of the Meanings of Sahih Al-Bukhari*, trans. Muhammad Muhsin Khan (Riyadh, Saudi Arabia: Darussalam, 1997), 1–9. See also https://sunnah.com/bukhari/.

20 Robert J. Mueller, "What Do Stories about Resurrection(s) Prove?" in *Will the Real Jesus Please Stand Up? A Debate Between William Lane Craig and John Dominic Crossan*, ed. Paul Copan (Grand Rapids, MI: Baker Books, 1998), 80.

21 Maulana Muhammad 'Ali, *Introduction to the Study of the Holy Qur'an* (Dublin, OH: Ahmadiyya Anjuman Ishaat Islam [Lahore] U.S.A., 1992), 81.

22 Ali Dashti, *23 Years: A Study of the Prophetic Career of Muhammad*, trans. F. R. C. Bagley (Costa Mesa, CA: Mazda Publishers, 1994), 86.

23 Damien Carrick, "What It's Like to be in a Polygamous Marriage? Muslim Malaysians Share Their Stories," ABC Radio International, August 16, 2020, accessed October 6, 2021, https://www.abc.net.au/news/2020-02-15/polygamous-marriage-debate-malaysia-shifting-cultures/11814258.

24 Helene Ijaz, "When Muslims Intermarry," The Interfaith Observer, November 15, 2018, accessed October 7, 2021, www.theinterfaithobserver.org/journal-articles/2018/11/13/when-muslims-intermarry.

25 Fatma Tanis, "Saudi Activist Who Led Campaign to Legalize Driving for Women is Released from Jail," NPR, February 10, 2021, accessed October 7, 2021, https://www.npr.org/2021/02/10/966258281/loujain-al-hathloul-saudi-activist-jailed-for-driving-has-been-released.

26 Georgia Aspinall, "Here Are the Countries Where It's Still Really Difficult for Women to Vote," Grazia, March 8, 2021, accessed October 7, 2021, https://graziadaily.co.uk/life/real-life/countries-where-women-can-t-vote/.

27 Katherine Schaeffer, "Key Facts about Women's Suffrage Around the World, a Century after U.S. Ratified 19th Amendment," Pew Research Center, October 5, 2020, accessed October 7, 2021, https://www.pewresearch.org/fact-tank/2020/10/05/key-facts-about-womens-suffrage-around-the-world-a-century-after-u-s-ratified-19th-amendment/.

28 Alan Smith, "Allah, the Best Deceiver (Qur'an 3:54)," WikiIslam, June 6, 2021, accessed October 7, 2021, https://wikiislam.net/wiki/Allah,_the_Best_Deceiver_(Qur%27an_3:54).

29 R. C. Sproul and Abdul Saleeb, *The Dark Side of Islam* (Wheaton, IL: Crossway Books, 2003), 66.

30 John Ankerberg and John Weldon, *The Facts on Islam* (Eugene, OR: Harvest House Publishers, 1998), 42.

31 Nabeel Qureshi, *Seeking Allah, Finding Jesus: A Devout Muslim Encounters Christianity*. 3rd ed. (Grand Rapids, MI: Zondervan, 2018), 255.

32 Embracing the World.org Editors, "Amma: Sri Mata Amritanandamayi Devi," Embracing the World, 2021, accessed October 7, 2021, https://www.embracingtheworld.org/about-amma/.

33 Amanda Leigh Lichtenstein, "A Small, Catholic, Midwestern Farming Town Embraces an Indian 'Hugging Saint,'" The World, August 13, 2019, accessed October 7, 2021, https://www.pri.org/stories/2019-08-13/small-catholic-midwestern-farming-town-embraces-indian-hugging-saint.

34 Wayne W. Dyer, *Inspiration: Your Ultimate Calling* (Carlsbad, CA: Hay House, 2006), 35.

35 Shilpa Kannan, "How McDonalds Conquered India," BBC News, November 19, 2014, accessed October 8, 2021, https://www.bbc.com/news/business-30115555.

36 Joshua J. Mark, "Hinduism," World History Encyclopedia, June 8, 2020, accessed October 8, 2021, https://www.worldhistory.org/hinduism/.

37 A. C. Bhaktivedanta Swami Prabhupada, "Binding the Butter Thief," *Back to Godhead*, October 1977, 13.

38 Mahanidhi Swami, "Krishna Steals Gopis' Garments," Mahanidhi Swami, 2015, accessed October 8, 2021, https://www.mahanidhiswami.com/krishna-steals-gopis-garments/.

39 Gautham Subramanyam, "In India, Dalits Still Feel Bottom of the Caste Ladder," NBC News, September 13, 2020, accessed October 9, 2021, https://www.nbcnews.com/news/world/india-dalits-still-feel-bottom-caste-ladder-n1239846.

40 Madasamy Thirumalai, *Sharing Your Faith with a Hindu* (Minneapolis, MN: Bethany House, 2002), 42.

41 Sujatha Gidla, *Ants among Elephants: An Untouchable Family and the Making of Modern India* (New York: Farrar, Straus and Giroux, 2017), 4.

42 Sture Lönnerstrand, *I Have Lived Before: The True Story of the Reincarnation of Shanti Devi*, trans. Leslie Kippen (Huntsville, AR: Ozark Mountain Publishers, 1998).

43 Dalai Lama, *How to Practice: The Way to a Meaningful Life*, ed. and trans. Jeffrey Hopkins (New York: Pocket Books, 2002), 12.

44 Ibid., 2.

45 Hans Wolfgang Schumann, *Buddhism: An Outline of its Teachings and Schools*, trans. Georg Feuerstein (Wheaton, IL: Quest Books, 1993), 23–24.

46 Barbara O'Brien, "Rebirth and Reincarnation in Buddhism," Learn Religions, January 15, 2019, accessed October 11, 2021, https://www.learnreligions.com/reincarnation-in-buddhism-449994.

47 Melvin McLeod, "What are the Four Noble Truths?" Lion's Roar, March 12, 2018, accessed October 10, 2021, https://www.lionsroar.com/what-are-the-four-noble-truths/.

48 Halverson, 63.

49 Shetty, xvi–xvii.

50 Ibid., 41.

51 Ibid., 69–71.

52 Ibid., 103.

53 Ibid., 190.

54 Ibid., 257, 269.

55 Ibid., 273.

56 Halverson, 63.

57 Bhikkhu Cintita, "What Did the Buddha Think of Women?" The Open Buddhist University, 2012, accessed October 12, 2021, https://buddhistuniversity.net/content/essays/what-did-the-buddha-think-of-women_cintita.

58 Secret.tv Editors, "Rhonda Byrne," TheSecret.tv, accessed October 12, 2021, https://www.thesecret.tv/rhonda-byrnes-biography/.

59 Biography.com Editors, "Deepak Chopra," Biography.com, May 25, 2021, accessed October 12, 2021, https://www.biography.com/personality/deepak-chopra.

60 Sylvia Browne, *Spiritual Connections: How to Find Spirituality Throughout All the Relationships in Your Life* (Carlsbad, CA: Hay House, 2007), 39.

61 Charles Stang, "Flesh and Fire: Reincarnation and Universal Salvation in the Early Church," Harvard Divinity School, March 19, 2019, accessed October 12, 2021, https://hds.harvard.edu/news/2019/03/19/flesh-and-fire-reincarnation-and-universal-salvation-early-church.

62 Deepak Chopra, *Life After Death: The Burden of Proof* (New York: Three Rivers Press, 2006), 127.

63 Ellen Debenport, *The Five Principles: A Guide to Practical Spirituality* (Unity Village, MO: Unity House, 2009), 35.

64 Rhonda Byrne, *The Secret* (New York: Atria Books, 2006), 164.

[65] Deepak Chopra, *The Third Jesus: The Christ We Cannot Ignore* (New York: Harmony Books, 2008), 183.

[66] Byrne, *The Secret*, 46, 68.

[67] Byrne, *The Greatest Secret*, 10. See also her comments on page 45.

[68] Browne, *Spiritual Connections*, 82.

[69] Deepak Chopra, *How to Know God: The Soul's Journey into the Mystery of Mysteries* (New York: Harmony Books, 20002), 57. Chopra doesn't believe the serpent is Satan, but Christians do believe that the serpent is Satan.

[70] Elaine Pagels, *Why Religion?: A Personal Story* (New York: HarperCollins, 2018), 56. Pagels doesn't believe the serpent is Satan, but Christians and some New Agers regard the serpent as Satan.

[71] Gary H. Kah, *The New World Religion: The Spiritual Roots of Global Government* (Noblesville, IN: Hope International Publishing, Inc., 1998), 26.

[72] Chopra, *Life After Death*, 104–105. Blavatsky founded Theosophy, which Chopra refers to in his book as the beginning of the New Age movement.

[73] Helena Petrovna Blavatsky, *The Secret Doctrine: The Synthesis of Science, Religion, and Philosophy. Volume I—Cosmogenesis* (Pasadena, CA: Theosophical University Press, 2019), 198.

[74] Helena Petrovna Blavatsky, *The Secret Doctrine: The Synthesis of Science, Religion, and Philosophy. Volume II—Anthropogenesis* (Pasadena, CA: Theosophical University Press, 2019), 282–283.

[75] Ibid., 243.

[76] Ibid., 111.

[77] Kah, 24.

[78] Eknath Easwaran, *Original Goodness: A Commentary on the Beatitudes*. 2nd ed. (Tomales, CA: Nilgiri Press, 1996), 14.

[79] Deepak Chopra, *Life After Death*, 99.

[80] For example, see Browne, *End of Days*, 226–234.

[81] Chopra, *The Third Jesus*, 16.

[82] Elizabeth Clare Prophet, *The Lost Years of Jesus: Documentary Evidence of Jesus' 17-Year Journey to the East* (Livingston, MT: Summit University Press, 1987).

[83] Deepak Chopra, *Jesus: A Story of Enlightenment* (New York: HarperCollins, 2009) and Deepak Chopra, *The Third Jesus: The Christ We Cannot Ignore* (New York: Harmony Books, 2008).

[84] Bart D. Ehrman, *Forgeries: Writing in the Name of God—Why the Bible's Authors Are Not Who We Think They Are* (New York: HarperOne, 2011), 252–254. See also F. Max Müller, "The Alleged Sojourn of Christ in India," *The Nineteenth Century* 36 (July–December 1894), 515–522 and J. Archibald Douglas, "The Chief Lama of Himis on the Alleged 'Unknown Life of Christ,'" *The Nineteenth Century* 39 (January–June 1896), 667–677.

[85] Chopra, *The Book of Secrets*, 124.

[86] Tim Challies, "What Kind of God Would Condemn People to Eternal Torment?" *Answers Magazine*, July–September 2012, 58.

87 Rice Broocks, *God's Not Dead: Evidence for God in an Age of Uncertainty* (Nashville, TN: W Publishing Group, 2013), 160.

88 Stephen T. Davis, *Risen Indeed: Making Sense of the Resurrection* (Grand Rapids, MI: William B. Eerdmans Publishing Company, 1993), 197.

89 Rebecca McLaughlin, *Confronting Christianity: 12 Hard Questions for the World's Largest Religion* (Wheaton, IL: Crossway, 2019), 58.

90 John Schwarz, *The Compact Guide to the Christian Faith* (Minneapolis, MN: Bethany House, 1999), 150.

Chapter 9: The Life Changer Is Still Transforming Lives!

1 Stephen Mansfield, *Lincoln's Battle with God: A President's Struggle with Faith and What It Meant for America* (Nashville, TN: Thomas Nelson, 2012), xvii. See also Allen C. Guelzo, *Abraham Lincoln: Redeemer President* (Grand Rapids, MI: W.B. Eerdmans Publishing Company, 1999), 434.

2 D. James Kennedy and Jerry Newcome, *What if Jesus Had Never Been Born?* (Nashville, TN: Thomas Nelson Publishers, 1994), 21.

3 Wendy Alsup, *Is the Bible Good for Women? Seeking Clarity and Confidence through a Jesus-Centered Understanding of Scripture* (Colorado Springs, CO: Multnomah, 2017), 3.

4 Ibid.

5 Rebecca McLaughlin, *Confronting Christianity: 12 Hard Questions for the World's Largest Religion* (Wheaton, IL: Crossway, 2019).

6 Henry G. Bosch, "Illustration 2679: Enriching Every Sphere," in *Encyclopedia of 7,700 Illustrations: Signs of the Times*, ed. Paul Lee Tan (Rockville, MD: Assurance Publishers, 1979), 647.

7 Josh McDowell and Sean McDowell, *Evidence that Demands a Verdict*, xxvii–xxix.

8 Josh.org Editors, "Josh's Bio," Josh McDowell Ministry, last modified December 18, 2019, accessed October 17, 2021, https://www.josh.org/about-us/joshs-bio/.

9 Strobel, 13–14.

10 Leestrobel.com Editors, "About Lee," Lee Strobel, accessed October 18, 2021, https://leestrobel.com/about.

11 Stoyan Zaimov, "'Cold-Case Christianity': The Gospel Through a Homicide Detectives Lens," *The Christian Post*, May 7, 2013, accessed October 18, 2021, https://www.christianpost.com/news/cold-case-christianity-the-gospel-through-a-homicide-detectives-lens-95382/.

12 Sarah Irving-Stonebreaker, "How Oxford and Peter Singer Drove Me from Atheism to Jesus," The Veritas Forum, May 22, 2017, accessed October 18, 2021, www.veritas.org/oxford-atheism-to-jesus/.

13 Doreen Virtue, *Deceived No More: How Jesus Led Me Out of the New Age and Into His Word* (Nashville, TN: Emanate Books, 2020), xv, xxii.

14 Ibid, 3.

15 Brandon Showalter, "New Age Writer-Turned-Born-Again Christian Steven Bancarz Exposes Demonic Deception of the Occult," *The Christian Post*, September 8, 2016, accessed October 18, 2021, https://www.christianpost.com/news/new-age-writer-turned-born-again-christian-steven-bancarz-exposes-demonic-deception-occult.html.

16 Scott Gillis, "From Atheist to Christian," *Creation Magazine*, January 2017, 16–18.

17 Stephen Baldwin, *The Unusual Suspect: My Calling to the New Hardcore Movement of Faith* (New York: Warner Faith, 2006), 3–7.

18 Hasset Anteneh, "Brazilian Nanny Led Actor Stephen Baldwin and Wife to the Lord," God Reports, March 12, 2017, accessed October 19, 2021, https://www.godreports.com/2017/03/brazilian-nanny-led-actor-stephen-baldwin-and-wife-to-the-lord-by-singing-about-jesus-to-their-baby/.

19 Dan Harris, "A Baldwin Brother's Journey to Jesus," ABC News, November 22, 2006, accessed October 19, 2021, https://abcnews.go.com/Nightline/story?id=2662535&page=1.

20 You can check out her Instagram profile at https://www.instagram.com/yamilexisfernandez/. Yami's TikTok profile can be found at https://www.tiktok.com/@yamilexisfernandez? Her clothes can be purchased at https://www.yamilexisfernandez.com.

21 Bethanyhamilton.com Editors, "Biography: Learn about Bethany," Soul Surfer and Co., accessed October 19, 2021, https://bethanyhamilton.com/biography/.

22 To check out Ally's many encouraging Instagram posts, please see https://www.instagram.com/allyyarid/.

23 Newsroom Staff, "Klamath Falls Woman Continues to Beat Terminal Illness," KOBI-TV NBC5/KOBI-TV NBC2, February 1, 2019, accessed October 21, 2021, https://kobi5.com/news/local-news/klamath-falls-woman-continues-to-beat-terminal-illness-95105/.

24 Cheryl Broyles, "Cheryl Broyles' Inspirational GBM Brain Tumor Survivor Story," Cheryl Broyles, October 2016, accessed October 21, 2021, https://www.cherylbroyles-gbm.com.

25 Cheryl L. Broyles, *Life's Mountains: What a Brain Tumor Survivor Learned Climbing a Mountain and Battling 'Terminal' Cancer* (Scotts Valley, CA: CreateSpace, 2012).

26 Mickey Seward, "The Tenacity of Hope," *Point Magazine*, May 2019, accessed October 21, 2021, https://converge.org/point-magazine/story/may-2019/the-tenacity-of-hope.

27 Vaneetha Rendall Riser, "My Polio Had a Purpose," *Christianity Today*, July–August 2021, 95–96.

28 ———, *Walking Through Fire: A Memoir of Loss and Redemption* (Nashville, TN: Nelson Books, 2021).

29 Tom Schad, "Sydney McLaughlin Sets World Record; Dalilah Muhammad Wins Silver in 400 Hurdles," *USA Today*, August 4, 2021, accessed October 21, 2021, https://www.usatoday.com/story/sports/olympics/2021/08/03/womens-hurdles-sydney-mclaughlin-dalilah-muhammad-tokyo-olympics/5478327001/.

30 Andrew Holleran, "Look: Sydney McLaughlin's Boyfriend Reacts to Her Gold Medal," The Spun by Sports Illustrated, August 4, 2021, accessed October 21, 2021, https://thespun.com/more/top-stories/look-sydney-mclaughlins-boyfriend-reacts-gold-medal.

31 Sydney McLaughlin, Instagram post, August 5, 2021, accessed October 21, 2021, https://www.instagram.com/sydneymclaughlin16/.

Chapter 10: The Life-Changing Message

1 Jerry Bridges, *The Discipline of Grace* (Colorado Springs, CO: NavPress, 2006), 46.

About the Author

Josh Peterson is the founder and director of HOLA Ministries. He enjoys working with Latinos and people from a variety of countries and backgrounds. Hundreds of people whom Josh has talked with have found their joy, peace, and purpose through a vibrant relationship with God. Josh's cross-cultural experience includes visiting five countries and talking and corresponding with people from many different countries. He also lived in Uruguay for about four years. His wife, Rosy, is a naturalized U.S. citizen who was born and raised in Brazil. They have two children. Josh is an avid nonfiction reader, and he enjoys playing sports with his kids and with Latinos. Josh has a BA in psychology from the University of Minnesota and four advanced degrees, including an earned doctorate degree from Luther Rice College & Seminary.